NAZARETH

ALONG THE BANKS

OF

THE GANGES

NAZARETH
ALONG THE BANKS
OF
THE GANGES
1947-1990

SISTER EUGENIA MUETHING

HARMONY HOUSE
PUBLISHERS-LOUISVILLE
1997

Cover Design and Production Direction: Robert Williams
Library of Congress Number: 97-074184
(Softbound) ISBN 1-56469-036-9
(Hardbound) ISBN 1-56469-035-0
©1997 Sisters of Charity of Nazareth
First Edition Printed Summer 1997
by Harmony House Publishers
P.O. Box 90 Prospect KY, 40059 USA
(502) 228-2010
Printed in the United States of America

CONTENTS

FOREWORD

When I retired after forty-eight years of teaching, thirty-four of which were spent in India, I was requested by the provincial, Sister Shalini, to tackle an unfamiliar job, the writing of the history of the Sisters of Charity of Nazareth in India. Having come out to India in 1952, I had shared all but five of those years with the pioneers. I was hesitant, as I felt incompetent for the job, but putting my trust in the Holy Spirit, I accepted.

I set out to gather material by visiting almost all of the missions of the community in India, travelling throughout Bihar, to Bombay and to the Himalayas both in Bengal and Uttar Pradesh, where I read the annals and noted down the salient facts about each place. Being possessed of some gypsy blood, I found this part of the work enjoyable and interesting. In all the places, I received a warm welcome and the utmost cooperation from the Sisters, and to them all I owe many thanks.

In the compilation of the material I was greatly helped by the hospitality accorded me particularly in three places—our mission stations in Sangsay, West Bengal, and Almora in Uttar Pradesh, both of these in the Himalayas, and finally at Koyal Kunj in Hazaribagh, in the Bihar Plateau. Sisters Vinaya, Maria, Beena, Arpita, Shobhana, Jyoti, and Rajni at Sangsay; Sisters Mary Chackalackal, Usha, Geeta, Ancilla, and Maneesha at Almora; and finally Sister Lucia Grabner of the Holy Cross Sisters and the boys and girls of her Children's Home at Hazaribagh provided for me a quiet place, a good typewriter, and excellent food and lodging, which enabled me to bring to fruition the task assigned to me. To all of them I owe my sincere thanks and gratitude for their generous assistance.

To Sister James Maria Spillane, author of *Kentucky Spring* and *Summer Winds,* living at the motherhouse of the SCNs in the United States, I owe a deep expression of gratitude for her interest and encouragement and also for corrections and suggestions that she offered while willingly perusing portions of the book, despite a heavy burden of work in the composition of her third book of SCN history.

For the many hours spent in typing, editing, and preparing the manuscript for the press, I extend my sincere appreciation to Sister Mary Collette Crone, Archivist at Nazareth, and to all those who worked with her.

Lastly, I thank Sanjay Sahay, a former student of Nazareth Academy, Gaya, for his generous contribution for the publication of the book. His appreciation of literary effort is the fruit of his own talent in the artistic field in prose and poetry and in his recent production of the film *Patant,* which has received national recognition as of exceptional merit.

To all those persons, named and unnamed, who have helped and encouraged me, I extend my gratitude, and it is my hope that my efforts will not be disappointing to them. All for the honor and glory of God!

VENTURING OUT

The first SCNs bound for India pose on the front steps of the Nazareth Motherhouse: left to right—Sisters Florence Joseph Sauer, Charles Miriam Holt, Ann Cornelius Curran, Crescentia Wise, Ann Roberta Powers, and Lawrencetta Veeneman.

The second group going to India—Sisters Ellen Maria Ballew, Ann Bernadette Ormond, and Mary Jude Howard—share their feelings after receiving the mission cross.

Chapter One

VENTURING OUT

Just how did this mammoth project—Nazareth in India—begin? As with most projects, the beginning was small, almost like a whisper uttered in the dark. Although the pioneer group left for India only in late 1947, the first inkling had come through a request for SCNs for India by Father Charles H. Cloud, S.J., provincial of the Chicago province, on the occasion of a visit he made to Nazareth, Kentucky, on 9 September 1931. No agreement was made, but Mother Mary Catharine Malone promised to "think about it" and to keep the project in her prayers.

Mother Mary Catharine's prayers must have been effective, but much time elapsed before God gave an answer. In December 1945, Father Dan Rice and Father James Cox (both future Jesuit priests destined for the India mission) suggested to Bishop B. J. Sullivan, S.J., bishop of Patna, that the SCN community be requested for the mission of Father Marion Batson, S.J., which was in Bishop Sullivan's diocese. Father Rice's interest had been prompted by his contact with St. Joseph Infirmary and particularly with Sister Charles Elizabeth (later Sister Lucy Carrico), with whom he had discussed the missions and from whom he had received great encouragement.

Five months later came the final message, which can best be narrated by quoting from a newsletter of Mother Ann Sebastian Sullivan, headed Motherhouse, Nazareth, Kentucky, May 7, 1946:

Dear Sisters,

. . . And now for the atomic bomb! We are entering foreign missions! The Patna District of India! The Jesuit Bishop of Patna, Most Reverend B. J. Sullivan, S.J., has asked us to build and operate a hospital in Mokameh Mission, Patna, for which purpose he has secured thirty-seven acres of land adjoining the Jesuit mission. In 1947 we expect to send at least six Sisters to open a dispensary and to do catechetical work. The Fathers hope the dispensary will soon develop into a hospital. Bishop Sullivan believes that later we shall see our way to open a central grade and high school at Mokameh. He even offers us a leper home in time, if you please, provided we are interested. The leper work is vast and most exciting, he says.

1

. . . Do your best praying that God will support every step of our way in these new foundations. Our confidence must not fail Him.

Lovingly yours in Our Lady,

(Signed) Mother Ann Sebastian

Then followed days of anticipation, days of eager questioning. Who would go? Who would be the first SCN foreign missionaries—"the lucky six"? On 11 April 1947 the letters of appointment reached the six SCNs who would become the pioneer band to India, the first foreign mission of the community:

1. Sister Lawrencetta Veeneman, a native of Louisville, Kentucky, music teacher at Good Shepherd School, Frankfort, Kentucky;
2. Sister Crescentia Wise, also a native of Louisville, Kentucky, pharmacist, Saints Mary and Elizabeth Hospital, Louisville, Kentucky;
3. Sister Charles Miriam Holt, a native of South Boston, Massachusetts, superior and principal at New Hope, Kentucky;
4. Sister Florence Joseph Sauer, a native of Henderson, Kentucky, nurse at Mt. St. Agnes Hospital, Louisville, Kentucky;
5. Sister Ann Cornelius Curran, a native of Bellaire, Ohio, nurse at St. Joseph Infirmary, Louisville, Kentucky;
6. Sister Ann Roberta Powers, a native of Cloverport, Kentucky, teacher at Holy Name School, Louisville, Kentucky.

A circular letter from Mother Ann Sebastian, dated April 24, 1947, informed the community about the members who would be turning their faces eastward. Mother's letter concluded with the following words: "We must pray for them that grace in abundance will be theirs to love eternal values with so much intensity that they may count the hard things of life as nought in the game of winning souls for God. . . . Six is the number chosen . . . but that does not bar the rest of us from sharing in the same apostolate." From that time forward a whirlwind of preparations began: medical examinations, passports, and visas had to be obtained. Necessary household goods and all kinds of supplies, including medicines, were collected, crated or boxed, and prepared for the long six-week voyage to the other side of the world. At that time, it was thought to be a departure for life, so there were visits home with final farewells to family, relatives, friends, and community.

An impressive and touching departure ceremony was held at Nazareth on 15 August 1947, attended by a large number of Sisters, as well as by families of the India missionaries. The six chosen ones received mission crosses at the hands of veteran India missionary, Father O'Leary, S.J. Between the hymns of Benediction, the entire congregation recited the *Itinerarium,* prayers for the journey.

By early October the six Sisters were gathered at Nazareth, where a number of programs were given in their honor. On Sunday, 5 October, to the lively ringing of the church bells, the Sisters, novices, postulants, and college girls gathered on the colonial porch and lined the steps and the walks to bid a fond and tearful farewell to the courageous band of missionaries that would make a new Nazareth half a world away. In the fully packed Cathedral of the Assumption in Louisville, the Sisters received the mission cross from Archbishop Floersh and were "sent forth" with all the blessings of Holy Mother Church.

JOURNEY TO INDIA

The group had to be divided for the voyage because they could not be accommodated on one cargo ship—the only type of ship sailing directly to India. Sisters Lawrencetta, Crescentia, and Ann Cornelius sailed on the *Steel Vendor;* Sisters Charles Miriam, Florence Joseph, and Ann Roberta on the *Steel Executive.* Thus two narratives of the voyages are preserved in the interesting letters written on the way. The two groups had been accompanied to New York in separate shifts. Mother Ann Sebastian had gone with both groups, but she had as her companion for the first trip Sister Bertrand Crimmins (later Mother Bertrand) and for the second trip, Sister Mary Anastasia Coady.

After leaving New York, the first group had a bonus ride along the eastern coast, having "loading stops" at Philadelphia (where they met the veteran India missionary and foundress of the Medical Missionaries, Mother Anna Dengel) and at Baltimore. There a sojourn of two days gave the departing Sisters the pleasure of meeting Mother Ann Sebastian's sister, Ella Sullivan, Sister Lawrencetta's mother and her sister Virginia, and of seeing several of the Maryland convents. Their farewell to the land of their birth was on 17 October, when the vessel really put out to sea.

Though marred by a few bouts of seasickness, the voyage was a truly delightful one. The presence on board of a chaplain, Father Harry Birney, S.J., gave the Sisters the privilege of daily Mass except when the ship rolled and pitched too much. As the *Steel Vendor* steadily plowed its way through the rolling sea, the world unfolded before the Sisters' eyes—Gibraltar, Tangier, Ceuta in Morocco, the Atlas Mountains, Algiers and Cape Bon, Pantellaria, Malta, Port Said, Suez, Jeddah, Djibouti, the Arabian Sea, Bombay (the first sight of India on 21 November), afterwards Cochin, Colombo (Ceylon), Madras, and finally, Calcutta—their longed-for destination—on 7 December.

The first real taste of life in India came at Cochin—featuring Indian money, a ride in a rickshaw, and a visit to a 300-bed hospital. By 6 December the *Steel Vendor*, with the pilot leading, started up the Hooghly River. When they arrived in Calcutta about noon the following day, excitement mounted with the announcement that someone awaited Father Birney and more exciting still the words, "There are three Sisters of Charity on the dock." Father Batson, the main guiding force at Mokama, was also present. The joy at meeting the three Sisters, whom they had not expected to see before Christmas, knew no bounds.

The second group—Sisters Charles Miriam, Florence Joseph, and Ann Roberta—boarded the *Steel Executive* in New York and was under way by the morning of 29 October 1947. Having saluted the Statue of Liberty as they sailed for the open sea, they bade farewell to their native land and turned their eyes eastward to the rolling Atlantic. Two priests were sailing on the same ship—Father Wyss, C.S.C., a veteran missionary of Bengal, and Father Holland.

The first portion of the sea voyage was marked by much rain and bad weather with little sunshine and brightness. The natural result was seasickness. Sisters Florence Joseph and Ann Roberta were greatly affected. By the time Gibraltar and the dim coast of Africa hove into view, however, all three Sisters were able to be on deck to see land after nine days of only water. Tangier, Ceuta, and Gibraltar were outlined in lights since darkness had already descended. The Mediterranean Sea was beautifully blue, and the Sisters enjoyed all the sights of this busy waterway. Especially lovely was the island of Crete.

The sailing days flew by with stops at Beirut, Alexandria, Port Said, Suez, and Djibouti. Through several excursions on land, the Sisters began to experience the life of the Orient: to know the different ways of the people in various places, the mystery that is the East. November 29 brought the *Steel Executive* to Karachi and the first direct experience of the Indian peninsula.

Next came the *real* India—the arrival of the *Steel Executive* in Bombay on 30 November 1947. Some decisions had to be made, as the dock strike was holding up all cargo ships for about two weeks. Should the Sisters wait and perhaps spend Christmas on shipboard, or should they cross the country by some other means? They decided to take the train and travel across country from Bombay to Calcutta. The journey was a long one, punctuated by an exciting and terrifying encounter with some thieves who entered the Sisters' compartment. Sister Ann Roberta became the heroine of that episode by getting the thieves out and stopping the train. To the amazement of all, the thieves were caught.

Because this train journey brought the second group to Calcutta even before the *Steel Vendor* had landed, it was possible for Sisters Charles Miriam, Florence Joseph, and Ann Roberta to be on hand, along with Father Batson, to welcome Sisters Lawrencetta, Crescentia, and Ann Cornelius. The happy six spent 8 December together, and many fervent prayers went up, thanking Our Lady for her constant protection and praising God's goodness in bringing them safely to their new land.

4

Some days were spent in clearing baggage and cargo through customs, but finally the group got under way for the overnight train journey from Calcutta to Mokama, under the able guidance of Father Batson, who was in charge of the mission in Mokama. The reception accorded the party on their arrival in Mokama at 4:05 a.m. on 13 December 1947 was tremendous. A warm and enthusiastic delegation awaited the new Sisters: Jesuit Fathers Richard Welfle, Philip Poovatil, Robert Stegman, and Edmund Burke; Father Burke's parents from Chicago; Mr. Gordon Murphy, a scholastic; and forty-five boys from the mission school. A band (drums and wind instruments) and fireworks accompanied the party from the station to the convent. Garlands of marigolds were presented, symbolizing the heartfelt joy and happiness that filled the hearts of all at the beginning of a new era in the life of Mokama.

Mass was offered in the early morning, and in the evening a Solemn Benediction at the Shrine of Our Lady of Grace was followed by a procession from there to the convent bearing the Blessed Sacrament, bringing God to dwell with the new missionaries.

The first day was completed by a welcome program offered by the boys of the school. When the Sisters finally got to bed on the "longest day" they found it difficult to sleep because of the bitter night cold. Since they had heard a great deal about India's burning heat, they were surprised and unprepared to experience penetrating cold.

THE NEW MISSION

Life began to take shape and to form itself into patterns. Some patients even began to arrive before Christmas, the first being the convent cook. Preparations got under way for the first Christmas, a never-to-be-forgotten one in its simplicity, away from the bustle, the commercialism, the worldliness of many present-day celebrations in the United States. Midnight Mass was celebrated in a large room on the ground floor of the convent. Beginning the day before, people trekked in from stations quite a distance away. They were prepared for the night, having brought along simple cooking utensils, bedding, and the means to sustain life while they spent Christmas away from home.

The Sisters were much heartened when on Christmas Eve they received Mother Ann Sebastian's Christmas letter. Nazareth in Kentucky seemed close to Nazareth in India. Homesickness faded away in the novelty of a new world and a new life to come.

Mention should be made of the great kindness of Father Batson and all the priests of the Patna mission. The fruitcake given by Father Batson (a treasure, indeed), the large supply of fresh foods paid for by his dear mother, and a fine turkey contributed by Father Poovatil all added to the beauty and enjoyment of the feast.

Slowly but surely the mission began to develop. The Sisters, along with several Jesuits, engaged in the study of the Hindi language under the direction of Father Vincent Gallagher, S.J., with regular classes every day. Celine Minj from Ranchi became the first lay person to assist in the dispensary. She occupied a small room on the roof. Housework, work with the sick, home visiting, language study, and various other occupations filled the day, and many were the interesting episodes that could happen only in "incredible India."

A transfer of significance at this time was that of Father Poovatil, who left Mokama for Bettiah and was replaced by Father Louis De Genova, S.J., brother of SCNs Theresa Mary and Louis Ann.

In mid January Father Batson returned from Calcutta, after securing from the *Steel Executive* the release of the baggage that the Sisters had left in Bombay. He brought a petromax and a kerosene lamp, which greatly improved visibility at night. Mokama at that time had no electricity. The refrigerator and a petrol-run washing machine that had been donated by Sister Florence Joseph's father, John J. Sauer, were also put to good use.

The Jesuits of the language school were untiring in their efforts to make themselves useful—unpacking boxes and furniture, putting things in their proper places, and sorting medicines and other necessary items. Mr. Eugene Hattie, S.J., and the boys of the hostel helped Sister Crescentia in arranging medicines and equipment for the dispensary and in setting up a reception room, treatment room, and pharmacy.

The medical personnel—Sisters Crescentia, Florence Joseph, and Ann Cornelius, along with Celine Minj (later to become the first Mokama nurse) who served as an interpreter—began going on sick calls to the villages near Mokama. This village work evolved into a kind of bi-weekly travelling dispensary. Means of transportation was very poor—mostly walking or riding in an oxcart or a *tum-tum* (a kind of flat-topped vehicle drawn by a horse or pony). The patients arrived in Mokama in the same manner. Permission was later granted to the Sisters to ride bicycles.

Sometimes disaster followed such expeditions. Sisters Crescentia and Florence Joseph had gone by *tum-tum* to see a twenty-year-old wife and mother who had developed a psychosis. After feeding her and giving her a sedative by nasal tube and asepto syringe, they left her sleeping. On the return journey their bag fell off the *tum-tum,* and the syringe was crushed under its wheels—a major catastrophe.

NAZARETH HOSPITAL, MOKAMA
1948

Nazareth Hospital at Mokama when Sisters arrived on
13 December 1947

Chapter Two

NAZARETH HOSPITAL, MOKAMA
1948

The second of February 1948 became a red-letter day when the first inpatient, an emergency maternity case, came to the dispensary. Hers was the first baby born at Nazareth dispensary, a boy born at 3:00 a.m. and baptized "Joseph." Joseph and his mother went home a few days later in the palanquin, a bird-cage type of conveyance used as an ambulance, suspended on a pole supported on the shoulders of two men.

This date was also Sister Lawrencetta's birthday, her first in India. Celine Minj, the dispensary assistant, came with six duck eggs on a plate lined with marigold petals, a card made by her tied with a ribbon, and a *mala* (necklace of flowers). On the same occasion Sister Florence Joseph received a *mala* plus a bouquet and a card. The donor read the card in Hindi and, according to Sister Florence Joseph, "read with much feeling on his part and little understanding on mine."

The dispensary, which was open daily from 10:00 a.m. to 11:30 a.m., served many poor, blind, undernourished people, suffering from diseases related to malnutrition. Although making progress in the Hindi language, the Sisters felt frustrated in not being able to speak to the people, to tell them about God's love for them. They also felt very much in need of a doctor. Sister Lawrencetta had been making strenuous efforts to find a doctor willing to work, and she had been buying supplies needed for a hospital in the hope that one could be opened soon.

On one occasion an outside call came for a maternity case. Going by motor car, the Sisters entered a courtyard full of buffaloes. The Sisters examined the woman, took care of her, administered a sedative, and were taking their leave, when the women folk (always in attendance in large numbers) came after them to say that the patient was dead, that she would not open her mouth to drink milk. The Sisters assured them she was only asleep. The patient recovered nicely.

SUMMER IDYLL

By the end of February the weather began to warm up, and Father Batson began planning for the time when the Sisters would go to Darjeeling, a hill station in the eastern Himalayas at an altitude of 7000 feet. Having prepared themselves to brave the summer heat, the Sisters were surprised at this new item on their agenda. They learned that, along with nine Medical Missionaries, they would enjoy the cool climate of Darjeeling in the Jesuits' villa, appropriately named "Loyola." The language school was also moving to Loyola, so the plan was to leave after Easter, about the middle of April, and stay until the monsoon broke in July. During that time the Sisters would continue language study and make their annual retreat.

The weather continued to grow hotter and hotter so that after Easter the Sisters were eager to depart for Darjeeling and the coolness of the hills. The day set for the exodus was 14 April. Because the Mokama establishment was to be closed for the duration, there was much packing and storing to do against the day of return. Moreover, all manner of supplies had to be taken: staple food supplies, bedding, kitchen and dining room utensils, as well as books, warm clothing, and personal belongings. The entourage resembled a great oriental caravan. Only the pack animals were missing, the train being the substitute. Celine Minj and Mary Magdalen Barla, a Hindi teacher who had been with the Sisters for several months, joined the excursion. The journey was overnight to Calcutta, then by another train through East Pakistan to Siliguri, and finally by motor vehicles up, up, up the hill to Darjeeling.

Loyola Villa was located on West Point, a high hill about a half-hour walk from Darjeeling proper. The Medical Missionaries and the Sisters of Charity proceeded to spread out all their paraphernalia and make their new abode comfortable and convenient. The coolness of the hills, the bracing air, the luxuriant flora, the magnificent scenery, and the good food quickly rejuvenated the heat-weary Sisters. They were ready for daily Hindi classes with Miss Barla and Father Gallagher, the latter having joined his Jesuit community at one of their nearby houses. Luxurious hot baths provided at the house of Mrs. Kearns, a benevolent resident of West Point, were a special blessing, sometimes an amusing one. Wandering late one afternoon along the mountain path above the Kearns' hillside bungalow, Sister Lawrencetta was stopped in her tracks by a well-meant but reverberating call from below from the mistress of the house: "Sister Law—ren—cet—ta—-you haven't had your bath yet—."

The sojourn in Darjeeling provided an ideal locale for the annual retreat. This first retreat in Darjeeling in 1948 was given by a Patna Jesuit, Father Richard Wrobeleski, S.J., a well known educator. His simple dress in old clothes and white cassock, his carefully combed hair, impressed the Sisters. They were even more impressed when Father appeared one day for a conference with the comb still in his hair, where it remained throughout the exhortation.

For many years a retreat was given in Darjeeling for those who could be there at the appointed time. That first year the last occupants of Loyola locked the doors on July 12, almost three months after the arrival of the first group.

The next big event—and it was indeed very big—was the opening of the hospital on 19 July. The preceding days were spent in frantic preparation of the ground floor for wards and other types of rooms. The layout of the hospital in general was as follows: on the ground floor were three rooms for dispensary and pharmacy; three wards—one with seven beds and two with ten each; three private rooms, the doctors' room, an operating room, and a delivery room; on the next floor and roof were the quarters of the Sisters, including the chapel, and those of the girls who worked in the hospital.

Bishop Augustine Wildermuth, S.J., the new bishop of Patna, blessed the hospital and declared it officially open. The day was aptly chosen—the feast of Saint Vincent de Paul, principal patron of the Sisters of Charity. Also present on the occasion were Father De Genova and three Medical Missionaries: Sisters Stephanie and Marcella from Patna, and Sister Ignatius Marie from Mandar.

The first patient of the hospital was admitted on 22 July. The next day a baby was born, and on 24 July a longed-for event took place—the arrival of the first doctor, Dr. Eric J. Lazaro from Madras. Thus the hospital staff became somewhat complete—Sister Crescentia, pharmacist and nurse, especially in the dispensary; Sisters Ann Cornelius and Florence Joseph, nurses; Sister Lawrencetta, superior; Sisters Charles Miriam and Ann Roberta, teachers, assisting in the hospital; Salomi Tirkey, a trained nurse; Celine Minj, a worker in the dispensary; and Rosalie, a worker in the hospital.

Patients with cholera, malaria, dysentery, abscesses, and many more diseases soon arrived in large numbers. The delivery room was adequately furnished, but there was no operating table. All activities were hampered by the lack of electricity. Gasoline or kerosene had to be used for the functioning of any machine or apparatus. The water supply was drawn by hand from a well. Two workers in the hospital and convent at this time were Doma, a hill girl whom the Sisters had brought from Darjeeling, and Seraphina, a girl of the locality.

This first year of experiencing the heat of India was hard for the new missionaries. Before leaving for Darjeeling, they had found the hot, dry, baking weather rather devastating, and when they returned from the hills, the humid, sultry temperatures of the monsoon left them soaked in perspiration and completely sapped of strength. Since Mokama was situated close to the Ganges, the moisture was intensified. The problem of washing, drying, and ironing clothes, especially the complicated cap, was an acute one.

An anecdote about a washing machine merits repeating. Mokama had a gas-propelled one, like most of the gadgets and machines at that time. The *dhobi* (washerman), who really did not like mechanical objects, operated this machine on Mondays. On one of these official washing days, this shaking, grunting, grinding machine came to a dead halt after four washes. A crowd gathered to watch Father Dineen examine the machine, go through a few maneuvers until the shaking, grunting, grinding recommenced. The secret of the mechanic's success finally leaked out: the machine had been "out of gas."

Throughout August and September the heat continued to plague the Sisters. The hospital became so busy that they could hardly manage the number of patients that poured in. Dr. Lazaro, the nurses, the Sisters, and the whole staff were busy day and night. Between the heat and the lack of rest and proper sleep, the newcomers began to fall sick. Both Sisters Crescentia and Florence Joseph were stricken and were incapacitated for a few days. By early October, however, because the weather grew better, the general health also improved.

Toward the end of October some major changes were made in the setup of the hospital, prompted largely by the fact that the operating room was entirely too small and presented some real problems for the doctor. Some shifting and cutting of walls and making of windows greatly improved the facilities. Thus began the evolution of the hospital that has continued throughout its existence.

In October the Sisters, through their friendship with Mr. and Mrs. Peter Havralant and family, Czech nationals, became associated with the Bata Shoe Company factory at Mokama Ghat. Mr. Havralant, the manager, gave invaluable assistance to the hospital and convent in every way that he could. His memory will always be held in deep gratitude and appreciation by the Nazareth community of Mokama.

The shrine feast in honor of Our Lady of Grace, which became a very big annual affair, was celebrated solemnly for the first time on 3 November. Present for it, in addition to the many priests and lay Christians who attended, were Mr. Leslie Martin, the donor of the shrine, and the architect, Mr. Lahiri. Father Joseph of Barbigha, with forty men and boys, walked eighteen miles to attend the feast. Their zeal and devotion were inspiring.

That first year transportation was considerably improved. A jeep donated to the hospital by Sister Catherine Arnold's father, Mr. Paul Arnold, had been in use for some time. It was not the only mode of transportation, however. On one occasion, Dr. Lazaro was transported to a distant village for a sick call on the back of an elephant.

The first anniversary of the arrival of the Sisters was observed by starting an outside dispensary at the village of Aunta about ten miles away. Dr. Lazaro and several Sisters and other assistants saw patients on the veranda of a house. Many came for medical help.

The work with orphans, so much loved by Mother Catherine Spalding, was growing in Mokama. There was hardly a time in the early years when some orphans were not in Mokama—abandoned children left in trains, in the nearby fields; poor children whose parents could not keep them; orphaned children; unwanted children.

Always there were such cases. Some who arrived very sick died; others survived and were enabled, through care and education, to get into the mainstream of society.

Mention should be made of the generous contributions of Father Edward Garische, S.J. During the first year twenty-five boxes of supplies, mostly hospital equipment and other medical needs, were obtained through his untiring efforts. The items even included an operating table. Through the years he continued this generous work.

This chapter would not be complete without recognizing the many others who helped the Sisters so much in finding their way and in getting established on a firm basis: Father Batson, Father Gallagher, Father De Genova, and all the other priests and brothers who assisted them so much in spiritual and material ways. The IBVM Sisters of Bankipore also gave much valuable assistance in buying, in advising, and in offering hospitality. A special word of gratitude must go to the Medical Missionaries, who offered every possible help, especially in the medical field, even to the extent of personal assistance through the untiring ministrations of Sister Elise, M.D., who came to Mokama despite heavy work in Patna, and aided in the operating theater when the load became too heavy for Dr. Lazaro.

Father Gallagher, the language guru, as well as great friend and helper, was transferred to the Jamshedpur Jesuits' language school at Gomoh. On Christmas he made a surprise visit and offered the midnight Mass in the beautifully decorated room used for a chapel. Just at the end of the festivities a child was born, fittingly commemorating the birth of Jesus on the day honoring the Nativity.

The year 1949 began in a special way with the arrival in Mokama on the morning of 8 January of Mother Bertrand and Mother Ann Sebastian, accompanied by Sisters Lawrencetta and Charles Miriam, who had met them at the airport in Calcutta. The visitors' presence, their understanding, their grasp of problems, their participation in the life and work of the mission inspired and encouraged the Sisters as nothing else could have done.

An eye camp organized eight days after their arrival, under the direction of specialists, Dr. Vertuno and Dr. Gardiner, gave the two visitors an opportunity to see at first hand the workings of an Indian medical team—how the members have to improvise in order to be able to carry out necessary operations and treatments.

On 9 February the two Mothers General were present for the Baptism and First Communion of Doma, the young girl from Darjeeling who had come with the Sisters. On the same night Sister Lawrencetta, Sister Crescentia, Mother Bertrand, and Mother Ann Sebastian left for Darjeeling to see the Kearns' place at West Point, which was under consideration for a summer home. (This home was later purchased and became Nazareth Cottage.) The two Mothers departed from there to return to the United States after a memorable visit, leaving a distinct void in those who were left behind.

Sister Crescentia had a series of heart attacks beginning on 30 March 1949. Dr. Lazaro said it would be a year before she would be ready for regular duty. This news was a severe blow to everyone, but most of all to her. She was literally carried all the way from Mokama to Darjeeling via Calcutta, even to the new cottage—Nazareth Cottage—and to bed.

While the Sisters in turns enjoyed some hard-earned rest in Darjeeling, a project was under way in Mokama. The wiring and fitting of fixtures—lights, fans, switches, etc.—were completed for the much-longed-for establishment of electricity to serve the hospital. Lights went on and fans began to whirl for the first time on 8 June. What a day of rejoicing!

This year saw a tremendous growth in the hospital. Patients continued to pour in. Many times all beds in the wards were occupied, and the overflow had to be accommodated on the verandas. The need for a new building became acute, and plans were made to commence the process before the situation got completely out of hand.

The growing number of patients increased the need for adequate, trained personnel. The obvious solution to the problem would be the institution of a recognized nursing school. Feelers had already gone out in late 1948, and contacts had been made. The fast-growing hospital needed expansion, and more space would be required for the nursing school. In July 1949 classes were started, the first nursing students being Celine Minj, Michael Gaetano, and Susan D'Cruz. This was the beginning of Nazareth School of Nursing, now internationally known, whose graduates have spread out through the nation and the world to carry the standards of the school far and wide.

An important concern of the nursing school was to obtain government recognition. Some time in November of 1949, Miss George, superintendent of nurses' training in Bihar, inspected the hospital and the existing facilities for the nurses' training. Although she was pleased with what she saw, it was obvious that some inadequacies would have to be resolved before recognition could be obtained. She did indeed boost the morale of all and gave assurance that recognition would come in due time.

An event in which the Sisters took active part was the arrival of the Sisters of Notre Dame of Cleveland, Ohio, in a town not far from Mokama—Jamalpur. For some weeks before they arrived, Sister Lawrencetta had been busy helping to get supplies, visiting the house they were to occupy, and preparing a fitting place for them to live. On the day before their arrival, Sisters Lawrencetta and Ann Roberta went to Jamalpur to put the final touches on the house and to be present to welcome them when they finally reached their destination.

Such kindness was common during those early days in India, and the SCNs were often the recipients. During the whole of this year of 1949, the Medical

Missionaries of Holy Family Hospital in Patna spared no effort to help the fledgling Nazareth Hospital to spread its wings and fly. When Nazareth Hospital needed doctors, Sister Elise, a surgeon, practically commuted between the two places; and Sister Marcella and Sister Benedicta also rendered great service. When needed nurses were sent, Sister Stephanie, administrator, arranged for the SCN nurses to be enrolled for midwifery at Holy Family, at the same time giving them the maximum amount of time for leave so that they could be of use to the much beleaguered Nazareth Hospital. The SCN debt to Holy Family Hospital can never be paid.

Contributions from other SCNs, their relatives and benefactors, the Notre Dame Sisters, the Jesuits, and other sources made this a year of great benefaction. Equipment, furniture, medicines, and supplies of all kinds poured in from all over the world, including gifts of money that could be used for many things that were needed as the hospital expanded.

A person who must be mentioned in this chronicle is Father Charles Scott, S.J., long since gone to his eternal reward. Without fail, Father Scott was on hand each month to direct the recollection day of the Sisters, to support them, and to assist them with his priestly ministrations. His faithfulness to the monthly day of recollection was a source of great inspiration. One cannot praise enough all the Jesuits who cared for the spiritual as well as the material life of the Sisters in those early years. Jesuit Fathers De Genova and Frank Martinsek, who were assigned to Mokama in those years, were especially untiring in their efforts.

A social event that marked the close of 1949 was the marriage in Our Lady's Shrine of Dr. Lazaro and Babs Gillard, daughter of an Anglo-Indian family of Calcutta. Babs had been working for some time at Nazareth Hospital as a registrar at the dispensary. Their marriage on 28 December brought to a close another year of mission work—laborious but happy.

1950-1951

The year of the definition, on 1 November, of Our Lady's Assumption into heaven, 1950, saw a number of important events in the calendar of Nazareth in India. The earliest of these was the visit of the statue of Our Lady of Fatima in March. The greater part of one day saw Our Lady present in a special way, first in the hospital and afterwards in the shrine. From mission stations all around, the faithful and non-Christians alike assembled to venerate the statue and to receive Our Lady's favors.

Progress in the hospital was very significant. Nursing examinations were taken in Patna by the male nurse, Michael Gaetano, and by the first nursing aide at Nazareth Hospital, Celine Minj. Official recognition of the nursing school was received in March with the condition that more hospital space and nurses' quarters would be provided. This recommendation made it necessary to plan and provide funds for immediate building.

The hospital suffered a severe loss in the departure for the USA of Dr. Lazaro in early July. He had received an appointment as a resident surgeon at St. Joseph Infirmary in Louisville, Kentucky. His place was taken by Dr. D'Silva. Through the goodness of Sister Elise, ever faithful friend of Nazareth Hospital, Dr. D'Silva stayed under her guidance at Holy Family Hospital in Patna in order to improve himself in surgery, while Holy Family generously loaned Dr. Gernon to Nazareth Hospital. Two other doctors—Sister Elise and Sister Marcella—continued to come periodically to Mokama to assist in the operating room and to give of their medical skill. It was with regret that the Sisters learned that Sister Elise was to be transferred to Rawalpindi as soon as her visa could be obtained. Nazareth Hospital was to lose two precious and faithful friends, as Sister Marcella also left later in the year to pursue higher studies in the United States.

In Nazareth Hospital a few more events of note occurred toward the end of the year. The first formal capping ceremony took place on 5 November. It was a simple but beautiful function that gave the feeling that the nursing school was on a solid foundation. The establishment in the nursing school of the Sodality of Our Lady took place on 16 November. Officers were elected, and Michael Gaetano became the prefect. The moving spirit behind the sodality was Sister Florence Joseph.

The new building, which had been completed in record-breaking time, was blessed on 18 November. Two great benefactors who had helped to make this possible were Mr. Havralant and Mr. Gillard (father of Babs Lazaro), who had been transferred to the railway division in Mokama. Both of these men made all-out efforts to get supplies, equipment, permits, and many other things necessary for building—manifesting a skill that was entirely new to the Sisters.

A great step forward in the catechetical ministry was the launching by Sisters Crescentia and Ann Roberta of regular classes in catechism for the women. Although the women were baptized and attended Mass, they could not be taught by men, so their knowledge had been woefully neglected. In the regular classes provided by the Sisters their understanding and appreciation of the great mysteries of faith opened up new vistas in their otherwise bleak lives. Seraphina, the young girl who worked in the hospital, gave valuable assistance by discussing the Sisters' teaching in a way that was simple enough for the students' comprehension.

Two encounters with the forces of nature in 1950 brought the Sisters close to peril. First, the year was one of terrible landslides in the hill areas because of excessive rains. Torrents of water rushing downhill threatened to engulf Nazareth Cottage in Darjeeling, but the Jesuit scholastics dug deep trenches and rechannelled the water, thus saving all from harm. Landslides cut off most of the motor road between Darjeeling and Kurseong, a distance of nearly twenty miles, making it necessary for

Sisters Lawrencetta and Crescentia, the last SCNs to leave, to make the descent almost entirely by foot, creeping over the broken roads, even climbing up and down ridges where the road was broken, before reaching Kurseong, where the journey could be continued "on wheels."

The second encounter occurred on 15 August, India's Independence Day and the feast of Our Lady's Assumption, when the hospital experienced its first earthquake. Panic seized upon those who felt the tremors, but no harm or damage was reported. Assam in northeastern India suffered extensive damage and some loss of life.

An outstanding event of 1950 was the arrival of three new American recruits for the mission: Sister Ann Bernadette Ormond, a native of Hyde Park, MA, teacher at Holy Name School, Louisville, Kentucky; Sister Mary Jude Howard, a native of Whitesville, Kentucky, nurse, pediatrics department, Georgetown University Hospital, Washington, D.C.; and Sister Ellen Maria Ballew, a native of Lowell, Massachusetts, teacher at Martin's Ferry, Ohio.

These Sisters were eagerly awaited, and after an interesting sea voyage that took them to England, then France, including Lourdes, they were received with great joy at Mokama on 27 November, having been met by Sister Charles Miriam, who escorted them from their port of arrival. Sister Mary Jude, an experienced nurse, was soon absorbed in the work of the hospital.

Meanwhile, new areas of service were opening up. Loreto Convent School at Gaya was a fully established institution. The Loreto Sisters, however, were under pressure to relieve their other schools that were understaffed, and they had petitioned the bishop to allow them to withdraw from Gaya. After several sessions were held with the Sisters on both sides, a request was made to the SCN Council to accept this school and thus to become involved in the work of formal education. Permission was granted, and by the end of the year 1950, after some preliminary visits to Gaya to learn directly from the Loreto Sisters something of the school and its administration, the first group went forth, arriving in Gaya on 28 December as permanent residents. The band consisted of Sister Charles Miriam, principal, Sister Ellen Maria, and Sister Ann Roberta. Sister Ann Bernadette also came to take charge of the parish school, Creane Memorial School. Thus the first branch house was established.

Father Batson, the great missionary of Mokama, who had been nearly two years in America because of illness, returned in early November, much to the joy of all. He was greatly impressed by the growth of the hospital and the mission. Unfortunately, the joy at his return was short-lived as he was transferred in December to Barh, which, though it was not far distant, removed him from Mokama.

As routine was established, the hospital and convent followed somewhat regular procedures and schedules. Several changes of doctors took place during 1951.

Dr. D'Silva received an appointment in the United States and was replaced by Dr. C.P.I. Smith. Dr. Schuler and the Swiss Holy Cross Sister, Dr. Hermenigild, spent some months at the hospital for experience. In August the first phone call jangled its raucous note within the hospital walls.

1952-1953

By the end of 1951, the normal census of the hospital had reached almost 100. In every way progress continued. On 31 July 1952, oxygen was used for the first time to the great relief of the patients. The Sisters continued to make their annual trek to Darjeeling for retreat and rejuvenation—always in turns, as the hospital could no longer be closed.

In August, Sister Crescentia, ever fired with initiative and enthusiasm, was able to obtain from the USIS both a movie projector and a slide projector, great educational aids for the nursing school. The treatment of lepers was also a product of her zeal and vision. The newly opened leper clinic received its first patient, the humble beginning of what was to become a most effective leper clinic, treating thousands of patients at regular two-week intervals.

In catechetical ministry, a program was begun in early September for the preparation of children for First Holy Communion. Eight little girls boarded at Nazareth Hospital and were taught by Sisters Lawrencetta and Crescentia, aided by some of the nurses. Seven of them persevered and received Holy Communion for the first time on 28 September.

The third group of SCN recruits, the first to travel by air, was welcomed enthusiastically in Mokama on 5 December 1952. These SCNs were Catherine Regina Rogers, Eugenia Muething, and Patricia Mary Kelley, all native Kentuckians. Sisters Catherine Regina was destined to remain for her ministry at Nazareth Hospital, while Sisters Eugenia and Patricia Mary were assigned to the teaching staff of Nazareth Academy, Gaya.

During the formative years of the hospital the Sisters involved in nursing went to Holy Family Hospital in Patna for necessary courses in midwifery. Although it was difficult for the hospital to have staff members and nursing school teachers out for midwifery, it was a *must* in their mission profession and was amply rewarded in the end.

Sister Crescentia began laying the ground for the inauguration of another courageous enterprise. Having attended a pharmaceutical society meeting in Kanpur in late December 1952, she took an active part in a similar meeting in February 1953 held in Patna. There she and Sister Jane Frances of the Medical Mission Sisters were appointed council members. These preliminaries were to flower in the opening of the school of pharmacy at Nazareth Hospital on 17 January 1954. The director was Sister Crescentia, the first graduate pharmacist of the SCNs in the United States.

Early in the year Sisters Crescentia and Florence Joseph attended a meeting in Patna held to organize a Bihar branch of the Trained Nurses Association of India (TNAI). In subsequent years Nazareth Hospital always took a very active part in all these associations and did much to promote their work.

The leper clinic got well under way during these early years. From a count of 200, the census soon went up by November 1953 to 625 patients seen in one day. A new building, very simple but utilitarian, was blessed in May 1955. Donations came both in money and in medicine. Father Patrick, superior of the T.O.R. Fathers of the Bhagalpur mission, assured a steady supply of medicine. Lepers travelled free on the trains for the simple reason that ticket collectors did not wish to handle the tickets of lepers. Ironically enough, other contagious diseases, such as cholera, smallpox, dysentery, and a few more, are far more contagious, with leprosy being one of the least contagious.

Other items of interest in 1953 should be included here. Nazareth Hospital received a recurring grant for the training of midwives' assistants from the Bihar branch of the Victoria Memorial Scholarships. More nurses prepared for examinations, and the success percentage was quite good. Ceremonies were held in the hospital for five graduates. To continue cooperation in all departments and organizations, Sisters Crescentia and Florence Joseph attended the Catholic Hospital Association (CHA) convention in Nagpur. Ground was broken for a new wing in late November. Once more there was a change in staff doctors; Dr. Smith resigned from his post and was succeeded by a husband-and-wife team, Drs. Orlando and Philomena D'Cunha.

An interesting natural phenomenon occurred, one in which it might be said that the supernatural vanquished the natural. The following quotation is from the Nazareth Hospital annals of 29 June 1953:

An immense swarm of locusts appeared over Mokama this morning about 5:30 a.m. At 9:00 a.m. it was still on its way. If the insects had alighted, there would have been not a blade of green untouched. Sister Lawrencetta took the holy water and sprinkled it about the compound. Then, waving the scapular in all directions, she invoked Our Lady's aid and she saved us, for the deadly army went on its way from Mokama without causing any damage.

Earlier in the year there had been a mild earthquake that caused no notable damage. Another very shattering phenomenon was the birth of a baby with two heads, delivered in the hospital with the assistance of Sister Ann Cornelius. Mercifully, the child did not live.

1954-1959

The fifties were years of great progress in the hospital. Its development was rapid and solid. The nursing school, the school of pharmacy, and midwifery training all received approval of the State of Bihar, and the trainees passed regular state examinations. In these they gave very creditable performances and achieved a good percentile standing in results. Sister Mary Jude passed the midwifery examinations with the highest standing in the State of Bihar.

Many achievements marked this decade. A new wing of the hospital was blessed on 19 July 1955. In the same year rural electricity finally reached Mokama. Then in January 1957, after the staff had experienced years of struggle and hard work, running water became a blessed reality at the hospital. At the close of the decade a new drying room annex was blessed by Father De Genova. At first this room had to be used for cholera patients as they were overcrowding the hospital.

Frequent changes of medical personnel occurred, but the fifties saw the arrival of three important members of the medical staff whose imprint would be long lasting. First and foremost was Dr. D. D'Cruze, who joined the staff in 1954 and soon rose to the position of chief medical officer. His name is synonymous with Nazareth Hospital. The thousands of patients he treated remember him with respect and high regard. Ever faithful to his profession, he maintained, through his skill and dedication, the high standards of the hospital.

In 1958 Dr. Maeve Kenney, an English surgeon, began commuting to Nazareth Hospital from Holy Family Hospital in Patna. She later served the hospital zealously as full-time staff member during two different periods, beginning in the late fifties.

A red-letter day dawned on 24 April 1959 when the only qualified surgeon in the SCN community, Sister Mary Martha Wiss, arrived in Mokama. Unfortunately, Sister Mary Martha's tenure as chief surgeon at Nazareth Hospital was destined to be brief, but her achievements during those years were staggering.

The hospital Sisters, notably Sisters Crescentia, Florence Joseph, and Mary Jude, continued to participate actively in the TNAI and the CHA. Sister Crescentia held offices in the TNAI and went as an official Bihar delegate to a national convention in Delhi. Both Sisters Florence Joseph and Mary Jude served as state examiners for a number of board examinations for nurses. All such examinations, both written and oral, were controlled and administered by the government.

The leper clinic continued to flourish under the able direction of Sister Crescentia. In 1955 a report of a TV appearance of Bishop Fulton Sheen, in which he stated that his March of Dimes project would go to leper work in Patna, gave a good morale boost to Sister Crescentia and her colleagues. The records show that on a clinic day in March 1959 more than 1300 patients were treated.

Nazareth Hospital has often taken on the heavy burden of a cholera epidemic. Handling 200 or more cholera patients at one time is an exhausting labor, since each patient requires almost constant attendance for 24 to 48 hours. In one such epidemic, Sister Mary Jude and Sister Josephine, a nurse from Banares, fell victims to cholera when attending patients. In God's mercy, both recovered.

Important SCN affairs went on concurrently with those of the hospital during the foregoing decade. Sister Ann Cornelius had for a long time been attracted to the contemplative life and had finally decided to embrace it. When arrangements had been completed, it was with heavy hearts that the little band of which she was a pioneer bade farewell to this faithful member on 1 January 1954, as she left for Calcutta, accompanied by Sister Lawrencetta. There the Sisters attended a religious conference, and on 10 January Sister Ann Cornelius flew out to Dacca in East Pakistan to enter the monastery of the Franciscan Sisters of Perpetual Adoration. God, however, had designed otherwise. On 21 January, to the surprise and joy of all, Sister Ann Cornelius returned, happy to be back with her SCN community, and life went on at the mission as before.

In the general chapter of 1954, the community in India followed a unique procedure. A delegate was to be chosen by vote, but she would not attend the session. Her votes on the main issues would be submitted by mail. Voting for the delegate and her substitute took place at a joint meeting of the Mokama and Gaya communities on 11 March. Sister Lawrencetta was elected delegate and Sister Charles Miriam, substitute.

At the close of the Marian Year, 1954, the SCN community was represented at the Bombay Marian Congress by Sisters Crescentia and Florence Joseph. After attending a CHA (Catholic Hospital Association) meeting in Bangalore, they proceeded to Bombay for the functions of the Marian Congress before returning to Mokama.

A special event took place on 1 May 1955—the donning of the new headgear by the Sisters in India. This headgear consisted of a simple white veil fitted to a plain starched piece to keep the shape—a great improvement over the old "Dutch Cleanser" cap with its complicated tailoring and ironing.

In 1956 Sister Catherine Regina, after three years of hard, patient, conscientious work in the missions, decided to return to the United States. Quiet, unassuming, and thoroughly dedicated to her religious life, she was an inspiration to all. She left India at the end of January to the deep regret of the entire community. A little more than a year later a new American recruit came for the Mokama mission, in the person of Sister Veronica Maria Brownfield. A native of Louisville, Kentucky, Sister Veronica Maria was a fully qualified nurse and became an integral part of both the service and teaching departments of the hospital.

A significant change of leadership in the community took place in September 1956. Sister Florence Joseph was appointed superior of Nazareth Hospital, while Sister Lawrencetta was named mistress of novices. The novitiate officially opened on 2 February 1957. Though it was temporarily lodged on the same premises as the hospital, its development, along with the convent, would form a sort of tributary that would later become a full stream in the SCN Indian history.

1960-1969

Looking at the Nazareth Hospital history decade by decade, one becomes aware of extraordinary progress, cohesiveness, and continuity. As the sixties began, Sister Mary Martha was hard at work as chief surgeon. She had completed a year in India and had learned to adapt herself to the Indian milieu and to the peculiar necessities of surgery practice in India. She performed remarkable feats with the scalpel and gained an enviable reputation, not only in Mokama but also far and wide. Open heart massage, tracheotomies, lung and abdominal surgery, amputations, skin grafts, bone repair, and many rare and unusual procedures were part of the day's work for her. One of these operations, one of only eighty cases in medical history, was on a man who had a volvulus of the stomach. The man had an uneventful recovery. She also had the opportunity to serve several Jesuits of the India missions. Fathers Dan Rice, Roman Lewicki, and Robert Slattery all came under her skillful knife and praised her ministrations most heartily. Many of the Sisters were treated by Sister Mary Martha. One of her prize patients was Sister James Leo, whose left kidney had to be removed. This operation was performed in Mokama by Sister Mary Martha, assisted by Medical Missionary surgeon Sister Frederick, who had been a classmate of Sister Mary Martha at Georgetown University Medical College. Another SCN to profit from Sister Mary Martha's skill was Sister Ann Bernadette, who was successfully operated on in 1963.

In 1964 Sister Mary Martha decided to return to the United States. She had spent only five years in India, but in terms of work and service, it seemed double or triple that much. Her loss to Nazareth Hospital could never be estimated, and she has ever remained a faithful and generous supporter of the hospital and of the country she had served so well.

The newly professed Sisters of the first group of Indian SCNs, all of whom had some medical training, joined the hospital staff. They were: Sisters Anne Elizabeth Elampalathottyil, Anne Philip Kappalumakal, Rose Sebastian, Elizabeth Emmanuel Vattakunnel, and Thomas Aloysius Velloothara. The latter two went to Jamshedpur to stay for one year while studying X-ray technology at Tata Main Hospital.

When things are going well, troubles seem to come. The child of a well known Mokama figure died in the hospital. A court case of "manslaughter" was instituted against Sisters Florence Joseph, Mary Jude, and Mary Martha. The charges, all completely false, were neglect leading to death, refusal to give up the body, and attempting to bury the body in the cemetery. After a year of litigation, 1961-62, the case was dismissed by the magistrate. Instead of the usual verdict "due to insufficient evidence," the dismissal was on the basis that "the charges are evidently false"—a clear definition that was much better for the name of the hospital.

In 1961 the mission suffered the loss of two great pioneers, Sisters Charles Miriam and Crescentia. Both were victims of progressive ill health. Sister Charles Miriam's story is largely connected with Gaya and is chronicled in its proper place. Sister Crescentia's departure was in October. She had instituted many of the notable projects of the mission, and despite debilitating infirmities and serious trouble with cataracts on both eyes, she had bravely carried on her work. Her loss to Mokama was incalculable.

A number of material facilities were added to the growing hospital during this decade. A new section, consisting of a second-story room above the carpenter's shop, provided a nursery for the orphaned babies. It was blessed by Father De Genova on 25 October 1961. On 1 February of the following year, the X-ray unit was inaugurated, a boon to any hospital. Sisters Elizabeth Emmanuel and Thomas Aloysius, trained in X-ray technology, demonstrated their efficiency and skill in the new department.

A special letter from Mother Lucille Russell received on 23 August 1963 granted permission to accept the offer of the German bishops for the building of a new hospital. Misereor, a fund-raising organization administered by the bishops of West Germany, would pay two-thirds of the cost, while the community would assume responsibility for the remaining one-third.

The cornerstone laying and blessing of an isolation unit had taken place on 4 May 1962. The completed structure was blessed on 6 January 1964, but it was not formally opened until 21 November 1964, when the pediatric and male patients were transferred to it. Brass memorial plaques were affixed to the walls of the isolation wing on the ground floor, honoring the donors who had contributed so much to make it possible: Misereor, (Rs 77,000); on the first floor, Mr. Phillipon (Rs 10,000); the second floor, Mr. Henry Miller (Rs 50,000). Other donations received during this decade were of tremendous importance, namely: a Gumco suction machine donated by Sister James Marian Curtsinger, Mt. Vernon, Ohio; a portable X-ray machine, donated by Saint Joseph Infirmary, Louisville, Kentucky; a Westinghouse refrigerator and later two large gas stoves, both gifts of Mattie Collins, Sister Crescentia's sister; and a new tube well for the Isolation Unit donated by Mr. Havralant, manager of the Bata Shoe Company. One cannot praise enough the untiring efforts of Mr. Havralant to help the hospital in all its needs and difficulties.

In addition, two new air conditioners were donated by Dr. Mary Wiss (the former Sister Mary Martha, who had left the community in 1965). The arrival of these in the month of June when the temperature stood at 114° Fahrenheit was like a gift direct from heaven. The old air conditioner was installed in the X-ray room.

An extraordinary gift, a T.B. ward with sufficient accommodation for twelve female and twelve male patients, was planned and financed by Dr. Joachim Reuss, radiologist, whose service is recorded among the accounts of the medical staff. It was named "Margaret Ward" in honor of Dr. Reuss's mother.

Three persons especially must be mentioned with gratitude and praise in connection with benefactions. Mattie Collins, who, throughout all the years of the India mission up to the time of her death, was an ardent and zealous worker, sponsoring and carrying out innumerable projects for the mission and its work. Sister Mary Martha's father, Mr. John Wiss, who had died of a heart attack in early 1965, had become an active member of the mission through Sister Mary Martha's work in Mokama. He had worked unceasingly and had spared neither time, money, nor labor in promoting the welfare of the hospital and the mission. Virginia Veeneman, Sister Lawrencetta's sister, has during all the years of the India mission been a faithful benefactor. In addition to her other sources of financial aid, she held an annual bridge party that netted a large contribution for India. These three benefactors deserve the undying admiration, gratitude, and prayers of the missionaries.

Significant changes and additions in personnel took place during the decade of the sixties. An appointment that had far-reaching effects was that of Sister Mary Jude as superior and administrator of Nazareth Hospital on 15 August 1962. Having already served with extraordinary dedication and efficiency during the twelve years of her life in India, she was destined to spend the next fifteen years as head of the same institution. It would not be possible to list or to estimate the work and influence of Sister Mary Jude during her tenure of office. Her name was synonymous with all that was good and worthwhile in the services rendered by the hospital. After stepping down from office in 1977 she remained actively engaged in the hospital, accepting and carrying out every task and assignment—nursing, teaching, clerical work—and, above all, manifesting interest in and concern for the poor, the needy, and the suffering. Until her death in January 1992 she continued to reside at Nazareth Hospital in "working retirement."

Dr. Joachim Reuss, a radiologist and native of Germany, began a two-year contract in 1963, his services to be shared between Nazareth Hospital and Holy Family Hospital in Patna. His interest in Nazareth Hospital led him eventually to serve there on a full-time basis. In addition to his skilled services, he contributed most generous material gifts: the T.B. ward, as already noted, was one of his many benefactions. He will also be remembered as a talented pianist.

SCN involvement in the hospital continued to grow. New American recruits in 1962 were Sister Marita Ann Nabholz, a fully qualified nurse, and Sister Mary Celeste Collins, who would be assigned to the educational field. In the same year Sister Marita Ann inaugurated a public health program that was the beginning of the hospital work in that ministry. The SCN community made another major step in

1965 when Sisters Anne Elizabeth Elampalathottyil and Ancilla Kozhipat were admitted to St. John's Medical College, Bangalore.

Sister Paul Therese Bohnert joined the teaching staff of Nazareth Hospital after her arrival from the United States in November 1966. She was one of very few in India holding the degree of M.Sc. in Nursing. Unfortunately for the hospital, both she and Sister Veronica Maria returned to the USA in 1969, a great loss. Sister Veronica Maria had been a tremendous worker for twelve years, despite frequent spells of illness, and had never spared herself in serving the hospital to her maximum capacity.

The position of chief surgeon had been difficult to fill. After the departure of Sister Mary Martha, the post was taken by Dr. Charles Cyrill, a competent surgeon and a native of Bettiah. However, in 1968 Dr. Cyrill departed for the United States for higher studies and, eventually, residence. Finally with the arrival of Dr. B.K. Setty, an English-trained F.R.C.S., the post acquired some permanence. He was accompanied by his wife, an Irish-Catholic trained nurse, and their two children, Sheila and Roy. A third child, Tara, was born after their coming to Mokama. Mrs. Setty also took her place on the teaching staff. Dr. Setty, a competent surgeon, was a native of Mysore. With the exception of a year's residence in Bangalore, Dr. Setty had been on the staff of Nazareth Hospital staff as chief surgeon since 1968. His services to the hospital and the reputation he had built, not only for himself as a surgeon but also for the hospital in general, can never be calculated. His innumerable patients looked upon him with awe and respect and with a deep sense of gratitude for the care they received from him. The integrity and firm principles that he brought to his profession made him an outstanding doctor and a true inspiration to those who worked under him.

Nazareth Hospital has been involved in a number of clinics. Since 21-22 January 1967 a regular feature has been the annual free eye clinics, which have been a great boon to poor people suffering from serious eye complications, especially cataracts. A team of eye specialists gives voluntary service for examination and operations; the hospital provides all necessary facilities, including nursing personnel; and volunteer services are given by the Rotary Club, Bata Company, local business men, and others. These agencies provide medicine, surgical supplies, food, mattresses, blankets, etc. for the lodging of the patients. The volunteers also attend to the needs of the patients day and night.

A new extension in hospital work began on 27 August 1963 when the first medical team, headed by Sister Florence Joseph, went to Jha-Jha and Mariampahari to conduct clinics. These mission stations, conducted by Father Rice, received free medical supplies from the Medical Mission Board in New York with the condition that the services of such teams would be available on a monthly basis.

So it was that Nazareth Hospital sponsored and staffed several clinics in outlying missions: Mariampahari in the Santal Parganas, Sheikpura, and Barbigha. The team, consisting of a doctor, a public health nurse, a Sister whenever possible, and some attending nurses, travelled by jeep to the station, taking with them necessary supplies and moveable equipment. The patients at the stations were organized and registered by mission personnel. They were then examined by the doctor or attended by the nurses. Treatment was given, and medicines were prescribed and supplied where available. When necessary, cases were referred to the hospital. Patients were seen throughout the day, and often the team was able to return late at night. Regular visits were made every two weeks. Much good work was thus accomplished, especially for the sick poor.

Another service of the public health program was the care of pregnant women who were too poor to go to any hospital. The jeep/ambulance brought the women to the hospital for prenatal check-ups. Medicines and treatment were given and powdered milk was distributed through the donations of the Catholic Charities.

The chronicles of the sixties would not be complete without an account of the great famine of 1967. Late in 1966, the specter of starvation stalked the land of India as it had many times in the past. All Catholic institutions rallied to the cause and began to mobilize their forces to see what measures could be taken to alleviate the suffering. Across the land Christians stood in the forefront of relief programs. Two wagon loads of flour were delivered to Mokama, sent by Bishop Wildermuth to be distributed to the famine-stricken people under an organized program. Help in the way of supplies and volunteer services poured into the affected areas, both from domestic and foreign sources. Nazareth Hospital also met the medical needs of the poor both at Mokama and at Gaya, where medical teams accompanied those who were distributing food supplies.

As previously stated, nature often provides anecdotes of interest. In 1963, on 16 August, an event of note was the birth of triplets in the hospital—two girls and a boy. These little ones survived, thanks to the incubators available at the hospital. The biblical quotation, "One shall be taken and the other left," is illustrated in the following incident. A bolt of lightning from the blue struck the companion of Kailesh, a watchman of the novitiate, when the two men were sitting together in a field near the shrine. The companion was killed instantly, and Kailesh was admitted to the hospital in a state of severe shock. Fortunately, he recovered. Another servant, Canisius, was bitten by a krait, one of the most venomous snakes. Timely action saved his life.

In the realm of the unusual and also dangerous, God's watchful care and preventing hand often appear. On the way to Darjeeling in 1968, Father Martinsek, chaplain at Nazareth Hospital, Sisters Mary Jude, Thomasine, and Elizabeth

Emmanuel, as well as their driver Jahri Mistri, were involved in a serious jeep accident, but God preserved the lives of all, and no serious injuries were incurred.

On the light side of life, it had become a tradition to have a costumed Mardi Gras party at Gaya to which representatives from Mokama always went. Mokama, keeping up with its "city cousins," as the Gayaites were called, staged its first Mardi Gras party in February 1962. From Gaya for the inaugural carnival came Sisters James Leo and Ann Bernadette.

This history would not be complete without a tribute to Mr. Leslie Martin, who was well known in Mokama. In 1965 this builder of the shrine to Our Lady of Grace at Mokama was laid to rest, as he had long requested, at the back of the shrine, in the Catholic cemetery. After his death in Calcutta in May 1965, he had been temporarily interred there. However, his nephew in England, Mr. Alexander Martin, made the necessary arrangements for the transfer of his body to Mokama. Accompanied by his wife, Mr. Martin arrived in Mokama on 20 July for the final interment of his uncle. A Solemn High Mass was celebrated by Bishop Wildermuth, attended by Mr. and Mrs. Martin and a large number of Sisters, lay people, and priests. Two years later, another nephew of Mr. Martin, Thomas Aquin Martin, and his wife, Jacqueline, came out from London to settle the estate of Mr. Leslie Martin. They visited Mokama and the final resting place of this great benefactor of the Patna missions.

Before the history of Nazareth Hospital in the sixties is closed, special mention of the nursing school should be made. Ever since its inception, the nursing program has put a high priority on the religious and moral training of the nurses. Daily prayers, Mass, the frequent reception of the Sacraments, the Sodality of Our Lady, holy hour, retreats, and the regular attendance of a chaplain, as well as instruction by priests and Sisters in the fundamentals of religion have always been part of the nurses' training. Many chaplains and spiritual directors deserve mention, but outstanding among them is Father George Ziebert, S.J., who has been engaged in ministry for nurses through most of the years of his priestly life.

1970-1979

Although the years from 1970 to 1979 were indeed important as Nazareth Hospital gained maturity, the events seemed to be less spectacular. Personnel changes and development during this decade, however, were notable. Sister Mary Frances (the former Sister Florence Joseph), after twenty-three years of service at Nazareth Hospital and a tremendous program of successful building, organizing and teaching, left Mokama for a new mission, Bakhtiarpur, where she would head the dispensary and hospital just erected there. She became once again a pioneer. Much of the history of the beginning and development of Nazareth Hospital was the result of her guidance. Her companions in the new mission were Sisters Joel Urumpil and Lucia Thuluvanickal. The mission formally opened on 11 February 1971.

During the same year Sisters Anne Elizabeth and Ancilla both passed the M.B.B.S. examinations at St. John's Medical College, Bangalore. Sister Ancilla joined Nazareth Hospital medical staff in March. Sister Anne Elizabeth, having passed her final examinations, returned to Mokama also, but spent two months (July and August) ministering to the medical needs of the Bangladesh refugees. Sister Mary Scaria Menonparampil, having completed the M.Sc. degree at Magadh University, Gaya, joined the teaching staff of the nursing school.

At the time of her last home leave, Sister Veronica Maria had remained in the United States. After a lapse of three years, she returned to Nazareth Hospital in 1972 to once again give her valuable service for three months.

Dr. Maeve Kenney, specialist in gynecology and obstetrics, returned to the staff of Nazareth Hospital in November 1973 after an absence of several years in Australia. Sister Mary Joseph Pamplaniel, one of the earlier professed Sisters and a graduate nurse of Nazareth School of Nursing, went to the United States toward the end of 1973 for a year to study anesthesia.

A great loss was sustained by Nazareth Hospital in 1973 with the departure of Sister Ann Cornelius for the United States. She left the SCN congregation in order to join the new community called Sisters of St. Joseph the Worker, founded by her sister, the former SCN mission procurator, Sister Ellen Curran. Sister Ann Cornelius had been one of the pioneers of the SCN mission to India in 1947. During all the intervening years she had served as a senior nurse and instructor at Nazareth Hospital. She excelled in her profession, and the training she imparted to the student nurses prepared them for competence in their field, especially in operating room technique, for which she became noted. The India mission will be ever grateful for her contribution to its success.

Both Sisters Anne Elizabeth and Ancilla spent time in medical studies abroad. Sister Anne Elizabeth for a half year in 1976 resided at a London hospital to study gynecology. Later, in 1979 Sister Ancilla left for study in the United States.

An important change in personnel took place in October 1977 when Sister Mary Jude stepped down from her office as administrator of Nazareth Hospital. As noted earlier, she had managed the affairs of the hospital with competence and skill, at the same time bringing to her office an understanding and a sympathy toward patients, staff, students, and servants that gave that human touch to all that she did. The debt to her cannot be measured. Sister Mary Jude was succeeded in office by Sister Celine Arackathottam, one of Nazareth Hospital's own nurse graduates and a fully trained administrator. One more SCN doctor, Sister Vinita Kumplankal, having finished her medical degree at St. John's Medical College, Bangalore, in 1979, came to Nazareth Hospital to do her internship.

December 1972 marked the silver jubilee of Nazareth Hospital—twenty-five years of joys and sorrows, of struggles, successes and failures all spent for the honor and glory of God and for the spiritual, moral, and physical uplift of India. As the pioneers and the early members of the India mission looked back to the Nazareth Hospital of 1947 and 1948, they could see the pageant unfolding—the small building growing bigger and gaining offshoots, the coming of electricity and running water, the growth of staff through the nursing school, the development of SCN medical staff. So much could be remembered in retrospect, so much could be envisioned for the future. The silver jubilee was indeed a time of rejoicing.

Development continued in the seventies on a large scale with the planning and commencement of the construction of the new hospital. By 1975 all agreements had been reached with Misereor of Germany. This organization would grant Rs 12,000,000, and the hospital would be required to contribute Rs 680,000 for the work. The contract for construction was finalized with Dalmia Construction Company, and on 12 February 1976 the cornerstone for the new Nazareth Hospital was laid by the provincial, Sister Teresa Rose Nabholz, formerly known as Sister Marita Ann.

A point of great progress was the permission for internship for doctors at Nazareth Hospital. The hospital was designated as a center for both written and practical examinations for the nursing school candidates. This arrangement relieved them of the trouble of going to Patna or elsewhere to sit for examinations and of finding suitable lodging during the required days. This permission also indicated the confidence placed in the nursing school authorities, who had to assume the responsibility for honesty and integrity in the administration of the examinations.

Mokama and its environs has long been known for its criminal activity. The 1970s saw the beginning of a long series of incidents that involved the hospital either directly or indirectly and that continue to harass and endanger the lives of Nazareth Hospital residents and patients.

A major robbery occurred on 1 September 1970 when the safe was stolen from Sister Mary Jude's office. The entrance was made through the bars of the window on the back side of the building. Losses included about Rs 11,000 in cash, the pay cards of the doctors and some of the graduate nurses, and a few important letters. The safe was recovered about twenty days later in a well, along with a small amount of money and some of the cards and letters.

In November, bandits attacked the personnel manager, Baptist Master, at his house. He and his son Anthony drove them off, but not without suffering shock and some minor injury. A few days later some criminals sent a letter threatening Sister Rose Kochithara's life. She left Mokama for some time and stayed in Delhi.

The Sisters have often been the unwilling witnesses of train robberies, beginning with the pioneer band in 1947, who were robbed in their first cross-country ride from Bombay to Calcutta. One of these episodes took place as Sister Mary Jude and an office secretary, Francesca Washington, were returning on a train from Delhi. But their guardian angels were busy: all their companions lost luggage and valuables, but nothing of theirs was taken.

The tragic culmination of this decade of criminal activity took place on 20 February 1979 when Father Martinsek, well loved chaplain of Nazareth Hospital and Convent, was attacked by armed miscreants when they came to the priests' house early in the evening, apparently with the intention of robbing. Father Martinsek, who bravely resisted them, received serious gunshot wounds and died in Nazareth Hospital on 24 February. His death was especially poignant for Dr. Setty, who had labored for long grueling hours in the operating room in a vain attempt to save his life. His funeral on 25 February was concelebrated by three bishops, fifty-three priests, and nearly 2000 lay people. Condolence and protest meetings were organized by various groups to mourn the death of Father Martinsek and to empha-size the sad lack of law and order that makes such criminal behavior possible.

Nazareth Hospital has always been ready to come forward with relief measures in time of disaster. One such incident occurred at the time of the conflict between Pakistan and the newly created Bangladesh, in which India was actively involved. Thousands of refugees had crossed from Bangladesh into India. They were in dire need of medical help, food, clothing, and shelter. Once again the Christian commu-nity moved to minister to the needs of the sufferers. Nazareth Hospital sent nurses and other personnel along with much needed supplies. As mentioned earlier, Sister Anne Elizabeth was among those who volunteered for two-months' service with these refugees.

A huge flood in August 1975 affected many of the Catholic institutions—Kurji Holy Family Hospital, Loyola School, Xavier Teacher Training Institute, Patna Women's College, and Notre Dame Academy. Mokama also saw much flood water. The Nazareth Hospital public health team, along with many of the hospital person-nel, worked long hours giving inoculations against typhoid, cholera, and small pox. At least 55,000 persons were inoculated against cholera in twenty-four days. The hospital also distributed food which had been prepared in the hospital kitchen. Daily the kitchen personnel cooked food for about 5000 people. This work done in coop-eration with the local authorities was really tremendous.

Although the 1975 flood posed problems, it was as nothing compared to the flood that Mokama suffered in 1976. Incessant rain beginning on 18 September turned the area around the hospital into a veritable lake. Water continued to rise inexorably, and as it did the problems increased. The ground floor in the old build-ing, the north wing, the T.B. ward, and eventually even the kitchen and storerooms had to be emptied. The collapsing of 350 yards of the back wall caused water to rush in with great force from the *tal* (low-lying meadow) area, making a quick evacuation imperative. People in outlying villages rushed to the hospital for refuge. The moving of furniture, medical supplies and equipment, as well as patients too sick to be dismissed, presented a major problem. The amount of work required was monumental. Staff, doctors, nurses, and employees worked round the clock. Volunteers came from the town, which had been less affected, and also from all the Catholic institutions nearby; from Patna, workers came bringing medical supplies and food. All patients who could be dismissed were sent away.

When the kitchen was no longer usable, an SOS had to be sent for food, and many merchants and friends, as well as people from far away, brought supplies in answer to the call for help. The storing of fowls, cows, and pigs was interesting. All were first brought to the kitchen, but it was necessary to move them again because of rising water. The cows eventually went to the municipal area; the chickens, upstairs on the top floor; and the pigs, on still another floor. After about four days the water gradually receded. Throughout the whole ordeal the courage, perseverance, and endurance of the entire hospital personnel were admirable. Because of the herculean efforts of all, the losses were remarkably small. It was a flood that will not soon be forgotten.

1980-1989

With the history of this decade, an attempt will be made to categorize events in order to have a more cohesive narrative. Personnel is, of course, a very important category. This decade was a time of many visitors from abroad, most of them Sisters. Some spent time as members of hospital personnel. In 1980 Sister Ann Kernen, who was destined for ministry in Nepal, spent some months working at Mokama. Sister Anna Marie Nalley came in the same year to take the midwifery course.

A loss to the staff in Mokama was the departure of Sister Ann Bernadette for the United States in November 1980, the thirtieth anniversary of her arrival in India. She had served in various capacities, beginning with the first group at Nazareth Academy, Gaya. She had been superior in both the Ranchi and Bangalore houses and had also spent several years in formation assignments. As a hospital visitor she had brought peace and consolation to the sick and suffering. In 1985 she made a "Golden Jubilee" visit to India to the great joy of all whom she had served so well. Her death on 28 October 1988 was a cause of mourning for the entire India mission, where she had been held in high esteem. Her name will ever be among the "greats" of the SCN missionaries.

Another pioneer of the India mission, Sister Mary Frances, left India for the United States on 28 June 1983 after thirty-six years of hard labor, most of which were spent at Mokama. As Sister Florence Joseph she had started with the original six and had contributed, through her skill and energy, to the development of the hospital and its resources. She had proven her talent in administration and building both in Mokama, where she had supervised the construction of the convent building, and again in the hospital and dispensary complex at Bakhtiarpur. Some of the important facilities of the hospital were initiated by her, notably the clinics that carried medical benefits to outlying mission stations. Her departure left a distinct void.

Sister Ancilla, who had gone to the United States for higher medical studies in 1979, returned to India in 1983. She rejoined the medical staff of Nazareth Hospital, fully equipped for her service after her stint abroad.

Two American SCNs gave valuable assistance to the administrative staff of Nazareth Hospital. The first, Sister Martha Discher, assistant administrator of St. Joseph Hospital, Lexington, Kentucky, visited India in 1984 and spent much of her time working with the Sisters in administration, sharing with them her valuable knowledge and expertise. In 1985-1986 Nazareth Hospital profited from the experience of another expert in hospital administration when Sister Philip Maria Fuhs came from the United States in October and remained for six months, studying the problems of the administration of Nazareth Hospital and offering solutions. Both of these administrators gave of themselves cheerfully and industriously, and the hospital was greatly indebted to them for their service. With Sister Philip Maria came Sister Josephine Barrieau, director of the SCN mission office, who visited Nazareth Hospital as well as the other missions.

Changes in administration are always important events. In April 1986 Sister Celine gave over the office of administrator to Sister Bridget Kappalumakal, who assumed the leadership on 1 May. Both Sisters Celine and Bridget, in addition to the usual problems that attend the day-to-day working of a large hospital, had to endure almost continual labor unrest, which began and grew considerably during this decade. They faced situations of harassment, threats, strikes, etc. with great courage and strength. Despite all the difficulties and anxieties, they maintained the hospital services and tried in every way to preserve normalcy in all the departments. Sister Bridget took an active part in civic affairs as a member of the railway consultative committee at Mokama and as the chair of the subcommittee of the Bihar Voluntary Health Association.

Three SCNs who had been long in service at Nazareth Hospital left for other fields of labor. In 1986 Sister Maria Palathingal went as a pioneer to a new mission, a remote hill place called Sangsay in the Darjeeling District of West Bengal. Sister Lata Thurackal, also a veteran worker at the hospital, took up studies for the B.SC. degree in nursing at Ahmedabad. Sister Mary Stella Ambrose, after eight years at Nazareth Hospital as staff nurse and supervisor, left also in 1986 to enter a new specialized field of labor—work with people with disabilities, especially blind people.

Two more veterans of the hospital left in June and July of 1988. The first, Sister Elizabeth Nadackal, had long been chief accountant of the hospital. Her work in that

32

department kept her fully occupied. It involved not only keeping accounts but also being required to submit all accounts to the exacting scrutiny of the auditor. Her efficiency and patience were outstanding in a profession where both virtues are hard to maintain. The second veteran to leave, Sister Mary Joseph, was one of the most competent nurses ever trained in Mokama. There was hardly any type of nursing in which she did not excel. After her training in the United States, she became the chief anaesthetist at Nazareth Hospital, a very important post in the operating theater. Both Sister Elizabeth and Sister Mary Joseph were a great loss to the hospital.

Another veteran was Sister Elizabeth Emmanuel Vattakunnel. She was in the first group of India SCNs, having made her vows in 1959. For most of the ensuing years she has been on the staff of Nazareth Hospital. As a licensed pharmacist when she made her vows, she spent a period of time studying X-ray technology at Jamshedpur. Following her licensing in that field, she returned to Nazareth Hospital, where she worked to full capacity as chief pharmacist, X-ray technician, and assistant in the dispensary and the outpatient department. Always conscientious and exacting in her work, she also trained many assistants. Of a quiet and retiring nature, she went about her work in such a way that her presence, except in her own department, was somewhat taken for granted. The hospital will ever remain indebted to her for her selfless service. The mandatory day of retirement came for Sister Elizabeth Emmanuel on 28 March 1989. It was marked by due ceremony and expressions of appreciation. But retirement was not to be for long, for she returned to service once more on a three-year contract—a continued blessing for Nazareth Hospital. (In India, one must retire at the age of 58, but after an interval of at least three months, the person may reapply for the position.)

Other Sisters of long-standing service in the community are the following: Sister Sunanda Urumpil, now deceased, who left the hospital staff in January 1988; Sister Teresa Kotturan in administration; Sister Bridget Vadakkeattam in community health; Sister Thomasine Kottoor, ward supervisor; Sister Lata Thurackal, nursing service director; Sister Mary John Nadackal, director of the nursing school; Sister Karuna Thottumarikal, operating room nurse; Sister Lucy Puthukkatt, operating room specialist; Sister Lucia Thuluvanickal, director of spiritual care; Sister Rose Kochithara, and Sister Benedicta (a Sacred Heart Sister), Sister visitors.

Sister Rose Kochithara deserves special mention as one of the most versatile sisters of the Indian community. Having joined as a fully qualified nurse, she practiced her chosen profession until ill health made a change of occupation advisable. Sister Rose acquired a degree in Business Administration in the United States and embarked upon a new career with equal efficiency both at Nazareth Hospital and subsequently at Nazareth Academy, Gaya. Nor did her versatility end there. When severe back and leg problems forced her to leave the academy, she spent much of her time of physical inactivity in making use of her artistic and literary talents to produce creditable works in the field of painting and literary composition in both prose and poetry. She also spent much time with the sick as a visitor and with all persons, young and old, who sought her advice and counsel. Her life, despite much physical infirmity, has been filled to overflowing with good deeds.

Another Sister of extraordinary versatility is Sister Xavier Valiakunnackal. In her days of candidacy in the late fifties, she entered Holy Family Hospital at Mandar to qualify as a laboratory technician. After she was professed, she obtained a B.A. Degree at Patna Women's College. Having been appointed to a post in Nazareth Hospital, she took leave to prepare herself as a certified dietitian and then assumed that post on the hospital staff. While in service she obtained, through summer courses, the degree of Sangeet Prabhakar (B. Music) in Hindustani Music (vocal). She also pursued studies on the Indian sitar. Subsequently she made use of her musical ability in the catechetical field in which she worked both in Mokama and, in more recent years, in her chosen field of retreat director and teacher of religion in far-flung areas of India, where she is in constant demand in both urban and rural parishes and missions.

Two veteran doctors of Nazareth Hospital, Dr. D'Cruze, chief medical officer, and Dr. Setty, chief surgeon, both retired in 1988, but were reappointed on a contract basis. By their competence, skill, and integrity both doctors have placed the medical services of the hospital on a very high standard. Their reputation for medical excellence did not stop at the hospital doors, but is extended throughout the Mokama area and much beyond, where former patients still sound their praises far and wide. During all the years when they might have attained eminent success and material gain, they have remained faithful in caring for the people of Mokama and the needs of Nazareth Hospital. Too much praise and gratitude cannot be given to these doctors who have given their all to the medical profession.

At this juncture it is fitting to give honorable mention to Mrs. Agnes D'Cruze and to Mrs. Setty, who loyally supported their husbands in their careers and did not ambitiously look to more comfortable or lucrative posts that would bring a higher status in life. Although Mrs. D'Cruze is not qualified in medicine, Mrs. Setty, a graduate nurse from Dublin, Ireland, has used her medical knowledge in the nursing school, where she has often held teaching posts. Both women should share in the laurels of their husbands.

Another person to be honored is Rosakutty C.V., who began her studies at Nazareth Nursing School in 1959 and has served Nazareth Hospital faithfully and devotedly as a senior nursing tutor for more than thirty years. Still another name that comes to the fore when personnel is mentioned is that of Mukhar Zaman. A young and energetic man, he has taken on a great burden of responsibility, that of director of personnel, with honesty, integrity, and patience. He has fully supported those in authority and has fearlessly tackled the many serious problems that inevitably obstruct the path of anyone appointed to such a position. The hospital has reason to be grateful for his loyal and efficient service.

A number of employees of Nazareth Hospital retired during this decade after long years of service. Baptist Master had first served on the teaching staff of the mission school and later became personnel manager at Nazareth Hospital. In the dual roles of teacher at the mission and personnel manager at the hospital, Baptist served at Mokama for almost forty years. In 1981 he retired from service and subsequently made his home with his son William in Begusarai, where he died in 1988.

In January of 1983 several employees were given a farewell party on the occasion of their retirement. One of the last of the long-serving employees was Jahri Mistri, who retired on 31 January 1987. Though a man of simple background, he became amazingly efficient in every way. Clothed in his characteristic *dhoti, kurta,* and turban, he was indeed a familiar figure. He could be entrusted with the most responsible duties. Several times he was the victim of criminal attacks but remained loyal and faithful. He was a valued member of the staff, and his memory will ever be held in high esteem at Nazareth Hospital.

A number of employees, many of them still on active duty, who have given outstanding service to the hospital are Seraphina and her husband Emmanuel, who between them can account for nearly ninety years of work; Stanislaus; John Baba; Joseph Chottey; Paul; Agnes Mirandi; Gabriel Ganauri; Savapati; Barotti Hansdak; Raphael Laldhari; and Rasidah Khatoon. Later in the decade two employees of long-standing service, Marykutty Andrews and Sara John, left the hospital service. They too had contributed much to the nursing and pharmacy departments.

When personnel is mentioned, certain deaths draw special attention. Two simple people held in high regard at Nazareth Hospital died in early 1985. Nepal, *chowkidhar* (nightwatchman) and one of the oldest employees of Nazareth Hospital, died of cancer. His body lay in state in front of the maintenance department, and a special prayer service was held for him. Miss Anna Joseph, who had been a patient at Nazareth Hospital for two years and had endeared herself to all at Mokama, died on March 8. Anna was homeless and lived at Nazareth Academy for about thirty years. A large delegation came from Gaya to attend her funeral.

The whole Patna mission suffered a great loss in 1987 with the death of its veteran architect and builder, Father Robert Stegman, S.J. Most of the buildings of the diocese and the missions built during the last twenty-five years had been planned and executed by him. Although plagued by ill health, he had worked tirelessly for the mission. The buildings in Mokama, except for the newest one, bore the stamp of his skill and long-range planning. The SCN community was greatly indebted to him.

During a severe flood in 1987, three of the five volunteers who lost their lives in a boat accident in Khagaria were connected with Mokama. Sister Sandhya Baxla was a Sister of Charity of Nazareth, Helen Enoch was a graduate of Nazareth School of Nursing, and Peter, a young college student, had been born in Nazareth Hospital. On 24 August 1987 in the convent chapel of Mokama, a memorial Mass was offered. When the victims' bodies were finally recovered on 29 August, the funeral service and burial were conducted by Bishop Osta in the presence of a large number of priests, Sisters, relatives, and friends who were present in Mokama to pay tribute to those true martyrs of charity.

Shree Ramon Roy, the former labor lawyer in Patna and long the principal lawyer for Nazareth Hospital, died of a heart attack in Calcutta on 8 September 1988. His death too was greatly mourned at Nazareth Hospital.

A number of developments in hospital service took place in this decade. The pharmacy and outpatient departments were made separate units under the direction of Sister Archana Valiaparambil and Sister Mary John Nadackal respectively. In 1986 Sister Bridget Vadakkeattam, head of the Community Health Centre, launched an impressive village health program that included the training of village health workers and the training of boys in basic health and social change. The community health team expanded this work in 1987 to include courses in tailoring and literacy in thirty-three villages.

Nazareth School of Nursing maintained its standards of excellence throughout its long history. Typical of its achievements were the results attained in the examinations of April 1986:

Midwifery—third in the State of Bihar;

General Nursing (final year)—first, second, and third in the state;

General Nursing (first year)—first and third in the state.

Pastoral care had been growing in importance as a branch of hospital service. By 1986 it was constituted as a regular department with Sister Lucia Thuluvanickal as director, assisted by Sister Rosemarie Lakra. Sister Mary Lynn Fields, visiting from the United States, joined this department for some months.

Other important projects of the time were a three-day workshop for paramedics on team building, conducted by Sister Mary Lynn; and evaluation of the nursing school and nursing service by Miss Manochari Sigamony of Nagpur, 21-25 April 1987.

Developments of a material nature were also notable in this decade of the eighties. Although not a part of the Nazareth Hospital complex, Martinsek Hall, directly connected with the catechetical center, was an important addition to the whole compound. It was opened on 5 December 1980. The first block of the new hospital building was handed over by the contractor on 14 April 1983. In 1984 came the outstanding event of the year—the blessing of the complete new hospital complex. Preparation for this event had begun at least a month before. With the cooperation of all departments and groups the work progressed, and when the BIG DAY, 20

May, finally came, all was in readiness, with lights, paper, flowers, and bunting making the whole building beautiful and festive.

At 6:30 a.m. Bishop Osta celebrated a Solemn High Mass. In mid morning the exhibition, depicting the history of Nazareth Hospital from 1948 to 1984, was formally opened by Bishop Wildermuth. The Central Reserve Police Band from Mokama Ghat arrived at 3:30 p.m. Promptly at 4 p.m. the governor of Bihar, Dr. A.K. Kidwai, was received at the main gate by Sister Celine, administrator, Sister Teresa Kotturan, assistant administrator, other staff, and local groups. The official party was led into the hospital to the stirring music provided by the CRP band.

The meeting got underway at 4:15 p.m. Sister Celine welcomed the governor and paid tribute to Misereor and the German bishops for their generous help in contributing to the building of the hospital. The chief guest, Governor Kidwai, praised the hospital for the great service rendered to suffering humanity. All the guests toured the hospital and viewed the exhibition. High tea was served, the guests departed, and the day ended with feelings of great joy and achievement. On 3 June, the moving day for the patients, the Central Reserve Police gave much valuable service.

In 1986 Nazareth Hospital continued its modernization with the installment of a much needed intercom system. In 1987 another valuable addition was the ECG machine, a gift of Father Rice. It was installed next to the laboratory. There were several other important changes or additions. New quarters for the staff nurses had been constructed and were blessed by the chaplain, Father Rice. In 1987 a new hospital chapel, made possible through donations gathered by Father Rice, was opened on 6 April. With that, the presence of Jesus the Healer became the center of the hospital. That same year the hospital Sisters set up in the old hospital building a new apartment consisting of community room, dining room, and kitchen. To express their appreciation for the hospital kitchen personnel's care in providing for their food for the past forty years, the Sisters invited them to lunch in the new quarters.

Annual eye camps were conducted at Nazareth Hospital. The Rotary Club and other benefactors of Mokama donated the services of the camp to a large number of poor people who required cataract and other operations. Devadas Bhadani, Niraj, and Rampiant Kattor were regular donors of food and eyeglasses for the patients. Police of the Central Reserve rendered services as stretcher bearers and helped in other capacities. The hospital provided all the requirements for the patients—rooms, bedding, nursing care, and treatment as needed. Dr. Rohatgi of Patna was the regular leader of the team, and with him were three or four assistant surgeons, all donating their labor and skill for the benefit of these poor people. All operating tables and other facilities, as well as the operating nurses and aides, continued to be provided by the hospital.

In the month of April 1988, a milestone was reached with the government, when Nazareth Hospital was granted permission to conduct the state nursing examinations in their own center at Mokama. There have also been significant developments in community health care programs with training courses and other projects, e.g., a health care outreach program that was being tried at Barauni.

By 1989 administration had once more passed into new hands. Sister Anupa Moozha, after studying administration in the United States, became the administrator of Nazareth Hospital, and Sister Vimala Karakkattu was appointed first assistant.

Two courses of importance were held in mid 1989: a seminar in medical ethics conducted by Father George Lobo, and a talk on indigenous medicine given by Brother Francis Thattaparampil, S.J. Both proved profitable and interesting. (Brother Francis's sister is an SCN graduate nurse, Sister Jyoti.)

The Mokama Rotary Club has taken an active interest in the work of Nazareth Hospital and has given valuable assistance. On the occasion of Nurses' Week in August 1989, the club offered a cup and a cash award to the best student nurse of the year and to the best staff nurse of the year. The club has also been ever ready to help in times of emergency.

The 1980s was a decade of trouble, worry, and anxiety for the hospital personnel—administrators, staff, students, and employees. The trouble could be listed under two headings: labor problems and criminal activity.

In July 1982 the rumblings of unrest among the employees began. This condition was to continue throughout the eighties and even up to the present. All during July and August there were constant harassment, threats, and disturbances by individuals and groups opposing the hospital. The Sisters, doctors, and others had to appear in court. Though occasionally there seemed to be a slight abatement, the fires of discontent were always smoldering and ready to flare up. An atmosphere of fear and uncertainty prevailed. Employees were often incited by outside agents to go on strike.

In 1986 a welfare committee was set up on behalf of the employees. Nevertheless, the troubles continued. Daniel Rosario, formerly employed as a driver, caused many problems. On 30 September 1987, the employees seriously defied the hospital authorities, taking up the cause of a young girl who had been dismissed because of unsatisfactory work. They also prevented her from going home. Led by the same former driver, they filed a case against the administrator, Sister Bridget Kappalumakal, stating that this young girl had been attacked and forced to resign. This event prompted some men to attack the Sisters on their way home from the railway station. The advocate, Rajendra Prasad, was called and the matter settled.

All through the ensuing months of October, November, and December, the tension with the employees continued. Threats, harassment, court cases, meetings, and letters of complaint became the order of the day. The Sisters suffered constantly because of the many false accusations and threats of strike.

By 1988 a grievance committee had been set up. This consisted of four members elected by the employees and four of the management. Harassment by members of the union continued. Meetings were held, strikes threatened, and demonstrations staged at the hospital gate as a protest, creating constant tension. During the month of May, the employees' union with outside forces, many of them prompted by Daniel Rosario, made threats and wrote intimidating letters to Sister Bridget and to staff officers Mr. M. Zaman and Jeevan Kishore. On 13 July a hearing on the case, filed by Daniel Rosario, was held in the office of the deputy labor commissioner. Sister Bridget and Mr. Zaman represented the hospital. Because Daniel Rosario had taken all his dues and had signed all his papers, the commissioner declared there was no room for the complaints and dismissed the case. Subsequently a number of meetings with the deputy labor commissioner took place in which the demands of the employees and other problems were discussed. A final conciliation meeting was attended by Sisters Anupa and Vimala, and Mr. Zaman representing the management and others representing the union. The final signing of an agreement was accomplished at this meeting on 10 May 1989.

In this decade criminal activity, for which Mokama is notorious, seemed to keep pace with labor problems. Some of it may have been interrelated. A former patient, who had been nursed back to life through the fine medical care he had received at the hospital, suddenly turned into a sworn enemy. On the evening of 18 February 1984, in front of the hospital, he shot at one of the laborers. By God's providence no one was injured.

In 1986 the hospital suffered more harassment when Jahri Mistri was attacked and beaten on his way to the bank and robbed of Rs 14,000. He was admitted to Nazareth Hospital with cuts and a broken shoulder bone. Police were notified and began an investigation under the deputy superintendent of police. Eventually four men involved in the attack surrendered and were lodged in the Barh jail.

An attack was made on hospital personnel on 29 June 1987. Six masked men stopped Damien Madassery and Shiv Kumar, the driver, as they returned from the bank at mid-day. The men beat them and snatched the bag of money they had. It contained only Rs 2500 and not the Rs 80,000 that had been reported to them.

One of the worst attacks by criminals took place on 5 May 1988. Certain victims of enmity between two groups were patients in the hospital. At about 9:30 p.m. two bombs were exploded at the main entrance outside the hospital gate, and two gunshots were fired. Six people, relatives of the patients, were injured, one of them seriously. There was panic and chaos everywhere. The police responded immediately and remained several days, patrolling on a twenty-four-hour basis.

Sister Mary Jude had several encounters with armed robbers on the train. Once she was traveling in the Dinapur-Howrah Express when a group of bandits entered the compartment in which she was riding and robbed the passengers. She escaped all harm, and when they snatched the chain from her neck, she asked to keep the crucifix. They allowed her to do so.

On another occasion Sisters Elizabeth Emmanuel and Karuna were attacked as they returned from the railway station to the hospital at 9 p.m. on 9 December 1989. Some men carrying pistols and knives snatched their handbags, watches, and chains. Later in the month, however, the culprits were caught and some of the stolen goods recovered.

It can be seen from the events herein recorded that the Sisters and staff have had to suffer much from the bad environment in which Mokama is situated. It is known nationally as a notorious haven for some of the worst criminals and their gangs, and until the problems are seriously tackled and eliminated, the hospital will never be free from trouble, fear, and anxiety.

On a lighter and more cheerful side, there were many important visitors to Mokama. A memorable day in June 1980 might well be called "Bishops' Day," for on that day four bishops visited Nazareth Hospital as they returned from the consecration of Bishop John Baptist Thakur, S.J., first bishop of the newly created diocese of Muzzaffarpur. The distinguished group was headed by Cardinal Picachy, S.J., of Calcutta, who offered Mass in the convent chapel and visited the hospital. He was accompanied by Bishop Leo Tigga and Bishop Francis Ekka. On the same day Bishop Telesphore Toppo of Dumka stopped by, accompanied by Father Sachuna, S.J.

In the same year Sister Ann Whittaker and Pat Mische came for a workshop on global education. Then Sister Alfreda Crantz, an SCN who had been working in Nepal, paid a visit on her return journey to the United States. Another very important visitor was Sister Dorothy MacDougall, superior general, who came in October 1981, accompanied by Sister Mary Joyce Kernen. Still another visitor was Mrs. Mary John (nee Mary Paul), who had distinguished herself as an outstanding nurse of Mokama. She came with her husband and child from New York where she resided. Her visit brought back many memories of earlier Mokama days.

Other American SCN visitors of 1988-1989 were Sisters Emily Nabholz (sister of Sister Teresa Rose) on her first visit to India in her new office of president and Sister Judy Raley, vice-president, both of whom were present for the general meeting of the Mokama Nazareth Hospital Society.

Also in 1989 the state minister for urban development, Shree Shyam Singh Dhiraj, came to Nazareth Hospital for the inauguration of a new health project. He praised the hospital for its excellent work and especially underlined the exceptional volunteer services in times of such calamities as floods, storms, famine, and other disasters.

On 23 August 1988 disaster struck in a large area of northern Bihar and up into Nepal. People at Nazareth Hospital, sleeping peacefully at 4:40 a.m., were terrified when they awoke to find their beds shaking, doors and windows rattling noisily, and an ominous rumbling, like the growling of a huge monster, causing panic and fear. It was the worst earthquake in this area since 1934. In places closer to the epicenter there occurred serious damage, injury, and even loss of life. Some patients with injuries were brought to Mokama for treatment.

An episode of 1989 that is of considerable interest is the strange case of Dr. Chandra Shekhar, who had joined the staff in mid 1989, presenting his certificates for medical qualification from Banares Hindu University, a highly reputable college of medicine. The first intimations of trouble came when a dispute arose between Dr. Shekhar and another staff doctor, Dr. Praveen, which had to be brought to the administration for settlement. A second irregularity was detected when Dr. Shekhar made illegal use of a medical service book for his wife. Less than a month later a second dispute arose between Dr. Shekhar and two junior doctors, Dr. Rajiva Ranjan and Dr. Praveen, in regard to professional, medical, and relational aspects, which once again had to be referred to the administration. Two days later Dr. Shekhar tendered his resignation, which was accepted.

Thereafter the affair took a dramatic turn, with Dr. Shekhar questioning the validity of the hospital's acceptance of his resignation. A lawyer in Patna was consulted. Meanwhile, Mr. Zaman and Sister Anjali Olickal were dispatched to BHU to verify the certification of Dr. Shekhar. They came back with the information that the certificates belonged to a different person and that Dr. Chandra Shekhar was obviously an impostor. This information led to the filing of a case and his arrest.

To complicate this matter, a woman claiming to be his mother appeared at the hospital and created much trouble by protesting his innocence. The case was carried on for over two months, with the fake doctor in and out of jail and his mother causing annoyance and additional difficulties. When it seemed certain that they had no hope of escape through appeal, the pair finally left the area.

December 1984 marked the twenty-fifth anniversary of the religious profession of the first India SCNs. Since all these Sisters were in the medical profession and for most of these years attached to Nazareth Hospital, the hospital joyfully celebrated. The honored silver jubilarians were Sisters Elizabeth Emmanuel, Anne Elizabeth, Bridget Kappalumakal, and Teresa Velloothara. The silver jubilee of Sister Thomasine in 1987 was also celebrated with much joy at the hospital where she has served long and faithfully.

The jubilee of the decade was that of Father Rice, the much loved and respected chaplain of the hospital, who on 30 November of the same year observed the completion of fifty golden years as a Jesuit. The hospital celebrated the occasion with much fanfare and joy. Father Rice had been connected with Nazareth Hospital since 1946, when he suggested to Bishop Sullivan, S.J., that he request the SCN community for the Mokama mission. It was suitable that he should be in Mokama for this golden jubilee.

This chapter of the narrative closes with the decade of the eighties, but it is certain that the history of Nazareth Hospital does not end there. By the year 1998 it will have completed fifty years of medical service. Its scope is not limited to the area in which it is located, but through the nursing school its humanitarian labors have been extended throughout India and even beyond its borders to foreign lands, where its nurses uphold the high standards of their profession.

Like "the mustard seed" and the "mighty oak" of the Gospel, the small one-wing hospital of 1948, without running water, without electricity, and with meager resources, has grown into the large, fully equipped hospital of today, a memorial to the Sisters of Charity, followers of Jesus Christ, the Divine Physician, who planted the seed so many years ago.

Graduate nurses at Nazareth Hospital, Mokama, 1994

NAZARETH NOVITIATE AND CONVENT

1957

Formation and Development of
the Indian Community

Novices and Novice Director Sister
Jane Karakunnel travel to a village in a
tum-tum.

Sisters set out for a mission by train.

Chapter Three

NAZARETH NOVITIATE AND CONVENT 1957

Formation and Development of the Indian Community

Until the latter part of the fifties, life in India, with the exception of Nazareth Academy in Gaya, had been almost entirely limited to Nazareth Hospital in Mokama. With the opening of the novitiate in 1957, a real milestone was reached, and a period of expansion began that has never stopped.

1957-1959

Slowly the ground had been prepared for the opening of the novitiate. The final stage just prior to the formal inauguration was the trip to South India (Kerala) by the newly appointed mistress of novices, Sister Lawrencetta, accompanied by Sister Eugenia, from 26 December 1956 to 13 January 1957. The return journey brought a number of nursing students and two candidates. These two, who later became Sisters Theresa Martin Thundyil and Anne Marie Thayilchirayil, remained as candidates for some time so that they could study English and Hindi.

The feast of the Purification of Our Lady, the second of February, was chosen for the solemn dedication of the novitiate of the Sisters of Charity of Nazareth in India. Bishop Wildermuth officiated at the ceremony. Others who were present were: Fathers Francis Martinsek, S.J., vicar general of Patna; Louis De Genova, S.J., pastor of Mokama; George Ziebert, S.J., assistant pastor of Mokama; Michael Adam, pastor of Sheikpura; Gregory Thekel, pastor of Barh; Sisters Lawrencetta, Florence Joseph, Mary Jude, Crescentia, Ann Cornelius, Charles Miriam, Eugenia, and Ann Roberta. Five postulants began their novitiate: Annama Abraham Elampalattyil, Bridget Philip Kappalumakal, Mariakutty Sebastian, Theresiamma Thomas Velloothara, and Marykutty Emmanuel Vattakunnel. All were from South India and were engaged in either nursing or pharmacy work. The opening of the novitiate marked a new phase in the development of the community in India. Mary Zachariah (later Sister Xavier) had come in the group escorted by Sister Lawrencetta in January, but joined the candidature months later. In September she went to Holy Family Hospital, Mandar, to take a course in medical technology.

A very big day came on 7 December when the first postulants received the habit at a Solemn High Mass celebrated by the vicar general, Father Martinsek. The new Sisters were: Anne Elizabeth Elampalattyil, Anne Philip Kappalumakal, Rose Sebastian Sebastian, Thomas Aloysius Velloothara, and Elizabeth Emmanuel Vattakunnel. Sisters Charles Miriam and Ann Roberta came from Gaya for the occasion.

Five new postulants were admitted on 6 January 1958, the feast of the Epiphany: Anna Joseph Thayilchirayil, Annama George Mukalel, Aleykutty Kuriakose, Lilly Rita Thundyil, and Rose Augustine Kochithara, who was a staff nurse at Nazareth Hospital. These postulants received the habit and their new names on 8 December: Sisters Ignatius Marie Thayilchirayil, Ann George Mukalel, Aloysia Mary Kuriakose, Theresa Martin Thundyil, and Augustine Marie Kochithara. The indigenous community was beginning to grow.

St. Vincent's Day, 19 July, was chosen to break ground for the new building. At this time the novitiate was quartered in a section of the hospital, and separation and expansion were needed. Father De Genova officiated at the groundbreaking.

The highlight of the year was the visit of Mother Bertrand Crimmins and Sister Agnes Geraldine McGann on 23 November. They received a warm and sincere welcome. After a number of days spent in seeing Mokama and environs and getting oriented, they proceeded to Gaya to see the first offshoot of the Mokama mission. They returned in time to celebrate Christmas at the hospital, where they experienced the simple beauty of this lovely feast in the setting of an India mission.

A large group of SCNs gathered on 26 December to celebrate the presence of Mother Bertrand and Sister Agnes Geraldine; hospital, novitiate, and Gaya Sisters joined for a happy get-together. On the following day the visitors bade farewell to Mokama and headed for Gaya for a final visit there.

The first profession of SCNs in India took place on 8 December 1959 at the Shrine of Our Lady of Grace, Mokama. Bishop Wildermuth officiated. Others attending were: Jesuit Fathers Robert E. Mann, Joseph Wilmes, Hubert Schmidt, Louis De Genova, George Ziebert, and Robert Donohue; Father Joseph Kottoor, brother of Sister Thomasine; and Brother George Thomas, brother of Sister Thomas Aloysius. Sisters from Gaya and other friends attended the profession. The newly professed Sisters, all of whom were medical personnel, joined the hospital staff on 13 December, the twelfth anniversary of the arrival of the SCNs.

1960-1969

New candidates in 1960 and 1961 included two future provincials, Margaret Rodericks and Shalini D'Souza. The new novitiate/convent building was completed by the end of 1960 and was blessed by Father De Genova on 6 January 1961. This structure, a fine three-story building of ample proportions, remains a credit to Father Robert

Stegman, S.J., master builder and architect, and to Sister Florence Joseph, under whose discerning and watchful eye the construction was carried on. Bishop Wildermuth officially opened the convent on 19 July 1961, the date coinciding with the silver jubilee of Sister Mary Jude.

In 1960 Sisters from India had representation at the General Chapter in the United States for the first time. The two elected delegates, Sister Florence Joseph, superior of Nazareth Hospital, and Sister Charles Miriam, superior of Nazareth Academy, left for the United States on 5 May. Feeling the need of a broader leadership in the face of community expansion, the General Council appointed Sister Lawrencetta regional superior the same year. This decision initiated the move toward a separate province in India, which became a reality a few years later. In the following year, 1961, Sister Lawrencetta made her first return visit to the United States. She accompanied Sister Charles Miriam, who had been advised to return to the United States permanently because of persistent ill health.

During the early years of the novitiate, all candidates except a few from Bombay and Bangalore were from Kerala. In 1961 Cecilia Tuti (Sister Mary Juliana), a qualified nurse and midwife, became the first tribal member to enter the community. Agnes Tudu had the distinction of being the only candidate from Gaya, as well as the first candidate from among the Santhals, another tribal people.

Sister Patricia Mary, after temporary assignments in the novitiate, was permanently appointed to the novitiate in Mokama. She replaced Sister Lawrencetta when the latter visited the United States in 1961. When the juniorate opened in July 1962, Sister Patricia Mary became the director. Two more recruits who had arrived from the United States in 1962, Sisters Marita Ann Nabholz and Mary Celeste Collins, were both destined for formation. In August Sister Marita Ann, who had been assisting with the candidates, replaced Sister Patricia Mary as candidate director. Sister Mary Celeste joined the formation group in 1963.

During the years between 1957 and 1969 the community developed and expanded. The number of professed Sisters greatly increased. Their training in various careers and professions made it possible to open new houses and take up new types of ministry. The India province was slowly taking form. In 1961 Sisters Anne Philip, Rose Sebastian, and Anne Elizabeth went to the United States to study—the first India Sisters to do so. Sisters Augustine Marie, Ignatius Marie, and Ann George followed them in 1962. In 1964 Sisters Jean Marie Menoparampil, Marietta Saldanha, Margaret Mary Rodericks, and Sarita Manavalan turned westward for study in the United States. These "foreign" students began a program of exchange that has continued in varying forms up to the present time.

Father De Genova, who had succeeded Father Batson as the pastor of the Mokama mission, was appointed provincial of the Patna Jesuit province in 1962. His long and dedicated service in Mokama had won the devotion and respect of all: the parish and mission, the nursing school, the hospital, and the SCN community.

The year 1962 marked the sesquicentennial celebration of the founding of the Sisters of Charity of Nazareth on 1 December 1812. The convent, the novitiate, and the hospital duly observed the event, and the arrival of the mother general, Mother Lucille Russell, and the community historian, Sister Mary Ramona Mattingly, made the celebration complete. They were received on the evening of 3 December 1963 with much fanfare, fireworks, music, *malas* (garlands of flowers), candlelight guard of honor, and the singing of the "Te Deum" in the chapel. During the ensuing weeks, the visitors divided their time between Mokama and Gaya, absorbing the sights, sounds, and customs of Hindustan (India). Their final departure was on 13 January 1964.

The first official feast of Our Lady of Divine Grace of Mokama was celebrated on 22 October 1963. For the occasion Sister Mary Celeste composed a choral drama that was performed several times by the novitiate and won wide acclaim. An Apostleship of Prayer Promoters Association was formed for the nurses and the junior Sisters. One of the principal activities was to visit five nearby villages every other Saturday in order to motivate the Christian women toward prayer and faithfulness to Sunday Mass. For that purpose the junior Sisters were formed into groups, one group to each village. To report on their progress a meeting was held each month.

The SCN community owes undying gratitude to the Sacred Heart Sisters of Bettiah for the services rendered to the SCNs during their formative years. Beginning with Sister Anastasia in Gaya, the Sacred Heart Sisters regularly lent some of their Sisters for teaching Hindi to both Sisters and students.

In 1964 junior Sisters began attending classes in Mokama College, which is within walking distance of the convent. An amusing incident occurred in regard to education in this local college. Five Sisters—Josephine Kisku, Sophia Kalapurackal, Francine Moozhil, Teresita Theruvankunnel, and Mary Magdalene Chackalackal, the first ever to attend—had taken examinations in March. Eagerly they awaited the publication of the results in June. On 26 June a visit from the principal of the college gave them considerable anxiety when he informed them that because the handwriting of all five Sisters was alike, he suspected some "foul play." (Of course the handwriting was similar since they had all been taught handwriting in the novitiate.) When results were published on 29 June, however, all five names were included among the successful examinees.

Also this year the International Eucharistic Congress was held in Bombay from 29 November to 6 December. Sisters Florence Joseph, Thomasine, Caritas Pamplaniel, and Josepha Puthenkalam represented Nazareth in India. Through the leadership of Sister Patricia Mary, the hospital and convent organized the Mokama Congress, which continued concurrently with the congress in Bombay. Various days were devoted to different religious subjects and to Mass, rosary, processions, holy hour with exposition of the Blessed Sacrament and benediction. Through her devotion and zeal Sister Patricia Mary had provided a local Eucharistic Congress for those who could not go to Bombay.

The end of 1964 marked several important events. After Christmas Sisters Patricia Mary and James Leo left for the United States, the former for a visit, the latter for medical treatment. About the same time new appointments were made in the novitiate. Sister Marita Ann was named novice mistress, and Sister Mary Celeste, candidate mistress. In the novitiate several new projects were undertaken. In March 1965 the novices began a weekly program of catechism teaching at the mission school. In 1966 they undertook the teaching of the women servants, most of whom were illiterate. The formation program of the novitiate was blessed with the services of a number of priests who were available for the teaching of religion and related subjects.

The decade of 1960-1969 was a period of many jubilees: the silver jubilees of Sisters Florence Joseph (1965), Ann Cornelius (1966), Patricia Mary (1967), Veronica Maria (1968), and Ann Roberta (1969). All jubilees were celebrated joyously. The celebrations of convent, hospital, and parish were a fitting tribute to all these Sisters, but especially to Sister Lawrencetta, the great leader who spent her life so totally for God and who had led the community in India with so much love and zeal through all its joys and sorrows. Her golden jubilee was celebrated in 1966. Especially touching were the simple gifts of the parishioners, the poor people, many of whom she had taught to make the Sign of the Cross or to receive the sacraments. Some offered one or two eggs, fruit, sweets, flowers, even a cock. No one came empty-handed.

Community development continued apace during the sixties. An international order came on 10 October 1965 with a letter from Nazareth containing the information that the community in the United States had been divided into four provinces. India remained a region for some time. Revised Constitutions came with this change. Sister Lawrencetta, elected to the General Chapter of 1966, attended the sessions in the United States at which Mother Lucille was reelected mother general. Another important decision was the appointment of Sister Ellen Curran, sister of Sister Ann Cornelius, as full-time procurator of the missions. Sister Ellen had long been a zealous worker for India.

St. Xavier's School in Mokama had been an established institution since the early days of the mission. In 1966 six Sisters began teaching in the school, and they have continued to hold posts as teachers and principals. Another first in Mokama occurred on 15 August 1966 when a Hindi High Mass composed by Sister Eugenia was sung. Sister Theresa Pinto had also composed a High Mass. These compositions had received episcopal approval and were recorded by Bishop Wildermuth, who presented them to the Music Commission of the Bishops' Conference of India in Delhi. Another milestone was reached in 1966. Upon the transfer of Sister Mary Celeste to Gaya as teacher, the first India candidate mistress, Sister Teresita Theruvankunnel, succeeded her.

Two important visitors, Sisters Marie Victoria Fitzsimmons and Margaret Vincent Blandford, arrived on 23 November 1966. Sister Marie Victoria, the retired administrator of Memorial Hospital in Chattanooga, Tennessee, had been awarded a parting gift by the City Council—a trip to India for herself and a companion. Sister Margaret Vincent, her companion, began a series of talks to help the Sisters in India understand the new direction taken by the community resulting from the proceedings of the General Chapter of 1966.

Sister Marie Victoria sustained serious cuts, bruises, and dislocations as the result of a fall from the veranda into some barbed wire, and she was incapacitated for several days. She also suffered shock and sorrow on hearing of the sudden death of her father, but carried on bravely. The two visitors received a grand send-off as they turned their faces westward to travel back to the United States.

Sister Lawrencetta, returning from one of her frequent trips to Goa for meetings of the Conference of Religious of India, stopped in Calcutta to complete the purchase of property in Ranchi for which negotiations had gone on for some time. This purchase was the remote preparation for the opening on 18 April 1967 of Nazareth Convent in Ranchi—the third SCN house in India. Sister Ann Roberta, appointed superior, was for a third time a pioneer in a new mission.

Almost simultaneous with the opening was the first session of a summer school of religious Hindustani music conducted by Sister Eugenia and Sister Lucia of the Holy Cross Sisters at Ursuline College, Ranchi. To help the Sisters and others attain a knowledge of Hindustani classical music for use in liturgical worship in the Church, a course was requested by the archbishop of Ranchi and by Bishop Wildermuth of Patna. After the first session in Ranchi, the venue was shifted to Hazaribagh and continued there for the next ten years. Sisters Lucia and Eugenia prepared for this summer school by studying Hindustani classical music at the Sangeet Sadhana Mandir, founded by Father Edmond, O.F.M. Cap., a Canadian missionary. This institution was a center of the Prayag Sangeet Samiti, a foremost music school of northern India, affiliated with the Allahabad University. The two Sisters attained the Sangeet Prabhakar, or Bachelor's Degree, in 1963. Other SCNs who acquired the same degree were Sisters Theresa Pinto, Xavier Valiakunnackal, and Rekha Kerketta.

Additional community events of this decade were: the appointment of Sister Anne Marie as the local superior of Nazareth Convent, Mokama, 1968; the regional chapter of SCNs held at Mokama in April 1969, attended by twelve delegates and a number of observers; the attendance of Sisters Rose, Patricia Mary, and Anne Marie at the special general chapter held at Nazareth in the United States in August 1969; the arrival of Mother Lucille and Sister Ellen, the mission procurator, on 29 November of the same year; the return of Sister Margaret Rodericks after five years of study in the United States; the death caused by hepatitis on 24 August 1969 of a candidate, Aleyamma T.M., the first of the Indian SCN family to be buried in the Mokama cemetery.

An event of the utmost importance was the establishment of the India province in 1969. As noted earlier, India had been a region until that time, and with its advance to the status of a province, Sister Teresa Rose Nabholz (formerly Sister Marita Ann), who was the regional superior, became the first provincial of the India province.

Events of a general nature that took place during the sixties included the outbreak of hostilities between India and Pakistan on 6 September 1965. United States citizens were offered evacuation by their own government if the need should arise. Holy Family Hospital in Delhi was commandeered by the Indian government. Blackouts were ordered as a precautionary measure throughout the country. Threats came from China of a possible attack on India. Much to the relief of all, a cease-fire between India and Pakistan was declared. The Chinese intervention seemed to have been only rumors.

Of national concern, particularly affecting Bihar, was the famine of 1967, which was very widespread and which prompted heroic charity, not only from India but also from many foreign lands. Huge quantities of foods were shipped from abroad, agricultural and irrigation technicians arrived, and medical teams and social workers both within and outside the country rallied to give assistance.

Through the relief work of both hospital and academy, SCN participation gave evidence of the tremendous amount of cooperation between the two institutions. The generous assistance rendered by religious and lay men and women from all over India and abroad alleviated the sufferings and prevented the large-scale starvation that might well have resulted without the massive relief operations. The Church and the Christians in general stood in the forefront of those who recognized the calamity and set about vigorously to tackle the problem.

1970-1979

The decade of the seventies could be considered the era of the East-West exchange program. From the United States a number of Sisters came, beginning with Sister Barbara Thomas, then a provincial, who arrived late in the year 1970. She gave workshops on prayer, religious life, and the new form of government.

In 1972 Sister Mary Holt (formerly known as Sister Charles Miriam), one of the pioneers of the mission, returned to take part in the silver jubilee celebrations of the mission and to renew the associations with her "second country." She returned to the United States in early 1973 with veteran Sister Veronica Maria, who had made a brief return visit to India.

In 1974 Sister Bridget Kappalumakal went to study in the United States. In the same year Sister Sunita Edattu returned to India after completing her studies. With her came Sisters Eula Blandford and Mary Bennet Cecil, both mission procurators, who spent six weeks experiencing the India mission for which they were working. The biggest influx of visitors from the United States came through two projects called Justice, '75 and Justice, '76. The groups of Sisters were large—thirteen and twelve—

and they dispersed themselves among the various missions, taking active part in the life around them and in the mission programs arranged for them. They had their share of interesting, harrowing, and amusing experiences and went away feeling grateful that they had been granted an opportunity to participate directly in the life of India, if only for eight weeks.

In August 1975 Sister Mary Madeline Abdelnour came to spend some months in teaching the junior Sisters. Sister Barbara Thomas, now superior general, and Sister Donna Kenney, her personal assistant, came for a visit in October. Sister Barbara received the vows of Sisters Vandana Vandanath, Ann Scaria Menonparampil, and Anita Palavelil, the first time that vows in India were received by a superior general. The last visitor in the record year of 1975 was Sister Gail Collins (formerly called Sister Mary Celeste), who spent three months happily and profitably in her former mission land.

In the midst of the cleaning up after the great flood of 1976, Sisters Mary Ellen Doyle and Dorothy MacDougall toured the missions, giving special attention to the field of education. Sister Mary Ellen remained for some time in Mokama to teach.

Sister Anne Horrigan, a faculty member of Nazareth College, Louisville, Kentucky, and Miss Virginia Veeneman, Sister Lawrencetta's sister and an indefatigable worker for the missions, visited in late 1977, remaining until early in 1978. Virginia and Sister Lawrencetta must have realized on parting that this would be the last time they would meet this side of heaven.

Mr. Bernard Roberts, brother of Sisters Jean Bernadette, Agatha Maria, and Agnes Vincent, visited the Sisters in Mokama. Sister Mary Frances had been a classmate of his sisters. Feeling great pity for the poor and for those housed in such miserable dwellings, he gave Sister Lawrencetta a generous donation of a thousand dollars to be used for housing for the poor.

Other visitors of 1978 were Sister Isabel Green, Father Thomas Hamel, and Sister Barbara Thomas, who conducted a workshop on Canon Law. Sisters Barbara Peterson and Kathleen Mary Bohan came in June 1979 and attended the India provincial assembly. The last SCN visitors of the decade were Sister Mary Elaine Zehnder, director of the SCN mission office, and Sister Barbara Flores, a novice from Belize, making her second-year novitiate in India.

A local visitor was Mother Theodosia of the Apostolic Carmelite Sisters, foundress of Patna Women's College, and later mother general, who came to pay a visit to her good friend, Sister Lawrencetta.

In the realm of community leadership, from the late sixties onwards, the Indian SCNs began to take on more and more positions of authority and responsibility—the ideal to be achieved in any mission of this character.

In June 1970 Sister Anne Marie, after two years as superior of Nazareth Convent, Mokama, was transferred to Gaya to replace Sister James Leo as principal of Nazareth

Academy. Sister Margaret Rodericks assumed the administration of Nazareth Convent, Mokama. Her tenure was brief, however, as she transferred to the offices of the Catholic Bishops' Conference in Delhi in October of the same year. Her place was taken by Sister Grace Androth. In 1974 Sister Ann Palatty succeeded Sister Grace as superior of Nazareth Convent, Mokama.

When India was constituted a separate province in 1970, Sister Teresa Rose Nabholz was appointed the first provincial. Succeeding her in 1977 was Sister Margaret Rodericks, who became the first Indian SCN to fill this important office. In the same year Sister Teresa Rose was named director of the junior Sisters, and Sister Sarita Manavalan became superior of Nazareth Convent, Mokama.

New ministries and missions developed in the seventies. In 1974 SCNs began to give retreats to women in the villages and to other local groups. Another innovation was the Crescentia Grihini Course (named in memory of pioneer missionary Sister Crescentia), which was intended to prepare young girls for marriage, home and health care, and family life. The girls reside in the institute and have regular courses in reading, writing, arithmetic, cooking, gardening, house care, cleanliness, hygiene, and child care.

A development in the catechetical ministry was the decision of some Sisters to stay with families in the villages, while instructing them in religion. Mercy Thundathil, Pauline Paraplackal, and Agnes Tudu were pioneers in this program. In 1975 the first group of catechists completed the nine-month course in the Liturgical, Catechetical, Biblical and Pastoral Centre in Bangalore. Three Sisters—Mercy, Sushila Palatty, and Stella Chullyil—had labored actively in this ministry.

To provide adequate educational facilities for girls living in outlying villages, the parish in Mokama opened a hostel for school girls, called Maria Sadan, under the direction of Sister Rosita Kavilpurayidathil. A further step in education in the same year (1974) was the appointment of Sister Ann George Mukalel as education director for the entire province.

A ministry of a different sort was taken up when an intercongregational project called Apostolic Orientation Program (AOP) was set up in Lucknow. SCNs provided two directors for this program: Sisters Teresa Rose and Marietta Saldanha.

Other community developments included two new foundations—Bassein, the state of Maharastra near Bombay, and Kathmandu in the Kingdom of Nepal. A first candidate from Bassein, Blanche Correia, arrived in May 1977. The permanent group assigned to Nepal—Sisters Anne Marie, Jean Kulangara, and Joel Urumpil—arrived there in April 1979.

A number of Sisters traveled to the United States for various reasons during this decade. Sister Teresa Rose attended the general assembly in 1974. In 1978 Sister Ancilla Kozhipat, a doctor, and Sister Philomena Kottoor, a nursing student, left for studies in the United States. The earliest Indian SCNs that visited the United States in the blossoming East-West exchange program were some veterans of the mission, Sisters Elizabeth Emmanuel Vattakunnel, Mary Juliana Tuti, Teresa Xavier Ponnazhath, Thomasine Kottoor, and Xavier Valiakunnackal.

An important event in 1972 was the twenty-fifth anniversary of the arrival of the SCNs in India. The main celebration in Mokama, coinciding with the 160th anniversary of the founding of the community in 1812, was widely attended by Sisters from all the missions. Five of the six pioneers, including Sister Mary Holt who had come from the United States especially for the occasion, were present. In 1976, to mark the 60th anniversary of her religious profession, Sister Lawrencetta, now 80 years old, welcomed five new postulants to the community. One of these, Sushila Baxla, later Sister Sandhya, was destined to be the first Indian SCN to die. The details of her death will be given in the chapter on Barauni. On February 2, 1979, a combined celebration included Sister Lawrencetta's eighty-third birthday, the twenty-second anniversary of the novitiate, and the anticipated celebration of Sister Teresa Rose's silver jubilee.

The month of September 1976 witnessed the worst flood in six hundred years. Many harrowing incidents plagued the convent—the four feet of water in the compound, snakes everywhere, and water on the ground floor requiring the mass shifting of the library, the moving of furniture, the housing of the hostel girls, the construction of stoves, and the colossal task of cleaning up the mess after the water receded. It was a never-to-be-forgotten experience and one that all hoped would never be repeated.

A major initiative was taken on 25 March 1975 with the opening of Nazareth Ashram at Kerwateri (Sokho). The first-year novices were to spend the year in a new setting and a new type of living. The first director, Sister Patricia Mary, guided the novices in this innovative program until December 1977, at which time she was succeeded by Sister Teresita.

The novitiate building was a large structure made of mud and a small amount of brick. There the novices could live a simple life in quiet and solitude, learning the rudiments of religious life. In the same area some mud dwellings were also erected for lay women and men, Sisters, Brothers, and priests who might wish to make retreats or spend some time away from the hubbub and turmoil of the world around them. Both Father Rice and Sister Lucia Thuluvanickal were regularly available for direction and counseling.

For the novitiate there were advantages as well as disadvantages. The quiet, solitude, and peace of the area made the place conducive to prayer, meditation, and a way of living close to God and nature. The presence of so many visitors coming and going, however, meant a number of distracting interruptions that militated against the very purpose of the ashram. A second very disturbing factor was the presence in the area of swarms of malaria-bearing mosquitoes. Many novices became victims of this debilitating disease and suffered relapses in subsequent years.

Sokho has always been a snake-infested region, and snake bite is a regular occurrence there. One of the earliest reptile visitors was a python, found coiled comfortably near the front veranda. It was ten feet long and weighed eight kilograms.

The Sisters of the ashram also engaged in rural development. They began literacy classes and also helped the people with the planting and harvesting of crops. Sister Evelyn D'Souza was actively engaged in this latter ministry.

The proximity of a river that was prone to sudden floods gave the novices experience in combatting the forces of nature. There were times when the river was swollen and the current swift, making it impassable. At such times it was necessary to remain on whichever side one happened to be. A dam had been constructed by the poor people of the area working under a "Food-for-Work" program, but unfortunately it was broken several times. There were times when the river had to be crossed either by wading or by swimming. Many were the experiences with snakes, scorpions, centipedes, and other such frightening creatures.

A touching episode was the miraculous escape from drowning of three children with their goats. Sister Teresita, standing on the shore, watched helplessly as she saw the children and goats being carried away in a sudden rush of water. Two children managed to save themselves, but the third disappeared. Sorrow was turned into joy when the lost child reappeared in the evening, hale and hearty. She had clung to an overhanging tree branch and held on until the water receded.

Many human interest stories can be told about Kerwateri and its people and the Sisters who worked there, as well as about Father Rice and the many who had been associated with him. When he became seriously ill at the ashram, the villagers came around to give help and to pray on their knees in the courtyard, beseeching God for his recovery. As he began to improve, they turned from the spiritual to the temporal, bringing milk, eggs, and chicken to help in his recuperation.

The novitiate in Kerwateri was for some time a matter of controversy in the community. In response to a negative vote of the community members, the ashram was closed for some time. It was later reopened for the novices and functioned until the end of 1982 when it was permanently closed. Now the buildings of the novitiate and the retreat huts stand in crumbling ruins—mute evidence of the days of yesteryear and the activities of the ashram.

1980-1989

In the early years of the decade, certain deaths drew special attention. Three of the stalwarts, "the elders of the SCNs," died in close succession. Sister Mary Holt died in the United States on 3 July 1982. As Sister Charles Miriam, she was one of the pioneer group who helped to lay the foundation of the mission. After three years of service in Mokama in the rugged days of the early mission, she moved on to lead the SCNs as principal of Nazareth Academy, Gaya. Because of ill health, her years in India numbered only fourteen, but India ever remained the great love of her life.

Another Nazareth Academy "great" was Sister James Leo Goldsborough, who died in the United States on 24 November 1983. Her twenty-five years in India (1954-1979) were spent entirely in Gaya. In Mokama she was known as a remarkable patient, having successfully recovered from major and minor operations as well as from serious bouts of illness.

The revered leader of the first band of SCNs was the great and beloved Sister Lawrencetta, who had been continually in Mokama from the foundation of the mission in 1947. She died in Mokama on 14 July 1984, at the age of 89, surrounded by the Sisters from all the branch houses, priests, and the people whom she loved. Sister Lawrencetta's dedication to her chosen mission field was an inspiration to all. Having come to India as the superior, she had faced with courage and steadfast purpose all the problems of adjustment and incorporation into a new and completely different culture that would have daunted a weaker soul. Although she was not trained in medicine (she was a music teacher), she tried to understand the needs and problems of the hospital and its personnel and to address them to the satisfaction of all.

As mistress of novices Sister Lawrencetta put a particular stamp of religious devotion and community charism on all those Sisters who were fortunate enough to come under her guidance. Until a few years before her death, she was still actively participating in community life and worship, and when old age deprived her of her full mental faculties, she retained the same sweetness of character. Her very presence was a privilege. Just as her mortal remains in the Mokama cemetery attract the devout in prayer, so does her spirit hover over this mission, blessing it from her heavenly home.

Growth and expansion of the community in India continued throughout the decade of the eighties. Mokama remained the center of the community. For the novitiate and junior and senior groups of Sisters, many courses, seminars, and studies were followed: the Global Education Workshop by Sister Ann Whittaker and Mrs. Pat Mische; courses in hydropathy and naturopathy by Father De Britto; and an intercongregational seminar at Nazareth Convent that brought together novices from the Holy Cross, Sacred Heart, Notre Dame, and SCN congregations.

In 1983 Sister Mercy Thundathil directed a four-day vocation camp for the senior class and other educated girls at Mokama. A second camp was held the following year, conducted by Sisters Jane Karakunnel, Marcelline Indwar, and Mercy. Development within the community included community-building sessions by Sisters Teresa Rose and Shalini in 1984, and SCN Days that brought a large number of Sisters together to share their hopes, their differences and difficulties, their plans and mutual interests. Junior programs organized on a regular basis from year to year were usually of a month's duration and consisted of workshops, seminars, retreats, and related courses. Profession Days marked achievements in community growth. Two days in 1988—8

May, the profession of twelve Sisters, and 15 May, the final vows for ten Sisters— brought large numbers in attendance, including villagers from Barh and Mokama.

Development of ministries and missions continued "to bloom and grow." A new mission was opened in February 1983 in the small town of Barauni, a half-hour ride from Mokama. A province mission-planning committee began to function at about the same time. A new step in development was the division of the community into the various ministries of education, health, and sociopastoral work. Meetings for each group are held at regular intervals.

A big move of 1986 was the transfer of the provincial administration to Patna. The first establishment was in two floors of a rented house in Banskoti, Kurji parish. Property was later bought on East Boring Canal Road, and the provincial administration settled there. New missions that were opened in 1986 were Sangsay in the Darjeeling District of West Bengal, Madhepura in Bihar, and Bangalore in Mysore State.

Sister Shalini succeeded Sister Margaret Rodericks in the office of provincial in 1983. In 1984 Sister Janice Rathappillil was elected coordinator of Nazareth Convent, Mokama. Sister Teresa Rose, so long based in Mokama, moved to Bakhtiarpur in August 1986. Nazareth Convent, Mokama, received a new administrator in the person of Sister Sarala Anithottathil in April 1988. The last major change of the decade was the installation in June 1989 of the newly elected provincial, Sister Sarita Manavalan.

During the eighties a number of assemblies took place both in India and in the United States. India delegates to the general assembly of 1980 in the United States were Sisters Margaret Rodericks, Sarita Manavalan, and Olive (formerly Theresa) Pinto. The India province had an assembly in June of the following year. Another form of meeting was the Province Days of the Christmas season in 1982. A provincial assembly was held in October 1983, and in December of the same year Sister Shalini attended the general assembly in the United States. Sister Dorothy MacDougall, superior general, opened the India provincial assembly of October 1985, and in December 1988 Sister Emily Nabholz, SCN president, presided over the India provincial assembly.

As boundaries were broken and the world began to shrink, there were frequent visitors. Sister Dorothy MacDougall had made her first visit as education director in 1976. Later in her capacity as superior general she spent six weeks giving workshops on the Constitutions. Other visitors from the United States in 1983 included Sisters Mary Reisz and Alice Adams, both of whom attended the provincial assembly of that year. In the same year SCNs Agnes Crone and Katharine Hanrahan arrived in November. Another visitor was Sister Ann Bernadette, who came on a golden jubilee tour in 1985 to the land where she had spent thirty years in fruitful labor.

Sister Patricia Kelley (formerly Sister Patricia Mary) was welcomed to her former field of labor in 1986. She was accompanied by Sister Miriam Corcoran, who, true to her profession as drama specialist, produced several items of a dramatic nature in

Mokama and Gaya during her short stay. Visitors of 1987 were SCNs Mary Elizabeth Miller, Brenda Gonzales, and Theresa Knabel. Later in 1988 came three other SCN visitors from the United States: Mary Victoria Hayden, Mary Margaret Cooper, and Judy Raley. In October 1989 a returning veteran and pioneer of the India mission, Sister Mary Frances, made a three-month visit to India on the occasion of her golden jubilee. With her were Sisters Carmelita Dunn and Irene Locario, the latter an SCN from Belize who was preparing for final vows.

While some Sisters came from the United States under the East-West exchange program, a large number were traveling in the opposite direction—from India to the United States. Sister Teresa Kotturan went in June 1982, and Sister Margaret Rodericks left for ministry at Spalding University in the United States in 1988. A returnee was Sister Philomena Kottoor, who graduated in nursing in February 1984. In November 1984 Sister Elizabeth Nadackal also returned after a three-month "USA experience." There was a large departure for the United States in 1985: Sisters Shalini, Vinita Kumplankal, and Marianne Puthoor as delegates to the General Assembly; Sisters Sangeeta Ayithamattam and Anupa Moozha for study. In the same year, Sister Olive returned after serving one year in the mission office. The following year Sisters Jane and Teresita went for ministry in Belize and the United States, respectively. In mid June of 1989 Sister Josita Eniakattu returned after a year of ministry in the mission office in the United States.

The decade of the eighties had its share of jubilees and anniversaries. A special milestone was reached on 27 December 1984 when four Sisters who had been the first professed in the SCN community in India celebrated the silver jubilee of their vows. They were: Sisters Elizabeth Emmanuel Vattakunnel, Teresa Velloothara, Anne Elizabeth Elampalathottyil, and Bridget Kappalumakal. A double jubilee was observed on 30 December 1986: the golden jubilee of Sister Mary Jude and the silver jubilee of Sister Xavier. Sisters Elizabeth Nadackal, Marietta, and Mary Scaria celebrated their silver jubilee together in Mokama on 20 December 1987. Sister Margaret Rodericks celebrated her silver jubilee in Bassein on 21 December 1987. A "mass" jubilee celebration took place in Mokama on 28 December 1988: the golden jubilee of Sister Eugenia, and the silver jubilee of the provincial, Sister Shalini, the provincial-elect, Sister Sarita Manavalan, Sisters Rita, Mary Joseph, Teresita, Mary Chackalackal, Sophia, Francine, and Mary Stella Ambrose. Another golden/silver combination occurred on 28 December 1989 with the golden jubilee of Sister Mary Frances and the silver jubilee of Sisters Mary Juliana, Anne Philip, and Ancilla.

An incident in 1986 that caused widespread concern in the community occurred in Nepal. The news came that serious trouble from the authorities had been encountered when Father Thomas Vattikad, Sister Francine, Sister Gracy Thombrakudyil, and some Christian lay people were accused of attempting to spread Christianity. They were actually conducting a retreat for Catholics confirmed in their religion for several generations. The accused were arrested, jailed, and even beaten by the police. Sister Shalini rushed to Nepal to try to get legal aid. The community commenced a program of prayer and fasting. Alhough the group was released after some days, the case dragged on without conclusion for several years. Eventually Nepal became a democracy, and all cases against Christians were dropped by the authorities.

Often fear causes people to shake, but on 24 August 1988 it was not fear but the earth itself that gave a good shaking. Most of the SCN missions, except those in far-off Bombay, experienced some terrifying moments—the house shaking, windows rattling, things falling from high places, the awful rumbling, growling noise. Dharan in Nepal was heavily hit, but by the mercy of God no Sister received injury nor was any SCN property severely damaged.

Some events of general interest took place in this decade. On 28 May 1980 Bishop Wildermuth visited Nazareth Convent for the last time as bishop of Patna. During his episcopate the SCN community had begun work in the Mokama mission. Before his retirement the bishop visited Mokama and administered the sacrament of Confirmation to a number of parishioners at the mission. One month later many Sisters attended the episcopal ordination of his successor, Bishop Benedict Osta, S.J.

Two important commemorations were marked during this decade. The Mokama parish celebrated its fiftieth anniversary in May 1986. On the spiritual side the anniversary was blessed by fifty First Communions and two marriages. The SCN mission was an integral part of the parish for thirty-nine of those fifty years. On November 30 the commemoration of the 175th year of the foundation of the SCN community opened with a Solemn High Mass. Various programs followed throughout the year.

Time goes on, and therefore this history cannot be concluded. Further events must be left to another writer in another time. Hopefully the work done by their predecessors will be carried on by succeeding generations of Sisters of Charity as the Divine Plan unfolds. May God be ever praised and glorified.

Dancing the Jubilarians into the house are (left to right) Sisters Mary Basanti Besra, Mary Margaret Nirmala, Smita Karikkattil, Manjula Hansdak, Arpita Mundamattathil, Rosemarie Lakra, Lucy Puthukkatt, Amrita Manjoly, and Usha Saldana.

NAZARETH COTTAGE, DARJEELING

Sister Lawrencetta Veeneman looks on as the driver of an ox cart guides his team up the hill. The uphill road in the background leads to Nazareth Cottage, Darjeeling, shown in the picture below.

Chapter Four

NAZARETH COTTAGE, DARJEELING

D
arjeeling, that privileged haven high in the Himalayas, has a special place in the history of Nazareth in India. For a month or six weeks in the year, the Sisters were able to escape the burning heat of the plains, to enjoy the cool, clear air of the mountains, to revel in the magnificent scenery, to put aside the cares of duty, and to relax with congenial companions in quiet and peace.

Situated in the northernmost part of Bengal, bordering on what was then the mountain kingdom of Sikkim, Darjeeling may be described as a "vertical" town, clustered in a horseshoe shape around the side of the hills to which it clings. At the northern extremity is North Point, dominated by St. Joseph College, a Jesuit institution for boys. On the other extremity, West Point, Nazareth Cottage is perched on the side of a hill at least 500 feet above the road.

In the summer of 1948, when the Sisters first went to Darjeeling, they were granted the use of the Jesuits' house called Loyola Villa, which they shared with the Medical Missionaries. By the summer of 1949 the SCN community had purchased the house of Mr. Kearns, whose wife had died during that year. Nazareth Cottage was duly blessed and set up for a summer refuge, not only for the Sisters of Charity but also for a number of other communities—Medical Missionaries, Sisters of Notre Dame of Cleveland, Sisters of St. Joseph of Cluny, Presentation Sisters, Sacred Heart Sisters, and others. Adjacent to Nazareth Cottage were three Jesuit villas, used mostly by the priests of the Patna and Jamshedpur missions. Hidden in a curve of the same hillside was Forest View, the villa of the IBVM Sisters, particularly the Patna group. Eventually the houses below Nazareth Cottage were acquired by the Swiss Holy Cross Sisters and the Cleveland Notre Dames. The Medical Missionaries purchased a cottage on North Point.

In the town proper, the Irish Sisters of Loreto operated a very old and famous institution for girls, Loreto Convent. Since the school was always in session when the Sisters and priests of the plains came for the summer holidays, both Loreto Convent and St. Joseph College played host to the visitors, inviting them to school functions, movies, high teas, and the like. All these events were thoroughly enjoyed by the vacationers. Regular retreats were held in Nazareth Cottage, sometimes two in a season, and were attended by other communities "on the hill" as well as by

SCNs. Jesuits were usually available as retreat masters. Thus during their free periods, in surroundings that were conducive to raising minds and hearts to the heavens and to the Creator of all the beauty around them, the Sisters could renew themselves both spiritually and physically.

Social events, such as wiener roasts, steak fries, songfests, picnics, and outings to the many interesting and beautiful spots in the vicinity, hikes and excursions to nearby places of renown, such as Goom, Sonada, Kurseong, Kalimpong, and Sikkim, made the weeks pass pleasantly and profitably.

A "must" for all vacationers was a trip on foot to Tiger Hill. The usual plan began with Mass about 1 a.m., followed by a snack and a cup of coffee. Breakfast was often carried along with necessary pots and pans and cooked after arrival at the peak. The party would set out about 2 a.m. and trek across the upper paths of the mountain from West Point to Goom, the next town. From Goom the company would make the final assault on Tiger Hill, reaching the summit about 4 a.m. to view at sunrise, if they were lucky, the world's highest mountain peak, the majestic Mount Everest. Many times, however, Everest was hidden in cloud and mist, and the viewers went away disappointed.

In those days Everest, Godwin Austin, and Khanchanjunga, the three highest peaks in the world, were conquered, and the Sisters had the chance to meet some of the conquerors or those who had led or participated in the adventures or helped climbers, from the sidelines, to achieve success. Khanchanjunga, its magnificent triple peaks covered with eternal snow, was in full view of Nazareth Cottage on clear days, and its grandeur and incomparable beauty never failed to inspire thoughts of heaven and the Creator of all things.

These were great days, but this utopia could not last. Gradually fewer and fewer Sisters went up for the holidays. Because of excessive expense and lowered occupancy, the various communities, one by one, sold their villas. The SCN community followed suit, and with the sale of Nazareth Cottage in the early 1970s, the idyllic "Darjeeling Days" faded into a lovely memory.

NAZARETH ACADEMY, GAYA
1950

Sister Ann Roberta Powers talks with Sisters Ann Bernadette Ormond and Charles Miriam Holt as they set out for the bazaar in a rickshaw. Nazareth Academy, Gaya, is in the background.

Chapter Five

NAZARETH ACADEMY, GAYA 1950

Nazareth Academy in Gaya, Bihar, was the second foundation of the Sisters of Charity of Nazareth in India. When the first group of Sisters was chosen for the India mission, their number included three teachers, and in 1950, when three members joined the original band, two of them were also teachers. Thus when Bishop Augustine Wildermuth, S.J., of Patna approached the community about staffing the already existing school in Gaya, personnel was at hand, and permission was granted to take over the school at the end of the school year in December 1950. The pioneers were Sisters Charles Miriam Holt, Ann Bernadette Ormond, Ann Roberta Powers, and Ellen Maria Ballew.

The school had been started by the German Institute of the Blessed Mary (IBMV), the same Sisters who staffed the well known school St. Joseph's Convent in Patna, founded in 1853. These Sisters opened the Gaya school in February 1939, calling it St. Michael. In Gaya today (1990) there are women and men who attended St. Michael School and have vivid recollections of their school and of the first superior, Mother Engelbert. The IBMV Sisters first resided and taught in a house opposite the mission compound, but when enrollment increased, they shifted to a more spacious house across the road. When that house also became inadequate, they bought the currently used building, which had first been a Masonic lodge and later the home of a Muslim family.

The German IBMVs had only a short stay in their new school. World War II was in full swing, and the Sisters, most of whom were German, came under the class of "enemy aliens" and were asked to reside in their larger institutions for the duration of the war years. The Irish Loreto Sisters (IBVM) took over the growing school in mid 1943, which then became known as Loreto Convent. In time, the shortage of Sisters and the demand for more teachers in many of their long-established schools in India caused the Loreto Sisters to give up the Gaya school. This time the Sisters of Charity of Nazareth filled the gap, and the school received its third name, Nazareth Academy.

Sister Charles Miriam, principal and superior, Sisters Ann Bernadette and Ann Roberta arrived in Gaya on 28 December 1950. (Sister Ellen Maria, the fourth member, came later on 3 January 1951.) The three Sisters were welcomed by the pastor, Father Hubert Schmidt, S.J., Father Albert Wilzbacher, S.J., Mother Helena, superior, Mothers Raphael, Pauline and Victorine, and Sister Jude. Two other Sisters, Mothers Pius and Clare, had left for Lucknow the previous day. The twenty-ninth of December was an exceedingly busy day, as the Loreto Sisters tried to acquaint the new Sisters with the general setup of the school and convent, and the new arrivals tried to absorb all that they could of the customs and traditions of the school. In the early dawn of 30 December, the Loreto Sisters departed from this mission that they loved so well, and the SCNs began their new work in Gaya.

As the Sisters prepared to begin the school year on 18 January 1951, they were faced with several problems that loomed large on the horizon. Because the four SCNs were replacing seven Loreto Sisters, the faculty had to be increased by hiring a number of lay teachers. Among the first teachers were some who remained long in service at Nazareth Academy, notably Mrs. K. C. Remedios, Miss Vicky Murray, and Miss Alma John. By 12 May, after final examinations, the first "Proclamation Day" was held and reports distributed to the 160 children.

In the first year, serious sickness attacked the Sisters. Sisters Ann Bernadette and Ellen Maria suffered from dysentery, which necessitated their going to Mokama for treatment. Sister Charles Miriam fought off several attacks of gall bladder disturbance, but eventually had to shorten her stay in Darjeeling to enter Holy Family Hospital in Mandar to have her gall bladder removed by the Medical Missionary surgeon, Sister Barbara. During these times of sickness, the hospital Sisters, especially Sisters Ann Cornelius and Crescentia, came to the aid of their ailing Sisters in Gaya. The latter had interesting tales of her days in the kindergarten.

But the real blow fell on this new community with the sickness of Sister Ellen Maria. In early August she began to complain of headaches that continued throughout the month and became more frequent and more intense. The joint diagnosis of Dr. Tobias in Gaya, Dr. Smith in Mokama, and Sister Elise of the Patna Medical Missionaries, was a possible brain tumor. Removed to Mokama in early September, Sister Ellen Maria did not improve, and the medical consensus was that she should return to the United States. On 18 October, less than one year after her arrival, Sister Ellen Maria, accompanied by Sister Ann Cornelius, said farewell to her beloved India. Her loss was irreparable; in that short time she had endeared herself to all with whom she came in contact. Ever a bright and cheerful person, she seemed exceptionally well-suited for the mission she had chosen. To replace Sister Ellen Maria, Sister Charles Miriam was able to obtain the services of a teacher from Bettiah, Miss Clara Marchino, M.A.

Happier events of that first year were: a beautiful Corpus Christi procession on the feast of Christ the King; the celebration on 4 November of Sister Charles Miriam's feast day, especially by the school children; sports day on 11 December;

final examinations, the distribution of reports to two hundred students on 12 December, and closing on 20 December.

The first Christmas in Gaya was very quiet and simple, with Midnight Mass in the Church of the Resurrection, better known as the Railway Church because of its location on the railroad property, and morning Mass in the convent. Many parishioners and friends came during the day to extend Christmas greetings. The holidays included a visit to Mokama on 27 December. Sister Ellen Maria was greatly missed at this time.

The parish school, Creane Memorial, named in honor of the saintly Father James Creane, S.J., who had worked and died in Gaya, was always interconnected with the convent school. Sister Ann Bernadette succeeded Mother Raphael in Creane Memorial and was subsequently appointed principal, a position requiring a knowledge of the Hindi language. Under the tutelage of Mrs. Samuel Shah, a staff teacher of Creane Memorial, Sister Ann Bernadette learned quickly and well. Gaya was fortunate to have the two best linguists in the SCN community in India, Sisters Ann Bernadette and Ann Roberta.

During the second year, Nazareth Academy progressed slowly but steadily. By December, the enrollment had increased from 204 to 240. Only three Sisters were on the staff, and Sister Ann Bernadette had to divide time between Creane Memorial and Nazareth Academy. Sister Charles Miriam did yeoman duty, serving as principal, registrar, treasurer, clerk, and often Senior Cambridge teacher. A regular substitute was Sister Ann Cornelius, who answered the SOS signals sent out from Gaya.

Creane Memorial, though a much smaller school, faced the same shortage of teachers. The classes were often divided between two teachers. One of the most faithful teachers was Mrs. Samuel Shah, who eventually joined the staff of Nazareth Academy and became a renowned teacher of the Beginners Class. Often the priests had to take their turns at teaching also.

Certain persons deserve a place in the history of these early years. Among the teachers Miss Alma John, who served the institution for a total of thirty-six years until her death in September 1983, was outstanding. Mrs. Babs Lazaro, wife of Dr. Lazaro, the first resident doctor in Mokama, and Miss Vicky Murray gave faithful and dedicated service in the early years. After her marriage to Joseph Fernandes, Vicky emigrated with her husband and two children to Australia, where she died in 1988. Mrs. K. C. Remedios, a skillful and well loved teacher, retired to Bangalore with her husband, Kenneth Remedios, who had served the Indian railways for forty years.

Dr. Millicent Tobias earned the undying gratitude of the Sisters, the priests, the lay teachers, the servants, and literally the whole Gaya mission for her unselfish care of the sick during her forty years' residence in Gaya, without asking a *paisa* for her services. Every day she attended Mass, received Holy Communion, and offered her prayers in the convent chapel. In 1978, at the age of seventy-five, still serving the sick poor, she emigrated to England to reside with her sister and died there in 1990.

Not to be forgotten is Mr. Augustine Fernandez, who, though retired, gave unstintingly of his time and labor in any service to school or church. He was especially untiring in his supervision of the construction of the new school building in any weather—heat or cold or rain. This idea of service he instilled in the hearts of his children: Pat, Tony, Joseph, Kenny, and his only daughter Monica, who was one of the early teachers of the school.

Among the servants who served long and faithfully from the early days were the tailor, Abdul Shakur; the *mistri* (mason), Kuldip Jha; the cook, Mahesh Ram; the assistant cooks and bearers, Benedict Baleshwar Das and Mahavir Paswan.

The two priests who were at Gaya when the Sisters arrived, Jesuit Fathers Hubert Schmidt and Leon Foster, as well as their successors, Fathers Albert Wilzbacher, James Cox, and Joseph O'Brien, all members of the Patna mission, were outstanding in their care of the Sisters, both spiritually and materially.

The last important event of this year was the arrival of two new recruits from the United States, Sisters Eugenia Muething and Patricia Mary Kelley. Traveling with these two Sisters were Sister Catherine Regina Rogers, destined for Mokama, and three Notre Dame Sisters bound for Jamalpur. On 5 December, the sextet was received at the Patna airport by a large delegation. On 8 December, after a short sojourn in Mokama, Sisters Eugenia and Patricia Mary were escorted by Sister Lawrencetta to Gaya, where they received a very warm welcome from lay teachers, Sisters, priests, and students at Nazareth Academy and Creane Memorial.

As Nazareth Academy continued to increase in enrollment, lack of space made it necessary to plan a school building. Early in 1953 construction began. Because building in India is very different from building in the United States, the Sisters required some expert advice and direction, which they received from Father Schmidt and Mr. Fernandez, who labored untiringly and looked for no reward except the blessing of God. The new building of five classrooms was ready for use in mid 1954.

Teacher problems continued. Miss Alma John became ill in March 1953 and had to be hospitalized for some months. The difficulty of getting a Cambridge teacher was ever present. Creane Memorial faced the same difficulties. A poignant story is connected with this problem in Creane. One of the teachers, an only child, did not return to duty after his Christmas holidays in Ranchi District. Tragedy had touched him and his father when his mother was attacked, killed, and eaten by a tiger.

70

Gaya and its nearby jungles had been the realm of tigers and other wild animals, but fortunately the encroaching population was driving the animals farther into the jungle. Even at that, the eerie howling of jackals could frequently be heard at night, and the animals even entered the compound of the residents.

Genuine snake stories—encounters with cobras and kraits—abound. Sister Ann Bernadette, about to go to bed one night, noticed something brown near the leg of the bed. It was a krait, one of the most poisonous of snakes. A battle ensued, the snake on one side and Sisters Ann Bernadette, Charles Miriam, and Patricia Mary on the other. The snake, however, outwitted them by escaping through the bathroom drain.

Sister Eugenia was working late one night when a snake glided into the room and proceeded toward the open door of a bedroom where a student boarder was sleeping. The situation required immediate action. Sister Eugenia stood on a chair and aimed, one by one, two volumes of an encyclopedia at the intruding reptile, but to no effect. The creature retreated and coiled itself in cobra fashion in a corner near the door leading to the inside courtyard. Furtively, Sister Eugenia crept by the snake, roused Sister Patricia Mary from her room nearby, and summoned a night watchman. While Sister Patricia Mary held the dog that had accompanied the watchman and Sister Eugenia watched the cobra from her perch on the chair, the intrepid night guard skillfully disposed of the cobra with a heavy iron bar. A few years later a new candidate came quietly and with some diffidence into Sister Patricia Mary's room and hesitatingly announced, "Excuse me, Sister, there's a snake in the bathroom."

Kuldip Jha, the general handyman, had a unique and picturesque handling of the English language. There had been trouble with the flow of water into the storage tank, and Sister Charles Miriam wanted to know whether the matter had been corrected. She questioned the man in charge, "Kuldip, is the water now coming into the tank?" His affirmative reply was, "Yes, Sister, many, many waters always coming."

Because the large majority of students of the school were non-Christians (Hindus, Sikhs, Jains, or Muslims), the Sisters' range of experience was widened considerably beyond their Christian circumference. The contractor for the school building, Alimuddin, was celebrating the Muslim feast of Mohurram. He wished to include the Sisters in the celebration and asked that the front gate be left unlocked after its usual 9 p.m. closing. About 10 p.m., a group of one hundred people entered the compound with a band, lights, and a decorated replica of the tomb of the saint being honored. The band played vigorously, while sword dances, spear dances, and stick-fighting provided lively entertainment.

In January 1954, Sister Chàrles Miriam, after consultation with Sister Lawrencetta and Bishop Wildermuth, decided to discontinue the Senior Cambridge course of studies. Because the board examinations had to be taken outside Gaya and because it was difficult to obtain competent Cambridge teachers, this decision was a wise one. A little later in the year, to the delight of all, word came that Sister James Leo Goldsboro would join the staff. She left the United States by cargo ship in early September, and after an overland journey from Bombay with Sister Charles Miriam, arrived in Gaya on the night of 12 October to a tumultuous welcome, complete with fireworks, oil lamps, *malas*, and shouts of enthusiasm. Sister James Leo, a native of Leonardtown, Maryland, had a long teaching career before coming to India from Archbishop Williams High School in Braintree, Massachusetts.

Two outstanding teachers of the fifties were Miss Madeline Boyce and Miss Nancy Andrade. Miss Boyce joined the staff in her older years as a highly experienced and very competent primary teacher. A convert to Catholicism, she sacrificed herself completely for an invalid brother, and at his death emigrated to England, where she died at an advanced age. Miss Andrade was a "natural" when it came to teaching. Joining Nazareth Academy in her late teens, she demonstrated an extraordinary talent in pedagogy. She entered the Sisters of Notre Dame and distinguished herself throughout India in the field of education. In more recent years, as Sister Jyoti, she has given seminars to the teachers of Nazareth Academy.

Slowly adjustments were being made in the curriculum that would lead gradually to the Bihar Board examinations. Five Sisters were teaching in Nazareth Academy in 1955—Sisters Charles Miriam, James Leo, Eugenia, Patricia Mary, and Ann Roberta. Sister Ann Bernadette presided over the fortunes of Creane Memorial. Sister James Leo, although fifty years of age when she came to India, characteristically plunged into teaching on a new continent with her usual enthusiasm and amazing ingenuity. Under her tutelage, science and mathematics took on new dimensions.

Miss Christine Toppo joined the Nazareth Academy family in 1954 and taught for thirty-five years. After she retired, she resided at Nazareth Academy and was often engaged in private tutoring. She was ever a faithful and dedicated teacher. Miss Anna Joseph made her home at Nazareth Academy and helped in the primary classes until she was no longer able to do so. After a serious fall, she went to Nazareth Hospital, Mokama, where she remained until her death in 1986. An important addition to the faculty and convent was Sacred Heart Sister Anastasia from Bettiah. She became fully involved in the teaching of Hindi and other subjects in the school, and served as a tutor in Hindi for the Sisters.

Because Gaya was an important place of pilgrimage for Buddhists and Hindus as well as an international attraction, visitors constantly came and went, many finding their way to Nazareth Academy. Sometimes the school was asked to take part in civic receptions for distinguished visitors. Pandit Jawaharlal Nehru, President Rajendra Prasad, Prime Minister Indira Gandhi, the Crown Prince (later Emperor) and Princess of Japan, King Mahendra of Nepal and his queen, President V.V. Giri, President Zail Singh, President Venkataraman, Commonwealth Secretary Ranpal, and many others created for the students a pageant of history. Nazareth Academy was involved in many civic and interschool affairs, and the students usually performed very creditably in competitions and cultural shows.

In this connection an amusing, though frustrating, incident occurred. The civic authorities had organized a national integration program, one feature of which was to be a parade of floats from various schools to carry out that theme. Nazareth Academy prepared a float on an open van, artistically decorated, carrying a group of students dressed in the attractive and colorful costumes of different localities and communities of India. This float, which had been prepared with great enthusiasm by the students, the Sisters, and the lay teachers, had been both expensive and time-consuming. Arriving at the place of assembly, Nazareth Academy waited in vain for other floats to appear. They decided to have their own parade, all around the Gandhi *Maidan* (playground), through the main thoroughfare and on through a well-populated housing colony, until they returned to their own fort. Shouting and singing all the way, they attracted a good deal of attention, thus fulfilling their mission.

A feature of life at Nazareth Academy was the Sisters' excellent relationship with the Protestant community, who were mostly Baptists. Some of these Protestants were on the teaching staff, and a number were students of the school. The English pastor, Reverend Mr. Sidey, and his wife were familiar friends, as were Reverend Mr. and Mrs. Bihari, their successors. The Baptist mission operated a girls' school, and the English headmistresses were close friends—Miss Dorothea Phillcox, Miss Edith Hallett, Miss Dorothy Belham, and Miss Elsie Hope.

At the close of 1956, Sister Ann Bernadette withdrew from Creane Memorial and joined the Nazareth Academy staff. With her came Mrs. Samuel Shah, who has earned an enviable reputation as a teacher of the primary classes. Other well known teachers who began long and faithful service at this time were: Mrs. Helen Bose (1956), Miss Mabel Dwyer (1959), Mrs. Grace Norman (1958), and Mrs. Gloria Scott (1958).

In July 1956, the two final years of high school were begun in preparation for the matriculation of the Bihar Board. Sister Anastasia was a great help in revising the syllabus to prepare for this big step. Mrs. Helen Bose, who became the principal teacher for the matriculation, continued in her post for the next twenty years, until the time of her retirement. The love and respect that the students lavished upon her indicated the high quality of her pedagogy and the beauty of her character. Sisters teaching in the high school at that time were: Sister Charles Miriam, English; James Leo, science and mathematics; Eugenia, Hindustani Music.

The first matric class in the Bihar Board had six students who succeeded in the Board examinations of 1958—Anita Varma, Geeta Varma, Shakuntala Devi, Razia Haq, Noreen Du Bois, and Violet Lowther. Four of these girls became teachers. Geeta Varma, Razia Haq, and Noreen Du Bois served on the Nazareth staff both before and after marriage. Three are still (1990) engaged in teaching: Geeta (Varma) Kumar at Nazareth Academy; Noreen (Du Bois) Harris at De Nobili School, Dhanbad; and Violet (Lowther) Moss at Sacred Heart School and Little Flower School at Jamshedpur. Shakila Ghani Ali, a student of those years at the academy, also served on its staff before and after marriage and is still teaching at Nazareth Academy (1996). Many other former students of the academy have served on its staff. There are hundreds of students on the school register whose fathers and/or mothers were also students of the school.

Like a tree that begins as a sapling, Nazareth Academy grew steadily higher and wider with increasing strength and vigor. More room was necessary both for classes and for housing candidates for the community who were living in Gaya. Two of these candidates, Sisters Anne Marie Thayilchirayil and Ann George Mukalel, later became principals of Nazareth Academy. Toward the end of 1958, the community purchased the house and property next to Nazareth Academy. Because the acquisition coincided with the visit of Mother Bertrand and Sister Agnes Geraldine, the building was named Bertrand Hall. An amusing anecdote in connection with their trip concerned the converted name given by Abdul Shakur, the tailor, who in keeping with his profession called the new property "Button Hole" instead of Bertrand Hall.

In the short space that is available, it would be impossible to list all of the hundreds of visitors who passed through the portals of Nazareth Academy. They belonged to the high and the low, the rich and the poor, the young and the old, friends and strangers—a real kaleidoscope of people coming and going as in a huge railway station. One of the most distinguished visitors who honored the institution was the Apostolic Internuncio to India, Burma, and Ceylon, Archbishop (later Cardinal) James R. Knox of Australia. On 22 September 1959, in company with Bishop Wildermuth, Father Leonard D'Souza, secretary to the Internuncio, and Father Robert Donohue, S.J., the Archbishop spent the greater part of the day in Gaya, meeting the Catholic people and the students of both Nazareth Academy and Creane Memorial.

An interesting and somewhat eerie event of 1959 was a triduum of nightly visitors. This quotation from the annals describes the strange affairs most accurately:

> On the night of 7-8 August about 2 a.m., Sister James Leo discovered a man searching in her room. When she saw him leave, she began screaming loudly. The house was aroused. It was discovered that he had gained entrance by forc-

ing some bars on the rear classroom window . . . . He took a watch, two flashlights, cloth from the tailor's bundle, the chains from the incense thurible, and a violin from Sister James Leo's room. [Is the reader wondering why Sister James Leo had a violin in her room when she was not a violinist?]

At 11 p.m. 8 August, Kuldip, the janitor, was aroused by stones being pelted at him as he slept outside. He saw a man standing on a table in the pavilion. Kuldip and the dog Sher chased him unsuccessfully.

At 10:30 p.m. the next night, the house was aroused for the third successive night by the terrified screaming of a teacher, Grace Norman. She said she heard a knocking noise and saw a figure in her room. Since it was very dark and she was so overwrought, it may have been an hallucination, but there is more evidence to support the possibility that this was the devil. [The dark figure was seen by one of the Sisters before she heard the account from Grace Norman.] Father Foster will bless the house during the coming week. No one feels too safe at nightfall. [Subsequently a full-time night watchman was hired.]

1960-1969

The years rolled on, and the first decade closed almost imperceptibly. From a mere 160 children who received reports on the first "Proclamation Day," the number had swelled to over 500 when classes began in January 1961. Some drastic changes had come about. Sister Patricia Mary had become more involved with the direction of the candidates. Three of the Gaya candidates were destined to become the first India provincials: Margaret Rodericks, Shalini D'Souza, and Sarita Manavalan.

In January 1961, Sister Ann Roberta, a pioneer at Nazareth Academy, left for a year's study in the United States. Quietly and unobtrusively, she had worked through the early years of struggle and adjustment to lay a firm and lasting foundation in the primary department. Sister Ann Bernadette, another expert in primary education, succeeded her, and this section of the school became a credit to the talent and laborious efforts of these two Sisters.

At the opening of 1961, Nazareth Academy received its first quota of India Sisters: Theresa Martin Thundyil, Ignatius Marie Thayilchirayil, Ann George Mukalel, and Aloysia Mary Kuriakose. Except for the last named, they spent a number of years teaching in the school, and, as noted earlier, Sisters Ignatius Marie and Ann George both served terms as principals of Nazareth Academy.

The academy had its lighter moments. Prior to 1961 an annual Mardi Gras party had been instituted exclusively for the Sisters. These parties became gala affairs, with the Mokama Sisters ("country cousins" as they were called) attending enthusiastically when they could get time off from duty. Great ingenuity was displayed in the choice and "construction" of costumes.

Throughout 1962 there was much sickness among the Sisters and teachers. Sister Charles Miriam struggled with constant bouts of sickness that robbed her of strength and vitality. Sister Mary Martha had come frequently from Mokama on her behalf, and the ever-watchful Dr. Tobias had tried in vain to improve her condition. When it was decided that she return to the United States, she left Gaya on 16 May 1961 with Sister Lawrencetta as her companion. Because she was loved and respected by all, her departure caused general mourning, as it was realized even then that she would not return to India in ministry. Her leadership as a principal and her excellent qualities as a teacher left a lasting mark on Nazareth Academy.

Other cases of illness plagued the staff. A flu epidemic attacked a number of teachers. Mrs. K.C. Remedios, a teacher of long standing, had to resign because of repeated attacks of asthma, and Mrs. Fernandez resigned because of high blood pressure and a heart attack. The climax was reached, however, when Sister James Leo, who had become the principal after Sister Charles Miriam's departure, had to be operated on for the removal of a diseased kidney. Sister Mary Martha, the chief surgeon at Nazareth Hospital, was assisted by Sister Frederick, a Medical Missionary surgeon. Much to the relief of all, Sister James Leo made a splendid recovery and returned from Mokama to Gaya on 14 October. On 30 December she was appointed superior of Nazareth Academy.

Another blow fell when Sister Patricia Mary was appointed assistant mistress of novices, with residence in Mokama. Because she had spent nine years of distinguished service on the Nazareth Academy staff, it was with sorrow that her colleagues watched her depart with the candidates on the first of November. She had directed the candidates with great success, so her transfer was a gain for the novitiate at Mokama, but a great loss for the academy. Her talents as a teacher, a dramatist, and a director and advisor of students and candidates will always be remembered.

Although the year ended with one of the severest cold waves in living memory, there was a bright side. Coinciding with the cold wave came the return of Sister Ann Roberta after her study in the United States. A large contingent of Sisters and servants welcomed her at 9:45 p.m. on 18 December at the Gaya railway station. (The lay teachers had left for the holidays.)

A much "warmer" reception was accorded two new American recruits—Sisters Marita Ann Nabholz and Mary Celeste Collins when they arrived in India on 5 April 1962, with the temperature standing at 102 degrees. Sister Marita Ann, destined to be the first provincial of the India province, went to Mokama, while Sister Mary Celeste joined the Nazareth Academy staff in July. She tackled the classes with zeal and enthusiasm. Her work in Nazareth Academy, not only in the classroom but also in the organization of the library and in the planning of the new hall, will always be appreciated.

In the same year, a new health problem arose for Sister James Leo in the form of an abscess on her hip, which necessitated a protracted treatment that continued for a matter of years. Despite all kinds of diseases and injuries, Sister James Leo never slackened her pace. As an administrator and teacher for many years, the amount of work that she accomplished—the building, the buying, the duties of her office and classroom—remains an almost incredible record for a woman in dubious health, entering the India mission field at the age of fifty and spending the next twenty-five years in a veritable whirl of activity.

Although the high school students remained few in number, the total school enrollment continued to grow year by year. The problem of limited space could be solved satisfactorily only by building. Additions had already been made in 1953-54, and Bertrand Hall had been purchased in 1958. This space was soon outgrown, and in 1964 another addition was begun and completed under Sister James Leo's watchful eye. This structure added twelve classrooms to the existing facilities. Other buildings constructed in the sixties were a school hall, seating about 700 with two classrooms in the rear, and a library room that was built on the open veranda of the old building. Sister James Leo had really come into her own as a builder.

In the summer vacation of 1963, Sister Eugenia passed the final examination for a Bachelor's degree in Hindustani music (called Sangeet Prabhakar). Since 1956, she had pursued the course of the Prayag Sangeet Samiti, affiliated with Allahabad University through a center in Naini Tal District, held each summer in the months of May and June. Her colleague in study was Sister Lucia Grabner, a Swiss Holy Cross Sister from Austria. The two Sisters were destined to work together for more than twenty years. Besides teaching in their respective schools in Gaya and Bettiah, they composed church music in the Indian idiom and for eleven years carried on a summer school that strove to impart basic knowledge of Hindustani music to those engaged in teaching music in church and school. This school was attended for the most part by Sisters and lay teachers.

Two visitors heartily welcomed in 1963 were Mother Lucille Russell and Sister Mary Ramona Mattingly. The annals of Nazareth Academy 5 December described their arrival:

> In the midst of shouting and gesticulating in preparation for their arrival, Mother Lucille and Sister Mary Ramona arrived by car almost unnoticed, with the reception committee about the house. There was general excitement over the new headgear they were wearing. They were accompanied by Sister Mary Jude. In their luggage were a goose and a turkey.

Rumor has it that the turkey, apparently pleased with its distinguished traveling companions, promptly laid an egg in celebration.

Five teachers who joined Nazareth Academy in 1964 remained on the staff for twenty-five years or more: Mrs. Gladys Peterson, Miss Josephine Surin, Miss Josephine Xess, and Miss Teresa Toppo. Mrs. Shakila Ghani, who joined in 1963, had a similar record. Mrs. Shakila Ghani Ali, Mrs. Geeta Kumar, and Miss Teresa Toppo were still on the staff (as of 1991).

An historic day for Gaya was 28 August 1964 when Dr. Radha Krishnan, the president of India, laid the cornerstone for the new Magadh University at Bodh Gaya. Sisters James Leo and Eugenia attended the ceremony.

A real contribution to culture and the arts was made by Miss Mabel Dwyer, who, during her twelve years of teaching at Nazareth Academy, produced some excellent Hindi dramas that were much appreciated. Among these were "Garibon do Mahal," the story of St. Thomas at the Kingdom of Taxila, "Tyag Murti Damien," the life of Father Damien, "Chor," and "Kusum Kali." Dramas at that time, prior to the building of the school hall, had to be staged on a makeshift platform in the pavilion. On that stage Sister Patricia Mary had produced some excellent English dramas—"Our Lady of Fatima," "Alice in Wonderland," and "The Emperor's New Clothes." In 1963, "The Taming of the Shrew" was given on the same stage under Sister Eugenia's direction.

The year 1965 opened on a somber note. On the very first day of the year, Sister James Leo left for the United States. From 1962 on, she had been plagued by multiple abscesses of the hip. These had been frequently operated upon only to reappear. It was finally decided that she should go to the United States for treatment. Her resilience knew no bounds, however. Having spent most of the time in the States under medical treatment, 22 June saw her reappear in Gaya ready to resume her usual pace.

The next year, 1966, seemed to be filled with interesting and important events: national, local, church, school, and community. Only a few of these events can be mentioned here. Nationally it was the year of the death of Prime Minister Lal Bahadur Shastri and the nomination of Mrs. Indira Gandhi as his successor. It was the time of severe crisis for India, faced at the end of the year with one of the worst famines in her long history. A new experience for the school was the closing in 1965 and 1966 because of political disturbances.

An important step in the school was the formation of Nazareth Student League (NSL). A quotation from the annals follows:

Sister Ann Roberta began the organization of a student league that will undertake projects for the welfare of the students and that will also promote social action. One of the first endeavors will be the implementation of famine relief. Each child in school will be asked for at least one *paisa* a day. There will also be days set for the collection of foodstuffs—potatoes, rice, wheat, cornmeal, and other staple foods. The District Magistrate will assign one or two villages that will become the beneficiaries of these collections. Another project will be the formation of a group of patrol boys to control road traffic at the time of dismissal.

As will be seen, this pledge of famine relief was fully honored by the school.

New Sisters joined the Gaya community. Sister Theresa Martin, having completed her college studies, returned to the staff. Other newcomers were Sisters Mary Magdalene Chackalackal and Francine Moozhil. Sister Mary Magdalene eventually held important posts—principal of Creane Memorial School and vice-principal and supervisor of primary classes of Nazareth Academy.

The annals of 20 November 1966 relate the following social event:

All eight Sisters were motored by John and Arthur Wakefield, sons of Mr. John Gurney Wakefield, an English resident of Gaya, who served as the manager of the Tekari Raj, to Balwa on the Grand Trunk Road, thirty-six miles from Gaya, where Maharajah Fateh Singh of Tekari welcomed them to his hunting lodge, Sabalpur. After luncheon in the open, John Wakefield, with all the Sisters aboard, drove the open hunting jeep seven miles deep into the jungle. Armed with a rifle, John hoped to at least get a peacock. The possibility of seeing a tiger, leopard, or other wild animal was small, as these animals seldom leave their lairs in the daytime. . . . Maharajah, John, and Arthur were perfect hosts and made the picnic a delightful experience. [The sons, nephews, and nieces of the Maharajah were Nazareth Academy students.]

The year 1967 was dominated by the massive famine relief work that gained momentum as the year went on. Volunteers from all over India and from many foreign countries gathered in various centers where food distribution and medical treatment were being provided to those suffering from the effects of the famine. In the forefront were the Christian relief services. The great social leader, Jai Prakash Narayan, categorically stated that the Christians were the first to realize the magnitude of the crisis and to take practical and effective steps to relieve the suffering.

Nazareth Academy can look back with pride on its record of service in this and other national emergencies. Under the direction of Father Frank Loesch, S.J., Sister James Leo wholeheartedly launched into the program, mobilizing the faculty and students to take part in the daily feeding of some five thousand people. Sister Ann Roberta, as overall director, worked indefatigably, even as she pursued school work. It was in late 1966 that a jeep van was given to the school to transport the necessary supplies to Bengali Bigha, the center of distribution. The driver, Ghulam Mohammed Ansari, who was hired at that time, remained with the school for almost twenty years and left only when his eyesight became defective.

Just when the program was at its height, Sister Ann Roberta was called to continue her pioneering by becoming superior of the new house in Ranchi. Actually her pioneering did not stop there. As will be seen, she opened the house in Chatra and was in the original group to go to Patna. She had also viewed the lofty heights of Darjeeling with the first band in 1948. It was with heavy hearts that faculty, students, and servants bade farewell to Sister Ann Roberta on 24 June after she had given sixteen and a half years of devoted service at Nazareth Academy. She had already been given a touching farewell at Bengali Bigha.

Sister Theresa Martin succeeded Sister Ann Roberta as director of the relief work, which continued until 15 November, a full eleven months. The number of men and women, religious and lay, Christian and non-Christian, who came and went during those months could not be estimated. Teachers and students labored along with the outsiders, and many made big sacrifices in order to pursue this work of generous charity. Two teachers, Miss Josephine Xess and Miss Teresa Toppo, gave up their usual summer vacation at home in order to remain with the teams engaged in famine relief.

Rupa Varma and Raihana Haq began teaching at Nazareth Academy in 1967, and it is an interesting fact that each was the third in her family to join the Nazareth Academy staff. Both were members of large families who studied at Nazareth Academy. Rupa Varma was the younger sister of Geeta Varma, already mentioned, and Rajni Varma, who had joined in 1966. Raihana Haq, who was teacher and librarian, was the younger sister of Razia Haq and Rafia Haq, also staff members. All had been students of Nazareth Academy.

Miscellaneous events of interest in 1967 include the following: the first Sister from Gaya, Agnes Tudu, daughter of the personnel manager, Paul Tudu, made her profession as Sister Rosita in December in Mokama; the school acquired a telephone after many years of "paper communication"; and the library addition was begun. Also in that year, Father Joseph O'Brien, S.J., pastor of Gaya for ten years, was transferred. For one month his place was filled by Father John Baptist Thakur, S.J., later to become first bishop of Muzzaffarpur. The permanent pastor, Father Joseph Pascal, S.J., came in July.

Changes were many during 1968. Sister Anne Marie Thayilchirayil (the former Sister Ignatius Marie) had to leave at the end of January, when she became the superior-designate for Mokama convent. Sister Theresa Martin began a new regime as principal of Creane Memorial School and was later joined by Sister Sophia Karapurackal. Sister Shalini D'Souza assumed the vice-principalship at Nazareth Academy and also took over the direction of the Student League. Sister Ann Bernadette was named superior of the convent, while Sister James Leo continued as principal of the academy. After a term in Mokama as candidate director, Sister Mary Celeste returned to the academy staff. Mrs. Bibha Sen, a trained teacher and nurse, also joined the staff. She used her expertise in both fields to good account and remained on the staff for almost two decades. Her three daughters were students of the school, and two of them, Jayasree and Banasree, later joined the teaching staff.

A major event of 1968 was the completion of the school hall in November. The ribbon was cut by the District Magistrate in the presence of a large audience. The inaugural drama, "Himani," the Hindi version of "Snow White and the Seven Dwarfs," staged under the able direction of two talented teachers, Miss Josephine Surin and Miss Anna Mary Surin, was an unqualified success.

Before the end of 1968 a number of important changes of personnel again took place. In July, Father Edwin Saxton, S.J., replaced Father Joseph Pascal as pastor. In November, Sister Ann Bernadette was named superior of Ranchi, replacing Sister Ann Roberta. After eighteen years of zealous and efficient teaching in Gaya, Sister Ann Bernadette slipped away quietly on 17 November, with the gratitude and appreciation of all for her excellent service in Gaya—in the school, church, and community. Sister Eugenia succeeded her as superior of the academy.

Nazareth Academy was beginning to be recognized as an outstanding institution. In January 1969, Mr. Kenneth James Smythe, an educator from Australia, came as a guest of the government of India on a study tour of Indian educational institutions. Nazareth Academy was privileged to be one of the schools appointed by the government to be visited by Mr. Smythe.

Nazareth Academy has had long and friendly relations with the Indian army— its officers and soldiers and their families. Through the years, many students and teachers have come to the classrooms of Nazareth Academy from the army cantonment. The army post of Gaya, dating back to its American origin in World War II, has grown and developed into one of the largest training centers in the country. Some officers were also members of the Church: Brigadier Ronald Wood, Major Leonard D'Cruz, Lt. Col. A.B.C. D'Mello, Major Abraham, Lt. Col. (later Brigadier) C.A.G. Pais. The army often provided valuable assistance to the school: the army band for functions, specialized equipment for sports, personnel for training in marching and games, etc.

An interesting encounter took place when Mother Lucille and Major General Eustace D'Souza of the Indian Army met on the occasion of their simultaneous visits to Gaya and to the church. It was the general who humorously termed it a "confrontation."

In this second visit of Mother Lucille in December 1969, she was accompanied by Sister Ellen Curran, procurator of the mission. Sister Ellen found much to interest her in the country for which she had been working for many years.

Nazareth Academy suffered the loss of two valuable staff members before the end of 1969. Sister Mary Celeste, a competent teacher and librarian, left for the United States in September. Miss Anna Mary Surin, also a dynamic and hardworking teacher, left the staff in December after a tenure of seven years to get married in the same month in her hometown of Naotoli.

Sister Mary Scaria Menonparampil was the first Sister of Charity to become a student of Magadh University. Having acquired a B.Sc. in her studies in the United States, she gained admission to the M.Sc. course in the field of botany. In connection with the course, she made an interesting field trip to the Himalayan region—Naini Tal, Mussourie, and their environs.

1970-1979

As the new decade of the seventies began, some major changes occurred. Sister Mary Chackalackal (the former Sister Mary Magdalene) became the principal of Creane Memorial School in January, but left in June to study for the B.Ed. in Madras. Her successor was Sister Teresa Xavier Ponnazhath. A more drastic change was the resignation in June of the principal of Nazareth Academy, Sister James Leo, who assumed the maintenance management of the school as well as the duties of treasurer. Sister Anne Marie succeeded her in the school where she had first begun her teaching career.

The school continued to grow, and efforts were made to gain recognition by the Bihar Board of Secondary Education. Before the end of this decade, the school became completely coeducational when boys were admitted to the high school. The matric students took the exam as private candidates of the Bihar Board in one of the government-recognized schools.

Also in 1971, other important changes came about through transfers and appointments. Sister Shalini, who had become deeply involved in the school in several capacities—vice principal, primary supervisor, and Nazareth Student League Director—was assigned to the United States and left in July. She was succeeded in the primary department by Sister Mary Chackalackal, who had finished the B.Ed. examinations in Madras.

During this year trouble between the two Pakistans had erupted, and Gaya had received a number of needy refugees from newly created Bangladesh. The government erected a camp at an abandoned World War II airfield near Gaya. There at Panchanpur the refugees were fed and housed. Once again the Christian volunteer groups came to the fore. Holy Family Hospital in Patna sent a team of doctors, nurses, and other medical staff to help with the needs of these 27,000 unfortunates who had been forced to flee their homes and country. Some of the SCN nurses from Mokama also took part in this program. When war actually broke out between India and Pakistan, it had little effect on everyday life, except for nightly blackouts and air-raid practice.

A tragedy touched the domestic life of the academy on the first of December. Its narration in the annals is precise and graphic:

About 7:45 a.m. Sawalik, a faithful servant of the school for more than twenty years, jumped from the third-story veranda of the school building and was killed instantly. No one could ascribe any reason, and temporary insanity was suspected. Police came and investigated, after which his body was removed for police autopsy. About 1 p.m. his body was released and given over to his relatives for funeral rites and cremation. He was a Hindu. His wife survives him, but he has no children. Everyone felt very sad, as he was well liked by all.

At the end of the year, Mrs. Grace Norman, a popular and efficient teacher for the last fourteen years in residence at Nazareth Academy, left for Kanpur with her three children—Lynette, Jimmy, and Judy—to reside with her sister, Mrs. Irene Shear. She took up a new teaching post at St. Mary's Convent, Kanpur. She was greatly missed on the Nazareth Academy staff.

Visitors of note in 1972 were Mr. and Mrs. A.N. Banerjee, who had emigrated to England in the mid sixties with their eight children, seven of whom had been students of Nazareth Academy. They arrived in early 1972 with their English-born children, John (5) and Mary (2) for a happy reunion with friends of their Gaya days.

The visitor of 1972 causing the greatest excitement was Sister Mary Holt, formerly known as Sister Charles Miriam. Her arrival was noted in the annals for 2 December as follows:

Sister Mary Holt arrived from America at 3:30 p.m. in the jeep. Sisters, teachers, students, servants, and friends gave a warm and touching welcome to their old principal. All were delighted to have her once more in Gaya after an absence of eleven years.

A reception was held on 27 December to honor Sister Mary. About 250 people attended—old friends, former students, parents, and guardians. It was a highly successful affair. The school was privileged to have its first principal inaugurate an old students' association that was later given the name of Nazareth Old Students Association (NOSA). Sister Mary remained in Gaya for Christmas and departed for Mokama on 27 December, along with the Gaya community, to participate in the silver jubilee celebration of the SCN mission in India. (Sister Mary had been one of the pioneers.)

In the second half of 1973, a Sanskrit Master, who was to became a sort of institution in himself, joined the staff. Pandit Hari Gopal Mishra, better known as Panditji, belonged to a special caste of priests known as Gaya *wallas* and was a well loved and respected teacher of the traditional guru type. He continued as the principal teacher of Sanskrit until his retirement in 1988.

Sister James Leo's golden jubilee occurred in March of 1972. The festivities included a children's program, a High Mass, a dinner followed by a program given by the Sisters and lay teachers, a light supper, and a movie. A special feature was the band summoned by the servants to play immediately after Mass. For the occasion, Sister James Leo was "decked out" in a gold-colored saree lent by one of the teachers.

As enrollment increased and space diminished, building was imperative, both for classrooms and for science laboratories. Father Edwin Saxton invoked God's blessing on the newest building project in an impressive ceremony held on 23 August 1973 in the presence of the assembled school children. Sister Teresa Rose, the provincial, broke ground for the new building. Enrollment reached 900 in 1974.

The president of India, Dr. V.V. Giri, officiated at two major functions in Gaya. The first was the opening of the new Japanese Buddhist temple at Bodh Gaya. Twenty girls of Nazareth Academy's fifth and sixth classes formed a guard of honor for the president on this occasion. On the same day, 8 December 1973, Nazareth Academy was also represented when the president laid the cornerstone for the Magadh Medical College Hospital.

The year 1974 was to have an unprecedented number of nonscheduled holidays because of repeated political and civil disturbances. To begin with, school opened a week late because textbooks were not available. Transportation and all means of communication had been seriously disrupted as a result of a nationwide railway strike in mid December, and since buses were not running either, textbooks were long delayed.

A family of four—Maureen and Colin Du Bois, teachers at Nazareth Academy, and their sons Brian and Johnny, students at the academy—left to take up residence in Australia. Mrs. Noreen Harris (nee Du Bois) a sister of Colin, who had been a student and teacher, replaced her sister-in-law Maureen. Noreen had four daughters in the school.

Sister Anne Marie, elected delegate to the General Assembly in 1974, left on 25 May to join Sister Teresa Rose for the journey to the United States. In her absence, Sister Eugenia was acting principal.

In mid October, Father Saxton was transferred and was replaced by Father George Ziebert, S.J. Father Saxton might be called a "man for all seasons," as he had made contacts and friendships among all communities and was liked and respected by all.

Two important SCN visitors in October 1974 were the two mission procurators, Eula Blandford and Mary Bennet Cecil. Gaya was pleased to receive these two zealous and hardworking Sisters, who had come to see at first hand the many places about which they had only a "reading knowledge."

A critical situation arose in late August 1975. Patna suffered a devastating flood that engulfed all the main parts of the whole city. Relief operations were undertaken on a war footing. At the height of the crisis, Sister James Leo developed severe abdominal pain. After she was taken by road to Mokama, the doctors diagnosed an intestinal obstruction requiring immediate surgery. Because Nazareth

Hospital was without a surgeon at that time and Holy Family Hospital in Kurji was closed because of the flood, Sister James Leo was moved to Tripolia, a section of Patna, where the Holy Cross Sisters have a hospital. There she was operated on by the Holy Family Hospital staff surgeon, Dr. V. R. Sinha. She made an excellent recovery.

Among foreign visitors of 1975 were the SCNs in the Justice '75 program, superior general Sister Barbara Thomas and Sister Donna Kenney, who conducted a workshop, and Sister Gail Collins (who had changed her name from Sister Mary Celeste), who was welcomed to her former mission, Nazareth Academy. Of the Justice '75 group, Sister Frances Loretto Yowaiski stayed to teach in the school and to give good points in pedagogy to the teachers. Justice '76 members Julia Dullea, SCN, and Sister Gertrude Roethle, a Franciscan, also gave service to students and teachers.

The Nazareth Pre-School Centre for four-year-olds was officially opened on 12 July 1976, with Sister Shanti Kappalummackal the first director. Sisters Teresa Rose, Ann Roberta, and Ann George attended the opening.

Mrs. Helen Bose, the well-beloved high school matric teacher since its inception twenty years ago, retired from Nazareth Academy in December 1976. The Nazareth Student League gave her a very touching farewell. Mrs. Bose was indeed an exceptional teacher—devoted, kind, gentle, but firm in demanding the best of her students. Her name will ever be remembered in the annals of the school.

Sister Margaret Rodericks made her first visit as provincial when she presided at the annual meeting of the Gaya Nazareth Academy on 30 January 1977. Sister Margaret, having entered the community with a B.A. and T.D. (Diploma in Teaching), had taught at Nazareth Academy during her candidacy.

Sister Lawrencetta, her sister, Miss Virginia Veeneman, and Sister Anne Horrigan (the latter two visiting from the United States) and Sister Mary Jude, administrator of Nazareth Hospital, Mokama, attended the final performance of the drama, "The King Who Took Sunshine," their distinguished presence helping to make the drama a success. The American visitors enjoyed a stay of several months in India at the end of 1977.

At the sixth annual meeting of the Nazareth Old Students Association, 1977, the members honored Sister Eugenia, the convener, on the completion of twenty-five years at Nazareth Academy. School children marked the occasion with an enjoyable program and the presentation of gifts. Nazareth Academy bade farewell to the popular principal, Sister Anne Marie, at the end of the school term in May 1978. Sister Ann George was named her successor. Both Sisters had spent long years teaching at Nazareth Academy and were loved and respected by all.

Dr. Millicent Tobias, one of the finest and most loyal friends that Nazareth Academy had from the beginning, left to join her sister in England. Sister Eugenia accompanied her on the long journey, which she was making at the age of seventy-five. The following excerpt from the annals of June 1978 describes her departure:

Mass was offered by Father Francis, S.J., from St. Xavier's, Patna. He paid a lovely tribute and farewell to Dr. Tobias for whom the Mass was offered. All assembled at the Gaya railway station to bid goodbye to this noble lady who had given forty-three years of medical service to Gaya. She served the Sisters and the poor without charging any fee and was ever ready to help in any way. She was daily in the convent chapel for Mass and Holy Communion. The train left for Calcutta at 10:30 a.m. The London-bound travelers are due to leave at 1:30 a.m. on the 23rd.

At Nazareth Academy, the post of primary supervisor, often united with that of vice-principal, has always been an important one. The following Sisters have held the office: Ann Bernadette, Shalini, Mary Chackalackal, Sophia, Sujata Maliakal, and Ann Scaria Menonparampil. Directors of the pre-school have been very important in maintaining that earliest branch of school for so many little ones. After the first director, Sister Shanti, others have been SCNs Sujata Maliakal, Prema Muthukatil, Nisha Chemmanam, Aisha Kavalakattu, Maria Palathingal, Arpita Mundamattathil, Philomina Hembrom, and Anne Philip Gnavally.

In February 1979 Sisters James Leo and Ann George purchased an autorickshaw in Patna. The diminutive vehicle was mounted on the back of the jeep van and transported in pouring rain to Gaya. It provided many years of service.

In those later years, crime had greatly increased. A casual report in the annals dated the first of September illustrated what had become a common occurrence: Sister Theresa Martin, Sister Cecily [Velleringatt], Miss Josephine Surin, and Shampa Roy, a student, left in two rickshaws to get an early train to Patna to attend a science seminar in which Shampa was to compete. On the way to the railway station, they were set upon by robbers armed with pistol and daggers. Josephine lost a gold chain and a watch, the Sisters their watches, chains, and money. The Sisters returned to the house, while Miss Surin and Shampa carried on to Patna.

Despite the unnerving experience, Shampa secured second place in the state, which made her eligible to compete in Calcutta.

The Patna unit of the All-India Association of Catholic Schools celebrated its silver jubilee in the latter part of 1979. A unique function honored all personnel who had served twenty-five years or more in the same school. Nazareth Academy had the largest number, and all of them went to Patna for the conferring of awards. The honorees were: Sister James Leo (1954); Sister Eugenia (1952); Miss Alma John (1940 and 1951); Miss Christine Toppo (1954); the school tailor, Abdul Shakoor (1948); the chief cook Mahesh Ram (1950); the two assistant cooks-bearers Benedict Baleshwar Das (1950); and Mahavir Paswan (1954). Besides attending the meeting and dinner, all received certificates and plaques.

On 12 October 1979, Sister James Leo completed twenty-five years in India, all at Nazareth Academy. She was honored by the students, by the Nazareth Old Students Association, the teachers, and many friends. Later, when it was learned that she would leave India in December, the functions and visits were almost continuous. She was guest of honor at a regular meeting of the Rotary Club. A quotation from the annals states:

> The members, prominent citizens all, paid glowing tribute to Sister James Leo and her work in Gaya and lauded her achievements as teacher, principal, manager, and treasurer. . . . The farewells were very touching.

Just five days before Sister James Leo's departure, the new church of St. Thomas the Apostle, the crowning work of Father Ziebert, was blessed and dedicated by Bishop Wildermuth of Patna on 25 November 1979, the feast of Christ the King. Foundation Day for the community on the first of December became "D-Day" for Sister James Leo. The next day all the Sisters were ready by 8 a.m. to depart for Mokama, from where Sisters James Leo and Margaret would leave for Delhi and the United States. A large crowd of teachers, servants, and friends had assembled in the compound by the zero hour. Tears were shed by all as the jeep moved out, bound for the final farewell in Mokama.

1980-1989

A solar eclipse was an early phenomenon of the new decade. This spectacular occurrence took place on 16 February 1980. All took the opportunity to view it, using various means of shielding the eyes from damage—thick dark glasses, old and considerably dark X-ray films, even buckets of water in which the sun was reflected. The eclipse was total in some parts of India but only partial in this northern region.

Bishop Osta, the new bishop of Patna, paid his first visit to Gaya on 16 August 1980. He had a heavy schedule, moving from one place to another for Masses and receptions at the parish, Creane Memorial School, Nazareth Academy, and the Missionary Brothers of Charity. Everywhere, he was received with respect and admiration.

Sudden deaths struck two friends of the school in 1980. The first was the death by railway accident of Carlyle Du Bois, an assistant driver on the electric engines. Carl was a former student of Nazareth Academy, brother of Noreen Harris and Colin Du Bois, also former students and former teachers as well. Carl's three children—Lynn, Cheryle, and Sean—were students of Nazareth Academy at the time of his death. His wife, the former Mathilda Lewis, was a graduate of Nazareth School of Nursing, Mokama. His sudden death was a terrible shock and loss to his family and his many friends. The second death was that of Dr. (Lt. Col.) K.S.R. Swami, a highly respected citizen of Gaya and a loyal and faithful friend of the school. His four granddaughters were students of the school, and two of them, Mrs. Deepa Raghbavan and Miss Chitra Narasimhan, served as teachers.

Two Sisters left the staff in 1980. Serious health problems caused Sister Rose Kochithara, who had replaced Sister James Leo as treasurer, to leave her work in September. Her loss was greatly felt. In December, Sister Theresa Martin, a long-time member of Nazareth Academy staff, an efficient and greatly appreciated teacher, was transferred to Ranchi.

The year 1981 began as one of "great expectations." Sister Ann George and her assistants had been working strenuously, though quietly, toward an important goal, namely recognition of Nazareth Academy by the Central Board of Secondary Education (CBSE) in Delhi. For at least twenty years, efforts had been made by Sisters James Leo and Anne Marie to gain recognition by the Bihar Board of Secondary Education, through which the Nazareth Academy students passed as private candidates.

These efforts finally paid off. The first stirring of hope for the CBSE came when three inspectors arrived on 21 January 1982, delegated by the Central Board to report on their findings. They spent the day in the school, auditing classes, teaching, inspecting the buildings and equipment, the library, and laboratories. Apparently they were pleased with what they found, for 6 June brought the joyful news that Nazareth Academy had been granted affiliation with the Central Board. This affiliation covered all classes from one to ten. Much credit was due Sister Ann George, the principal, and her coworkers, especially Sister Sunita Vayalipara, who spared neither time nor labor to place the school on a firm footing. This affiliation was to be renewed periodically and could be made permanent after ten years.

Adjustment of courses and school sessions had to be made. The former Beginners Class was abolished and was converted into Class 1 when the new school year began at the end of June. All classes moved up accordingly, except Class 9, since the new syllabus for passing matric would require two years. Class 10 finished the preliminary Bihar Board examinations in December and was the last class for the final examinations in May 1982. A new era for Nazareth Academy had begun.

Nazareth Academy completed one year under the CBSE in May 1982. The school year at that time was from 2 May to 30 April. The new arrangement was a one-session school day from 7 a.m. to 12:30 p.m., the timing of which was adjusted according to the season. The year 1982-1983 would be momentous, especially for the students of Class 10 as they began final preparation for the first matric examination under the new board. The enrollment exceeded 1200.

On 3 July 1982, word was received of the death of Sister Mary Holt, beloved first principal of Nazareth Academy. On 11 July, the students held a prayer meeting for the repose of her soul. On 12 July, a condolence meeting was held for her former students and friends. Glowing tributes were paid by those for whom she had been principal, teacher, and guide. Her memory is eternally engraved in Nazareth Academy—in its buildings, its institutions, its traditions, and in the hearts of the people of Gaya whose lives she enriched so much.

In March 1983, eighty-five girls and boys took the All-India Secondary School Examinations in Central School No. 1. They were the first to appear under the Central Board of Secondary Education in Delhi. Results published in June brought the good news that all had passed.

In June 1983, Sister Roselyn Karakkattu became the supervisor of the primary section and vice-principal of the school. Creane Memorial School had been growing steadily and had become an important institution. Sister Josita Eniakattu as principal continued to enhance its ever-growing reputation.

On 1 September, Miss Alma John, a teacher for nearly forty years at Nazareth Academy, having been on the staff when the school was first functioning as St. Michael's, died at Nazareth Hospital, Mokama, after a brief illness. She was highly respected by all and held a warm place in the hearts of hundreds of students who had passed through her hands. She was always a conscientious and dedicated teacher as well as a woman of firm faith and devotion to her Catholic religion.

On 30 November, Nazareth Academy received word that it had lost another of its great teachers, as well as principals, when Sister James Leo died on 24 November. She had been seriously ill several times after her 1979 retirement from India, where she had served for twenty-five years. Even during her tenure in India, her health had often been precarious, but illness had never prevented her from giving the utmost of her talent and energy to the work of education in Nazareth Academy. In her time, the school grew in numbers, and she ever maintained and even enhanced the standard that had been achieved. All Gaya mourned her death, and hundreds came to offer condolence and to join in the prayer meetings that were held for her.

Two commendable social projects were initiated in 1984. On 26 January, Republic Day, it became an annual custom for Class 9 to conduct a sports competition for the poor children who were being taught by the Sisters of the pre-school in the late afternoons of the school days. The competition had been extended to other poor children of the area.

The second project was initiated on 11 February 1984. An Appreciation Day for the Nazareth servants was given by the students of the school, Class 9 taking charge. It consisted of a reception with garlanding and presentation of a gift to each servant. A lively variety program, with skits, speeches, songs, and dances, was followed by dinner for all the servants, prepared and cooked by students and teachers. Sister Sunita, teacher of Class 9, had been the moving power behind these projects, which eventually became traditional.

By the end of 1984, changes came in leadership posts. Sister Cassilda Castell, a well known teacher of Nazareth Academy, succeeded Sister Josita as principal of Creane Memorial, and in the pre-school Sister Aisha took over the post of director from Sister Maria.

In July, two deaths occurred that had a strong impact on the school. Mrs. Shobha Lalchandani, a former student and teacher on the staff, died suddenly, less than a year after the death of her husband. Popular as she was with friends and with her students, her untimely death saddened all who knew her. Only five days later came word of the death of Sister Lawrencetta, the beloved first superior of the SCNs in India. A school holiday was declared on 15 July, and the whole community departed to attend the funeral in Mokama.

On 14 August, the school received another great shock when Mrs. Bibha Sen suffered a severe heart attack while on duty with her class at the school assembly. She was attended at the school by six doctors who had assembled upon hearing the news. She was immediately removed to Magadh Medical College Hospital. For some days her condition was critical, but she gradually improved and was eventually able to return to school after a leave of about five months.

Television came to Gaya in 1984 with a transmitting station situated very near the school. Although it was a sensation initially, it soon became commonplace. The next year, Nazareth Academy had its own TV.

A memorable picnic, unique in Nazareth Academy experience, is reported in the annals of December 1984:

Class 10 boys and girls of both sections, Sisters Ann George, Roselyn, Eugenia, and five lay teachers went for a picnic to the Balwa jungle. On the return journey the bus with its approximately 90 passengers, got stuck in sand and rock at a small river crossing, about five kilometers from the main road, quite in the jungle. There was great anxiety among the parents when the bus failed to arrive on time, and it was nearly three hours later that a message finally reached Gaya that all were safe but stranded in the jungle. A relief bus was sent, and the D.I.G. (Deputy Inspector General of Police) with escort, two army trucks and about five private cars made their way into the isolated spot. The picnic party reached Nazareth Academy safe and sound about 2:00 a.m., lightening the spirits of all.

As the days of Sister Ann George's tenure drew to a close, she was feted by students, teachers, families, and friends. Students gave a farewell program on 27 December 1984, and a collection of Rs 1700 and other gifts were presented. By 3 January 1985, Sister Ann George managed to wind up "the affairs of state" and departed for Ranchi. With deep regret and heartfelt appreciation, Nazareth Academy bade farewell to a distinguished and well loved principal.

A change of leadership in any institution marks an important step. Sister Ann Palatty took up the reins of administration with vigor and enthusiasm when school opened on 7 January 1984. She became thoroughly acquainted with the organization of the Central Board of Secondary Education and skillfully guided the third group of candidates who were preparing for the AISSE (All India Secondary School Examinations) in which they would appear in March. The school enrollment continued to increase, creating a constant problem of accommodation. A note in the annals for 26 August 1985 is short but expressive: "Due to all kinds of shortage—water, electricity, gas—only one day of school was held this week."

An interesting visitor on 21 December 1985 was Sister Jyoti of the Notre Dame Sisters. As Miss Nancy Andrade, a young and exceptionally talented teacher, she had spent one year teaching at Nazareth Academy in 1956. In the intervening years she had attained high positions in the field of education.

The year 1986 saw a few personnel appointments. For the first time, two Sisters—Sheela Palamoottil and Evelyn D'Souza— took up direct social and pastoral work in the Gaya area. Sister Evelyn also had teaching assignments in the school. In September 1986, Sister Eugenia received a new assignment and resigned as teacher after thirty-four years on the staff of Nazareth Academy. She continued to reside at the school.

SCN visitors from the United States in 1986 were Sisters Julie Driscoll in July, Miriam Corcoran in October, and Mary Lynn Fields in November. In collaboration with Sister Miriam, a drama specialist, Sister Roselyn Karakkuttu produced a most entertaining drama in November. In the early part of 1987, another SCN from the United States, Sister Maureen Daugherty, editor of *SCNews,* the community paper, paid a visit to Gaya. From a journalist's standpoint, she found very much to interest her not only in the missions but also in the whole country with its varied peoples and cultures.

After nearly twenty years of use, the school hall was subjected to intensive repairing, cleaning, painting, and refurbishing. A second item of progress was the purchase of a Mahendra minibus that had been long awaited and much needed. The autorickshaw, despite its advanced age, continued to ply the streets of the town on its various errands.

A note in the annals for June 1987 gives a typical picture of a summer day in Gaya:

The heat for the last two weeks of May was very intense with daily temperatures reaching not less than 114 degrees F, 46-47 C. The roof is the one refuge at night, otherwise there would be no sleep. Both electricity and water have been in very poor supply so the suffering is increased. The heat continued with out a break for about five weeks.

Sister Sujata Maliakal joined the staff of Nazareth Academy in June 1987 as vice principal and supervisor of Classes 2 to 5. Sisters Stella Kaiprampatt and Priya Kalapurayil were added to the high school staff, and Sister Deepa Thekkecheruvil was assigned to teach at Creane Memorial. When Sister Cassilda Castell moved to an assignment in Ranchi in January 1988, Sister Deepa succeeded her as principal. Under the capable leadership of Creane Memorial's principals, the enrollment increased year by year. The school acquired a good reputation and a position of great importance in the town. On two successive nights, the parents of the students in different classes were entertained with a fine variety program, which was presented in the school hall.

A new student council was formed at this time, and trips were made by the students to two villages to assess the general poverty of the people and the effect of the damage caused by the incessant rain. It was also at this time that regular Parents Days were established for all classes.

The death by drowning of Sister Sandhya in 1987 had special significance for Gaya, as she had been a much loved and respected teacher at Creane Memorial for two years. By giving her life to relieve the sufferings of flood victims, she was an example to all of supreme charity.

In and around Gaya, there was havoc wrought by flood during September 1987. Class 10, through a number of projects, collected Rs 5770 for the victims.

Sister Ann Palatty, elected delegate to the General Assembly in the United States, departed with Sister Shalini for foreign shores in November 1987. For the first month of her absence, 26 November until Christmas, the former principal, Sister Anne Marie, replaced her. For the remainder of the time, until her return on 19 February 1988, Sister Sujata functioned as acting principal.

With the ever-increasing enrollment in the school, the existing facilities became inadequate. Plans eventually materialized into a large two-story building with offices on the ground floor and a library on the upper floor. The first step was the demolition of the fifty-year-old pavilion, the scene of so many and varied school activities, a nostalgia-evoking landmark to all old students. Another building project of the same year was the enlargement of the two classrooms at the rear of the hall made possible by demolishing the veranda.

Sister Eugenia's golden jubilee in the community on 19 July 1988 was celebrated joyfully by school and community. A purse of Rs 8000 for the relief of the poor was presented to her by students and teachers. Mass was offered in the evening of the jubilee day, followed by a supper which was attended by Sisters, priests, Missionary Brothers of Charity, and resident teachers.

The earthquake of 21 August 1988 was a national disaster, with the greatest damage occurring in Bihar and Nepal. In Gaya all experienced the terrifying shaking of the beds, the rattling of the windows and doors, and the low rumbling noise. By God's blessing, Nazareth Academy and Gaya in general received no serious damage. Sister Mary Chackalackal, who was visiting at the time, provided a humorous touch when she suddenly emerged from an inner bedroom to the quadrangle where the Sisters had gathered, with the belated announcement that there had been an earthquake. All had forgotten she was in the house. Some time later, announcements from TV, radio, and newspaper revealed the seriousness of this quake. School children contributed to relief funds, and teachers of both the academy and Creane Memorial decided to forego gifts and luncheon on Teachers Day to contribute further to the relief. In recognition of her cooperation in all Red Cross activities available for schools, Sister Ann Palatty was awarded an honorable life membership in the Bihar branch of the Indian Red Cross.

In late October, the community in India received the sad news that Sister Ann Bernadette had died in Kentucky on 28 October 1988 after a painful illness heroically endured. She had been the principal of Creane Memorial and later supervisor of the primary section of Nazareth Academy. Almost twenty of her thirty years in India were spent in Gaya.

In November 1988, under the direction of Sister Priya and other science teachers, students participated in a science fair at the town school. They won first place in the competitions for exhibits, which entitled them to participate in the state fair in Patna, where two of their exhibits won first place.

In response to a long-standing request, a Delhi unit of the Nazareth Old Students Association was begun in mid November 1988 at St. Xavier's in Delhi. The event was attended by Sister Eugenia, convener; Miss Josephine Surin, senior teacher; and Mrs. Geeta Kumar, staff teacher as well as old student of Nazareth Academy. The school, nearing its fiftieth anniversary, was the subject of several evaluation teams. A preliminary session was conducted in February 1988 by Sisters Marianne and Cassilda and attended by about nineteen other Sisters. In October, a five-day conference was held under the direction of Sister Teresa Rose and Father Bill Dwyer, S.J. A further seminar for teachers was held in December 1988, conducted by Sister Marianne and Father Robert Slattery, S.J. Sister Jyoti of the Notre Dame Sisters, an educator of national reputation, gave a four-day seminar to the teachers in late June 1989. Still later in July, SCN Marietta Saldanha, education director, made an inspection of both Creane Memorial School and Nazareth Academy. At the same time, she gave a number of valuable sessions on various aspects of education, especially on the teaching of moral science.

In the pre-school, Sister Arpita Mundamattathil, who had taken over as director in 1988, was transferred at the end of June 1988 and replaced by Sister Prema

Muthukatil. Other important appointments in 1988-1989 were Sister Stella Kaiprampatt, a staff teacher named as coordinator of the Nazareth Academy community, and Sister Elsy Vettickal assigned as administrator of Nazareth Academy.

A number of other changes slowly took place in the school. Because of the affiliation with the Central Board, the school terms, through successive stages, were brought into compliance with the AISSE programs. A notable addition to the school curriculum in July 1989 was the commencement of regular courses in Computer Science. By 1990, the school was in session from 1 April to 31 March. All examinations and terminal reports were completed by the end of March.

In September 1989, the first of several groups of international visitors came. Joseph Fernandez, a brother of Mrs. Monica Robbins, a resident of Nazareth Academy, arrived with his family for a short visit—his first since he had emigrated to Australia nineteen years before. Members of the Rotary Club from Great Britain visited the school in December.

Kaushik Kiran of Class 9, accompanied by Sister Sujata, attended an International Peace Council in Pondicherry in late December 1988. He was one of a privileged group selected to attend a similar council in Switzerland the following summer.

Jackie Lord and her husband Tony arrived from England in December. A former student of Nazareth Academy, she had left Gaya thirty-four years before. She is the niece of Arthur Wakefield, a lifelong resident of Gaya.

The golden jubilee of the academy was launched on the anniversary of its opening, 2 February 1939, and was to be celebrated throughout the jubilee year. A committee was formed consisting of Sisters Eugenia (convener), Ann Palatty, Sujata, and Stella; lay teachers Josephine Surin and Josephine Xess; guardians Dr. Alo Sircar and Mr. D.K. Jaia; former students Mohammed Hafeezuddin Ahmed, Abhay Kumar, and Pramod K. Gupta. Proposals for the observance of the jubilee were made, and committee members were given charge of various projects.

A jubilee souvenir booklet was planned and successfully published. Functions to be held in the new school year began in April and continued until the early part of September. There were competitions in drama, dancing, singing, speech, drawing, essay, poetry, and other forms of art. From September onward, the students practiced daily in preparation for the jubilee program in November. A special group of singers practiced daily on the school song, the words and music of which had been composed by Dr. Alo Sircar, who personally supervised the practice of this song along with other items which were part of the final program. A special feature was a selection of English and Hindi songs sung by sixteen young men and women, former students of the school. The cultural program included songs, dances, an historical pageant, and a one-act drama.

Guests began to arrive for the celebration. SCN guests were: Sarita, Teresa Kotturan, Teresita, Ann George, Cassilda, Janice, Marianne, Marietta, Geeta, Ann Roberta, Anne Marie, Priya, Irene Locario, Mary Frances, and Carmelita Dunn. (The latter three were visiting from the United States.) Mother Pauline, IBVM, stationed in Gaya from 1943 to 1950, arrived from Delhi. Sister Jyoti of the Notre Dame Sisters joined the group.

The zero hour arrived after feverish final preparations. All the Sister guests were pressed into service to give the finishing touches to costumes, scenery, decorations, etc. The program started about 4:45 p.m. with the chief guest, Brigadier Vijay Kumar, and his wife present. The presentations were given one by one and were well received by the full house. Awards were given to Sisters, lay teachers, and employees with twenty or more years of service. After the program, dinner was served to the VIP guests.

A Mass of thanksgiving was offered in the hall at 7:30 a.m. the next morning. After breakfast, many guests began to make preparations to leave, and by the end of the day, most had departed. School holidays were enjoyed on the 13th and 14th. Mother Pauline departed on the afternoon of the 14th after a happy return to her convent of thirty-nine years before.

The golden jubilee marked the ending of an era. As St. Michael's of 1939 had evolved into the Loreto Convent of 1943, and Loreto Convent into Nazareth Academy of 1951, so the traditions laid with skill and dedication will have to be carried on into yet another era of sacrifice and devotion in the field of education. The aim of Nazareth Academy must be to maintain the high standards so firmly established in the past, so that future generations can be developed physically, intellectually, morally, and spiritually according to the same God-given ideals.

Sister James Leo Goldsborough (deceased) embraces an employee who has come to greet her on her feast day.

Sisters Ann George Mukalel and Ann Palatty, former principals at Nazareth Academy, Gaya, "bargain" for tokens at an Educational Ministry Meeting.

Sisters Reena Theruvankunnel, the current (1997) principal at Nazareth Academy, and Teresa Rose Nabholz serve as panelists at a Community meeting.

NAZARETH CONVENT, RANCHI
1967

Candidates Josepha Baghwar and Anita Kujur prepare a meal
at Nazareth Convent, Ranchi.

Chapter Six

NAZARETH CONVENT, RANCHI
1967

Nazareth Convent, Ranchi, became the third foundation of the SCNs in India. Situated in the heart of a large city, it was very much an urban mission. Since it was in one of the few highly Catholic areas in India, it joined many other religious institutions. With the blessing of Archbishop Pius Kerketta, S.J., of Ranchi, it was formally opened on 23 April 1967.

The spadework began in 1966, and with the able assistance of Jesuit Fathers Binje and Zwifsen, the purchase at Station View, owned by Mrs. Gita Mitra of Calcutta, was completed in December 1966. The next months were spent in repairing, renovating, wiring, and cleaning. The big move began on 27 April 1967, when a truck bound for Ranchi rolled out of Mokama at night. Sister Lawrencetta with three postulants traveled in a station wagon provided by Mr. Havralant of the Bata Shoe Company, arriving on 28 April to a warm welcome by Sister Lioba of the Queen of the Apostles Sisters, Sister Genevieve of the Missionaries of Charity, and women and men of the parish. The first night was spent with the Ursuline Sisters. Led by Sister Celine Arackathottam, three more postulants arrived by train from Mokama the next morning, and by nightfall members of the community slept in their own house.

During the summer, two courses at Ursuline College were provided for the junior Sisters and novices: a course in classroom management by Sister Ann Bernadette and a course in Hindustani Music by Sister Eugenia, SCN, and Sister Lucia, CSC. On 24 June Sister Ann Roberta, the superior, and Sister Josepha Puthenkalam arrived. In August the last of the permanent community arrived, consisting of five candidates and two junior Sisters, Mary Magdalene Chackalackal and Mary Juliana Tuti. Coinciding with their arrival, a terrible communal riot that resulted in frightful destruction of property and loss of life raged from 22 August to 1 September. The Catholic institutions were in the forefront, giving solace and aid to victims of both warring communities.

The first Christmas in Ranchi was a holy and happy event, with Mass in the cathedral at midnight, followed by Mass in the chapel. In true Indian style, fireworks were set off on the front lawn. One rocket hit a window curtain and set it on fire, while another caused a fire in a heap of dried grass. Previously a palm leaf had caught fire during Mass. Perhaps all the conflagrations were to symbolize that Jesus had come to "cast fire upon the earth." A fitting close to 1967 was a day of recollection and midnight vigil on 31 December.

The first full year in Ranchi saw much development. The community seemed to take on certain characteristics that would become rather stable features of the place. Sisters Mary Juliana, Mary Magdalene, and Josepha, as well as the candidates, studied regularly in the colleges, especially at St. Xavier College and the rapidly growing Nirmala College. The group became involved in works and projects of an unusual type in collaboration with the numerous Catholic institutions in the area. Sisters, neighbors, and many other lay people became coworkers and friends. There were numerous opportunities for the pursuit of charitable works of mercy.

Sisters and candidates took active part in the parish Masses at Easter time. A further development was the shifting of the juniorate to Ranchi in July of 1968. The junior Sisters also attended college courses and availed themselves of the classes offered by the nearby Yogada Math. At the end of the year, the Sisters took an active part in the Regional Seminar of the Church in India.

The admission of a candidate from Naotoli, Mary Henrietta Hembrom, was the first fruit of the Ranchi convent. Sister Mary Juliana, who had been in the pioneer group, left on 20 July for a public health course in Delhi.

Rumblings had been going on for some time in regard to a plan for a high school for girls at Khalari, a place not far from Ranchi. Sister Ann Roberta was appointed superior, Sister Teresa Xavier, principal, and Sister Rosemarie Lakra director of the dispensary. Sister Ann Bernadette, named the new superior in Ranchi, arrived with Sister Teresa Rose on 20 November. The Khalari project had to be abandoned, however, and all the appointments for the mission were canceled. Eventually the convent in Chatra grew out of the Khalari withdrawal. Thus Sister Ann Roberta, in the following year, took charge of the new convent and left for Chatra with SCNs Anne Philip Gnavally and Rosemarie Lakra on 7 June 1969.

Nazareth Convent, Ranchi, had a record number of superiors beginning with Sister Ann Roberta in 1967: Sister Ann Bernadette, who served three different times, Sisters Lawrencetta, Anne Marie Thayilchirayil, Shalini d'Souza, James Leo Goldsborough, Teresa Rose Nabholz, Mary Joseph Pamplaneil, Marianne Puthoor, Sophia Kalapurackal, Bridget Kappalumakal, and Alice Chirackanal.

Materially the Ranchi convent had a number of developments. Major building and repairs were made only fifteen years after the first extension was blessed in May 1969. During that interval, improvements and renovations of a lesser scope took place. In September 1984, a second floor was added to the old building, and substantial repairs were made on portions of the building that were deteriorating.

In the center of a large Christian area, Ranchi was a metropolis, a focal point for Christian activity. As such, it always drew a large number of visitors, of which Nazareth Convent received a generous share. From the time of its establishment, the Mothers General of the SCNs and a few leaders of other communities visited the Ranchi convent. Mother Lucille paid a visit in December 1969. Sister Barbara Thomas, who had visited Ranchi in 1970, returned in April 1977 as superior general, accompanied by Sister Donna Kenney. The next superior general, Sister Dorothy MacDougall, paid two visits to Ranchi, first in January 1983 and then in October 1985. Sister Emily Nabholz, president of the congregation, visited in 1988.

The visits of the Indian provincials were always important occasions. Sister Teresa Rose, the first provincial in India, in previous positions a superior and junior director, had strong connections with Nazareth Convent. Sister Margaret Rodericks laid the foundation stone for a new kitchen on one of her visits. Sisters Shalini and Sarita both paid visits during their terms as provincial.

As an ecclesiastical province with a major seminary, Ranchi has been the venue for a number of large gatherings of the hierarchy. As a result, Nazareth Convent has played host to many bishops. Their local bishops, Archbishops Pius Kerketta and Telesphore Toppo, were received at the convent. Among others were the following Jesuits: Bishop A.F. Wildermuth of Patna (1974), Bishop Joseph Rodericks of Jamshedpur (1974 and 1983), Bishop Benedict Osta of Patna (1983 and 1984), and Bishop John B. Thakur of Muzzaffarpur (1984). A notable celebration in Ranchi, attended by sixteen bishops, was the commemoration of the centenary of Father Liewens, the famous Belgian Jesuit of the late 1800s and early 1900s, the pioneer missionary of Chotanagpur.

A number of Sisters served in various capacities in Ranchi Convent as teachers, administrators, and directors. Among these were Sisters Marietta Saldanha, who served as teacher and director at the convent and who gave of her expertise in courses to other Sisters, Brothers, seminarians, priests, etc.; Sister Ann George Mukalel, a teacher for a number of years; Sister Rita Puthenkalam, teacher; Sister Francine Moozhil, administrator of the house; Sisters Cassilda Castell, Sunita Vayalipara, and Ann Moyalan, teachers and directors.

An innovation came in January 1971 when Sister Ann Bernadette took a teaching post at St. Xavier's School in Doranda—English in Class 8. Incidentally, one of her students was a boy whom she had admitted at the age of five in the Beginners Class at Nazareth Academy in Gaya.

The convent received a gift of Rs 1000 in December 1973 from Urmilla Patel, a woman whom the Sisters had befriended when she was refused admission to Yogada Math. She had not forgotten the kindness shown to her.

When possible, the Sisters were active in civic affairs. Led by Sisters Marianne Puthoor and Rosita Kavilpurayidathil, they participated in a strike for the pay of minority school teachers in Ranchi in 1977. In 1979 candidates and Sisters attended a political procession related to the Religious Freedom Bill. An event of human interest was the visit in December 1979 of the former owners of Nazareth Convent, who were happy to see it used to such good purpose.

"Poisoning Day" caused a great flurry in the community. On the fateful day, 10 August 1983, most of the Sisters were laid low after consuming mushroom curry. Only the few who had not partaken of the curry were exempt from its dire effects. Fortunately, all recovered.

Nazareth Convent, Ranchi, celebrated its silver jubilee in 1992. It has served primarily in two aspects. It has been a house of studies for professed Sisters and candidates. Through the years a large number of Sisters have pursued their studies in St. Xavier College, Nirmala College, and Yogada Math. Many have attained degrees through these institutions. It has also been a house of formation. Candidates, novices, and junior Sisters have spent time under the guidance of various directors as they prepared themselves for religious life. They have attended many courses and meetings in the various other religious institutions in and around Ranchi that have provided them with competent teachers and guides. In their turn, the directors and teachers have also shared with the other institutions their knowledge and training in the religious fields.

Through the years, Nazareth Convent has often been a haven for travelers and for the sick or exhausted who needed rest and quiet, a refuge for the poor and the suffering in body and mind, and a warm place of hospitality for friends, relatives, and the passing stranger, where all received a smile and a hearty welcome. The high and the low have been received with equal warmth and graciousness.

The real social work that has been done cannot be measured. Where there was poverty, sickness, suffering, or death, the Sisters were ever ready to succor the needy. They did not wait for the poor or distressed to come; they went out to all in need.

NAZARETH NIKETAN, CHATRA
1969

First building at Chatra, 1971

Chapter Seven

NAZARETH NIKETAN, CHATRA
1969

Nazareth Niketan, Chatra, the fourth foundation of the SCNs in India, was the result of the aborted Khalari mission. Chatra, a sizeable town in Bihar, is considered a subdivision of the Hazaribagh District. At the time of its foundation, this district was still a part of the Ranchi archdiocese, but later became a part of the newly erected Daltonganj diocese. Negotiations for a convent in Chatra were carried on by Father Louis Lachal, S.J., an Australian of the Hazaribagh mission, which administered the Chatra mission. When the convent was opened in 1969, there was no resident priest and no church. A priest came for Sunday Mass and occasional weekday Masses from Hazaribagh, forty-five miles away.

Geographically, Chatra differed from previous foundations. The land acquired for the convent site was outside the town limits on the edge of a jungle, where there were many wild animals—tigers, leopards, panthers, bears, deer, and jackals. In the surrounding areas were ravines and hills, boulder-strewn and thick with shrubs and undergrowth, scenically beautiful and wild. Although the altitude of Chatra is 1400 feet, the climate is still hot and sultry during the summer months. The people from the area are mostly tribal people who live in the villages scattered in the jungle. The town people, who are Hindus and Moslems, are engaged in business or in government offices.

On a hot afternoon, 7 June 1969, the three Sisters arrived who were to form the nucleus of Nazareth Niketan. The house, which included the one-room school, was not fully ready, but nothing daunted Sisters Ann Roberta Powers, Anne Philip Gnavally, and Rosemarie Lakra, who set to work as true pioneers to make ready a new establishment of the Sisters of Charity of Nazareth. The Chatra house consisted of three rooms, one destined to be a classroom and the others to serve as bedroom, dining room, chapel, and whatever else would be required. The Blessed Sacrament was reserved in a corner of the bedroom, separated by a curtain. Kitchen and bathroom were contained in a small building outside.

Father Lachal welcomed the Sisters and offered Sunday Mass the next day on the veranda. More than two hundred people assembled, some walking through the jungle during the night. The people welcomed the Sisters after Mass with song, dance, flowers, speeches, garlands, the ceremonial washing of hands, and with gifts of rice, eggs, and other edibles.

As the days went on, the Sisters became acquainted with their new surroundings. Patients were brought even though there was no hospital, and Sister Rosemarie, a nurse, administered basic medicine and first aid, referring serious cases to the local government hospital. Furniture was acquired for the school. Although the land outside the low compound wall was a veritable jungle, the large compound itself gave ample scope for cultivation. Near the boundary wall was found a burial ground and cremation site. Long, exploratory walks into the jungle brought the Sisters to other interior villages where groups of Christians lived. The feast of Saints Peter and Paul, 29 June, was a big day for the mission of Chatra, when the new building was blessed by Archbishop Pius Kerketta, S.J., of Ranchi. A large contingent of people from surrounding villages, some of whom had begun to arrive the night before, assembled in the early afternoon for the 3 p.m. ceremony. Priests, Brothers, and Sisters from Mt. Carmel, Hazaribagh, and Nazareth Academy, Gaya, were in attendance, as well as friends and villagers.

The blessing took place under a *naruwa* (leafy roof), erected outside. After all the rooms had been blessed, the people gave a program of songs and dances. Then followed speeches and the offering of gifts: rice, eggs, cocks, vegetables, and even two goats. The ceremony closed with tea and *nasta* (snacks) for all.

Although school registration was set for the first of July, it was several days before the arrival of the first pupil, Saroj Kumari Saha, the daughter of a forest ranger. Gradually the admissions increased, so that on the first day of actual class, 8 July, thirty-six students in Beginners and Class 1 started their education at Nazareth Niketan. Each day brought more admissions. Children were seated on mats in front of small tables. Families from farm lands were granted admission for their children upon payment of one *maund* (80 pounds) of grain per family per year.

As early as December, final examinations were held and final reports distributed. In 1970 a number of new admissions were taken, notably from the Muslim population. During the year, Sister Anne Philip initiated a "Head Start Program" for underprivileged children. The Sisters began giving special tuition to needy village children.

To meet medical needs, the original plan was to have a type of clinic or dispensary. From the beginning Sister Rosemarie cared for the sick. She was succeeded by Sister Mary Juliana Tuti, who continued the work zealously. As time went on, however, it was found that because the government hospital was so close, medical work was not a great need at this mission. After a time, a nurse was no longer needed as one of the regular personnel.

The first Christmas gave the Sisters a real experience of the tribal manner of celebrating a feast. Midnight Mass was on the veranda. Singing and dancing followed the Mass and went on until dawn. Some Australian visitors shared the experience with the Sisters.

The Sisters had been in Chatra a little over two months, when Elizabeth Beck, daughter of the catechist, became the first candidate from Chatra to begin her candidacy in Ranchi. As Sister Abha, she made her final vows in the Chatra parish on 17 December 1982, an occasion of pride and rejoicing for the parish.

The convent building, begun under the direction of Brothers Francis Xaxa and Tarcisius in September 1969, was blessed by the pastor, Father Louis Lachal, S.J., on 19 July 1970. At the Mass on that auspicious day, Sisters Mary Juliana and Anne Philip Gnavally pronounced final vows, and Sister Teresa Xavier Ponnazhath renewed her vows. Still later, in February 1971, the convent was consecrated to the Sacred Heart of Jesus.

As early as December 1969, distinguished SCN visitors came to Chatra. Mother Lucille Russell, Sisters Teresa Rose Nabholz, Ellen Curran, and Ann Cornelius Curran had an interesting visit. They toured various villages and saw at close range the life and customs of the tribal people. A chilling experience on their first night was the presence of a tiger, prowling near the kitchen and bathroom. This beast returned in the early part of the year, his visit accompanied by terrifying roars and the frightened howls of the jackals.

During 1970, a charitable work was undertaken with the opening of a hostel for high school girls who had to walk very far in the jungle to reach the Chatra government high schools. Later, girls in the lower classes were allowed admission to the hostel. These girls lived very simply, sleeping on the floor, which was covered with straw. They brought and cooked their own food. Although the conditions were somewhat primitive, the advantages in time saved and shelter provided in a protected place greatly helped them in pursuing their education.

The *chota* (small) bishop, as the villagers called him, Father George Saupin, S.J., vicar of the archdiocese of Ranchi, came to Chatra in 1970 to confirm sixty parishioners, mostly adults. Before the end of 1971, Father Saupin had become their own bishop and the Chatra parish a member of the new diocese of Daltonganj. At the consecration of Bishop Saupin on 19 October 1971, Sisters Ann Roberta and Anne Philip represented Nazareth Niketan. At the program of entertainment for his installation in Hazaribagh on 31 October, children from Nazareth Niketan offered two action songs. Bishop Saupin's first visit to Chatra as the head of the new diocese on 25 November 1971 was an occasion of great celebration.

The Chatra mission never remained static, even though for a long time it had neither church nor parish house nor priest. By January 1974 the parish house, Shanti Bhavan, was blessed, and the first resident parish priest, Father Fulgens Kujur, was appointed by May of the same year. With the completion of the church, the Chatra mission became full-blown.

As admissions in the school increased, larger facilities became badly needed. On the occasion of the visit of Sister Mary Holt in the silver jubilee year of the Sisters of Charity in India, 1972, a new school extension was blessed. In November 1975, construction of three classrooms and a storeroom began providing additional space. In keeping with the government policy of vocational training, six sewing machines obtained in July 1975 helped older students, teachers, and village women to acquire a skill that was useful both at home and for outside income. In 1982, a boys' hostel was opened in the parish compound, operating on the same lines as the girls' hostel started in 1970. After a long struggle with officialdom and the recognition of the school, the teachers were paid by the government for the first time in September 1982.

The growth of the Chatra mission has been gradual but thorough. Because it bordered on jungle territory, the living was more primitive, but the early annals give evidence that the pioneer Sisters made good use of the natural materials and resources of the surrounding land. The three multipurpose rooms of the first building have developed into a set of buildings that will no doubt expand still more as the need arises. A further sign of Catholic growth is a full-sized church and rectory.

The school, from the original thirty-six pupils of 1969, now has an enrollment of over one thousand students from Beginners to Class 10 (as of 1995). It has provided a good education to hundreds of students who have come largely from the outlying areas. All of this has been accomplished with much sacrifice on the part of the priests, principals, teachers, parents, and students. With great difficulty the school obtained from the Bihar government recognition that placed it on a firm footing.

In the sociopastoral field, Chatra has blazed the trail for many other missions. Constant visits to villages and action in cases of the needy, the sick, the dying, the oppressed, and the troubled exemplify a vigilant awareness of social needs and a willingness to tackle the problems. In the pastoral field, the Sisters engage in religious instruction of both children and adults. The Sisters prepare them for the reception of the sacraments, organize the Mahila Sangh (women's organization) and other parish groups, and go wherever religious need arises. All activity has been marked by a joyous service and a willingness to sacrifice. Christ reigns in Chatra.

COMMUNITY HEALTH CENTRE
BAKHTIARPUR
1971

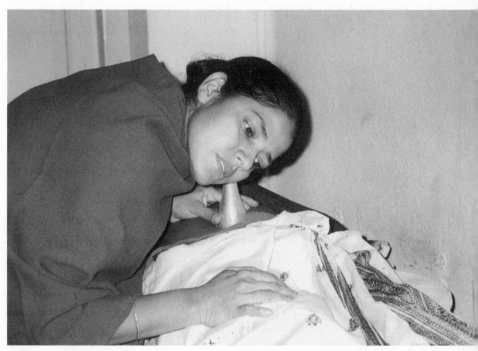

Sister Lucy Puthukkatt listens for a fetal heartbeat at the Community Health Centre in Bakhtiarpur.

Chapter Eight

COMMUNITY HEALTH CENTRE BAKHTIARPUR 1971

A clinic and convent, envisioned by Father William Goudreau, S.J., pastor of Our Lady of Perpetual Help Church in Bakhtiarpur, one hour from Mokama on the Patna Road, became a reality when in 1969 a contract for the proposed project was signed between Bishop A.F. Wildermuth of Patna and Sister Teresa Rose Nabholz, provincial. When Misereor of West Germany accepted the plans, the necessary funds were assured, and the building got under way.

Early in 1970 Sister Mary Frances Sauer was named administrator of the new undertaking, and she became the prime factor in the designing and executing of the building. For Sister Mary Frances it was a second "pioneer" enterprise, because she had been one of the original band of Mokama. Later in 1970, the two other pioneers were appointed: Sisters Lucia Thulavanickal and Joel Urumpil. All three Sisters were experienced graduate nurses.

The opening of a women's health center, Mahila Swastia Kendra, as it was originally called, took place on 11 February 1971 when several vehicles, escorted by Father Goudreau, conveyed the new Sisters and their accompanying party from Mokama to Bakhtiarpur. They were received by the school boys of the mission, and the assembled group went to the church to sing the Magnificat in thanksgiving for the new work of the Church.

Early days in new places usually have some difficulties and hardships. Bakhtiarpur was no exception. Because the well was not yet completed, there was no running water or proper bathroom facilities. Water had to be carried from the well in the mission compound across the road. A number of rooms were not finished; therefore, temporary rooms had to be arranged. Despite many shortcomings, the first patient was admitted on 13 February, and during the night Sister Joel attended the birth of a baby girl.

Before the official opening, the medical work slowly took shape. Dr. Parmanand, a local doctor, who had been seeing patients in Father Goudreau's house, began coming to the clinic. By the fifteenth of the month, the Sisters started visiting villages, one of which was Ragophur, where a public health center would later be located. A meeting on 3 March dealt with a possible T.B. control program to be financed by Misereor. As no other doctor was available in

111

Bakhtiarpur, Sister Ancilla Kozhipat came from Mokama for the first time on 15 March to see patients.

The official opening of the new convent took place on 25 March. After Sister Teresa Rose had cut the ribbon, the bishop blessed the entire building. The German consul was among the many guests. There were the usual songs, speeches, garlands, and high tea. It was a day of rejoicing both for the Catholic community and for the people of Bakhtiarpur and its environs.

A "dog story" of the early days provides a touch of humor. Raja, the watch dog, was still on duty early in the morning when Sisters Mary Frances and Joel were descending from their night's sleep on the terrace. Raja trapped them as they reached the ground floor. They managed to escape to the chapel and remained besieged on the window sill until they were finally rescued.

The hospital was the first shoot of a multifaceted mission. Its activities increased and developed, with emphasis on two fields—the care of T.B. patients and the improvement of mother/child care services.

Running water had become a reality in the dispensary by 29 March and throughout the whole building by 5 April. Brother George Cheru, S.J., who was largely responsible for all of the construction and other facilities of the new institution, left Bakhtiarpur in July. He had rendered invaluable assistance to the Sisters.

Sister Lucia attended a public health course in Delhi in 1972-73. Sister Mary John Nadackal replaced her during her absence. A new recruit in 1974 was Sister Lucy Puthukkatt, who took up duties in the dispensary. In the same year Sister Lucia made a step forward with the government and community when she accepted the chair of the Family Planning and Child Welfare Centre. This centre included six nurseries as well as fifteen camps a year to teach crafts to young women. Sister Lucia received no salary from the government, supervising these projects on a volunteer basis. Her work included counselling the women.

During the ensuing years, important transfers of personnel took place. The mission lost a veteran nurse and social worker in May 1974, when Sister Lucia was transferred to Sokho. A second veteran to go was Sister Joel, who left for public health work in Mokama in 1977. Sister Nirmala Mulackal succeeded Sister Joel, and Sister Mary John returned in September 1978 to take over as administrator from Sister Mary Frances, who departed for a year in the United States. Sister Teresa Velloothara replaced Sister Mary John in 1979. Also in 1979, Sister Karuna Thottumarikal, who had been working in the public health program, was replaced by Sister Mary Juliana.

Leprosy patients had long been treated at Bakhtiarpur. In 1970, after persistent efforts, these patients were able to obtain the necessary "Red Card" from the block office and were issued rations of wheat from government stores. Another important aid from the government was a subsidy of 45% of the total cost of a gas plant that became operative by 1 May 1980. The same month, a doctor from Holy Cross Hospital in Tripolia, Patna, began to come to the clinic on a weekly basis. After visiting the clinic, Dr. R. Hasan, an eye specialist, promised to be available once a month for eye cases. In July 1982 Sister Vinita Kumplankal, M.B.B.S., began a regular visitation from Nazareth Hospital on a weekly basis.

After a three-year stint in public health, Sister Mary Juliana was transferred to Tatanagar and was replaced by another veteran of public health, Sister Rosemarie Lakra. One more SCN recruit, Sister Marina Thazathuvettil, was assigned to public health in February 1982.

A sad day for Bakhtiarpur came in 1983 when Sister Mary Frances bade farewell to this foundation that she had helped to establish. After more than thirty-five years in India, she was returning to the United States. The people paid high tribute to her long years of service. Sister Elizabeth Emmanuel Vattakunnal was appointed administrator in 1983.

Through the hospital, dispensary, and other health services, the Community Health Centre has brought untold medical benefits to Bakhtiarpur. Very soon after their arrival in Bakhtiarpur, the Sisters also began to take part in pastoral activities. First they began the teaching of catechism after Sunday Mass. Another project was retreat work for women. They also took part in other pastoral works. An innovation in November 1979 was a charismatic retreat conducted by Sister Xavier Valiakunnackal for three different groups. In the school, the children were prepared for the reception of the sacraments of Penance, Holy Communion, and Confirmation.

Of great importance to the church in Bakhtiarpur was the consecration on 21 June 1980 of the new bishop of Patna, Benedict Osta, S.J. A number of Sisters and parishioners attended the celebration in Patna. On the day before this memorable event, Bakhtiarpur was honored by the visit of two bishops who were on their way to participate in the consecration: Bishop Telesphore Toppo, then of Dumka, and Bishop Leo Tigga of Raiganj.

Bishop Osta's first visit was on 7 September. He was accompanied by Father Jacob Kunnackal, S.J. The bishop was officially welcomed at the Bakhtiarpur parish on 8 October. On that occasion the program included First Communion and Confirmation during Mass, followed by speeches, songs, visits to several villages, and an elephant ride to bring the day to a close. A second official visitation of the parish was made by Bishop Osta on 5 February 1983. He included several villages on his tour and took time to listen to the problems of the people.

Parish work became one of the recognized ministries when Sister Rajni Hembrom joined the community in December 1980 as a full-time parish worker. A further step in parish ministry was the organizing of the Mahila Sangh by Sister

Mercy Thundathil, who joined the community in early 1982. Forty women were present at the opening. Later in the same year Sister Mercy held a vocation camp for girls of the Patna diocese. Sisters Rajni and Mercy extended their ministry to some distant villages, where they acquainted themselves with the needs of the people.

Two great events for the Christian people of Bakhtiarpur took place in 1986. One was the ordination of the first priest from the parish. On 2 April 1986, Bishop Raphael Chimath of Cuttack, Orissa, raised to the altar Father Anand Prakash of Pinarpur village. The occasion was graced by the presence of two bishops and twenty-six priests, who concelebrated the Mass with the newly ordained priest. A large crowd of Sisters, school children, and parishioners attended the solemn ceremony. The school children and parishioners marked the event with a short but very fine program, followed by *badha khana* (a banquet) for all.

Only a few days later, Bakhtiarpur mission had a second day of rejoicing, this time the golden jubilee of the mission. Six men who had been among those first baptized in the new mission were present to participate in the celebration. The golden jubilee Mass was concelebrated by Bishop Osta and a large number of priests. Thirteen children received their First Holy Communion. Another milestone had been reached.

Although Bakhtiarpur started initially as a medical project, involvement in all other types of mission followed almost automatically. As the community prepared more and more Sisters for these various works, recruits began to arrive. So it was with the parish school. By July 1972 Sister Rani Thundyil was sent to teach in the school, and the following year more Sisters were added to the staff. When Sister Rani went to Pune in June 1973, Sister Sushila Palatty replaced her. In September of 1974 Sisters Lalita Edapadieyil and Anupa Moozha joined the teaching staff, and in January 1976 Sisters Leela Vandanath and Suma Muthukattuparampil also came to Bakhtiarpur for the school.

The seventeenth of January 1977 was a "red-letter day," the fulfillment of a long-awaited dream—the blessing of a new school structure with additional classrooms. It was a day of double significance. At a Mass offered by Bishop Wildermuth, about 200 Catholics were confirmed. Following the Mass, the bishop blessed the new addition to the school. In the same year Sister Janice Rathappillil became headmistress.

When Sister Janice was transferred in May 1981, Sister Theresa Martin Thundyil joined the school as headmistress. In January 1982 Sister Deepti Ponnambal joined the staff of the school. Sister Theresa Martin initiated the process for government recognition of the school, which was finally concluded successfully several years later after many ups and downs. Subsequent head-mistresses and teachers have kept up the standards of the school.

It might seem that in order to have a complete experience, every convent must have its robberies. An unusual case was that of Sister Mary Frances, whose purse was stolen on November 1976 as she sat in the jeep waiting for the driver. She lost her passport, watch, cash of more than Rs 1000, and personal articles, including her teeth! On the night of 15 February 1977, thieves came over the wall and stole all the metal buckets and the lid of a large cooking pot. They climbed back over the wall when they realized they had been discovered by the night-watchman. From April through June of the same year, there was frequent harass-ment with stone throwing on the roof, yelling, and similar forms of disturbance. Finally, on 29 July, a second robbery took place. Thieves broke in and collected a number of articles. Once again the nightwatchman intervened. A fight ensued between the watchman and one of the thieves. The situation was saved by the timely arrival of Father Jacob, his nightwatchman, and some of the big boys of the hostel. Again the thief escaped.

An episode involving one dog and three cobras occurred the night of 5 October 1980. Two cobras that were detected in the kitchen and in the labor room were dispatched quickly. The third cobra was discovered by the nightwatchman through the furious barking of Jyoti the dog. In the ensuing struggle, the dog bit the cobra; the watchman mortally wounded the cobra with his heavy stick; yet the dying cobra still managed to bite the dog, who died from the poisonous venom. The Sisters greatly grieved over the loss of their faithful dog.

The Bakhtiarpur mission, with the same ethnic groups, the same scenery and climate, the same ministries but on a smaller scale, seems like an extension of the original SCN mission in Mokama. Although the usual hardships marked the beginning of the mission, yet with God's blessing it has grown and flourished. The dispensary developed into a small inpatient hospital, especially intended for delivery cases. The outpatient department took care of the needs of the town area and surrounding villages. Medical services and health care extended into outly-ing localities. Health care, hygiene, cleanliness, and child care were taught in order to promote more healthy, useful lives.

The Sisters fully participated in both the pastoral and educational ministries. As teachers of religion they instructed adults and children, bringing the truths of faith ever closer to their everyday lives. In school they filled the posts of head-mistresses and teachers with admirable skill and dedication and brought the school to a high peak of excellence.

In retrospect it is clear that much has been accomplished. Mistakes and fail-ures have occurred, to be sure, but they are greatly outweighed by the successes. The SCNs can look with pride at this offspring and feel that the feeble beginning, like a sapling, has grown into a strong, flourishing tree, spreading its branches to protect and shade the sick, the ignorant, the uneducated. The Sisters who have valiantly worked in Bakhtiarpur can for a few contemplative moments take a rest and listen to Christ's own words, "Well done, good and faithful servants."

Sister Anjana Kunnath holds a newborn child at the Community Health Centre, Bakhtiarpur, while Champa, an employee for many years, looks on.

NAZARETH NIVAS,
LUPUNGUTU (CHAIBASA)
1971

Teaching crafts at the Women's Centre in Chaibasa

Sewing leaves together to make plates

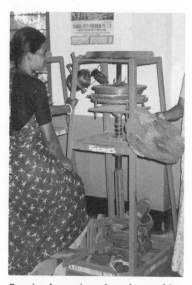

Showing the finished plate

Pressing leaves into shape by machine

Chapter Nine

NAZARETH NIVAS, LUPUNGUTU (CHAIBASA) 1971

T he sixth offshoot of Nazareth in India was Lupungutu, formally opened on 8 September 1971. Rumblings of the new birth began in late 1969, when the Jesuits of the Jamshedpur mission began scouting for a congregation of Sisters prepared to take up work among the Ho people in and around Lupungutu, where the Jesuits had been conducting a large school, St. Xavier, founded in 1953. Although Chaibasa, a good-sized town in south Bihar, is only two miles away, Lupungutu, nestled amid rolling hills, gives the impression of being somewhat remote. It is a stronghold of the Ho tribe and is a gateway to many more remote villages and small settlements.

Chaibasa is historically older than Ranchi as a mission, but because the work did not prosper, the missionaries pressed on to Ranchi and there met phenomenal success, the mission at Ranchi now being more than a hundred years old. This fact explains the fewer numbers of Christians among the Hos. Even now (1996) Lupungutu has no parish church, but the active programs fostered by the students, teachers, and directors of St. Xavier High School have done much to advance the people socially, economically, culturally, and spiritually. The educational institutions in the locality comprise a high school, middle school, and primary school.

Among the endeavors undertaken by the school before the Sisters' arrival were: l) adoption of villages and the running of night schools; 2) common labor in these villages on Saturdays for three or four hours; 3) Catholic Relief Service Food-for-Work projects in which the staff assisted villagers in house, well, and road construction; 4) procuring medicine for animals and poultry through government sources; 5) assisting in village schools to upgrade the standards.

Sisters were needed to organize and consolidate this village work and further develop it. Some prospects for work were: cooperatives, medical care, education for home life, midwifery, agriculture in theory and practice, night classes for children and adults deprived of education, and the teaching of hygiene and sewing.

When SCNs were first approached in early 1970 by Father Richard McHugh, S.J., there seemed little hope that the community would be able to take on this new place for at least two years. The invitation, however, held a strong attraction, and almost miraculously, through a persistent correspondence between Father McHugh and the provincial, Sister Teresa Rose Nabholz, Lupungutu became a household word among SCNs. By March 1971 approval that had already been given by the India SCN Council was confirmed by the Central Executive Committee.

In the contract drawn up, the first paragraph quoted here clearly defines in broad terms what SCN Lupungutu was to be: "A minimum of two Sisters are to be engaged in social and/or medical work in conjunction with the social work program set up by the administration of St. Xavier High School, Chaibasa. This service will center primarily on the general development of the villages through the involvement of village women. . . ."

Concrete plans and construction went forward all during the first eight months of 1971. Father McHugh and his collaborators in the mission worked untiringly so that all things would be in order by the proposed date of opening, 8 September 1971, the feast of Our Lady's Nativity. The convent was practically ready by that time—a fine structure of seven rooms, built around a quadrangle on three sides with inside verandas, providing bedroom, dining room, community room, bathroom, and chapel space.

The first Sister, Olive Pinto, accompanied by Sisters Teresa Rose and Teresa Kotturan, arrived on 2 September. Sister Mary Juliana Tuti was delayed because of the sudden critical illness of her sister in Khunti. By 8 September, all was in readiness. Bishop Joseph Rodericks, S.J., of Jamshedpur blessed the new convent in the presence of a large gathering of Jesuits, diocesan priests, Sisters, and lay people. Pioneer Sisters Olive and Mary Juliana began their work. By late 1971 the third member, Sister Agnes Tudu, joined the group. She was to participate in the social work program of the parish, while the other two Sisters would function with the program in the school.

A development in 1972 was the sending of the Sisters to various places where they could get specialized training. Sisters Olive and Agnes went to Ernakulam to learn cottage industries and handicrafts, while Sister Mary Juliana took a course in catechetics at Tongo. Accordingly Nazareth Nivas remained closed from early January to the end of March.

Events of interest in 1972 included the following:

1) A first delivery was conducted by Sister Mary Juliana, a qualified midwife, assisted by Sister Olive.
2) Sister Mary Juliana gave a retreat in the nearby village of Guira.
3) Sisters Mary Juliana, Olive, and Agnes went on a missionary expedition to three villages.
4) The Mahila Kalyan Kendra (Women's Handicraft Center) was initiated.
5) The Mahila Sangh had its first meeting on the same day that Father McHugh paid a first visit to the project, which he had launched so successfully.
6) Sister Agnes became co-director of the Boys Sodality.

By 1973, programs and projects were blossoming. Handicraft training for unmarried girls was thriving. Mother/child health care programs were started in the nearby villages. CARITAS, an arm of the Catholic Relief Service, came forward in 1975 with further funds for the health programs, thereby promoting them more vigorously. With the advent of Sister Teresa Madassery in 1977, the nutrition, education, and mother/child health care programs prospered.

Gradually a move into formal education developed. Sister Agnes took on the supervision of the night schools and also began teaching in the primary schools. Later, when various transfers had taken place, the Sisters took up regular teaching in the school. Bethany in Jamshedpur, begun in 1980, became strongly linked with Lupungutu in all programs—nutrition and health education, teaching in rural schools, marriage preparation courses, youth camps, retreats, and medical work. By 1985, the original band had been transferred, but work continued under new leadership. Two new Sisters were Prema Muthukatil, who became fully engaged in school work, and Beena Chirackal, a graduate nurse. The latter took over the charge of the dispensary and the general medical work.

During 1985, a move was made to change the nature of the Mahila Kalyan Kendra (Women's Handicraft Center). Considering the expenditure necessary to produce handicraft articles and the discontinuance of funds from Catholic Relief Service, the market was no longer profitable, and those involved favored a shift in the work in order to enhance its effectiveness. It was decided to fan out into more distant villages and to bring to the young women of those places a nonresidential *grihini* program that would include essentials, such as household management, elementary reading, writing and arithmetic, nutrition, health and child-care education, agriculture, and some sewing and handicrafts. The basic idea of advancement projects remained, but the emphasis as well as the venues shifted.

The foundation of Lupungutu, begun in 1971, has developed and flourished. By late 1986, a program involving trained health workers, one for each of thirty villages, brought health care and instruction to several thousand people. Monthly meetings of health workers brought about a pooling of effort and a good measure of coordination, greatly extending the work of the Sister in charge. By 1988, the Sisters were firmly entrenched in the life and work of the people and were actively participating in important projects. A full-fledged dispensary now stands on their premises. Sister Beena, the director, did not confine her work to those four walls. She visited sick patients in far-off villages, traveling by cycle or moped for long distances. She assisted in getting the sick or injured to hospitals when necessary, if at all possible.

The Sisters have constantly taken part in the ministry of education in the schools. It is mostly through their direction that the primary and middle schools run smoothly and efficiently, and they lend valuable assistance to the lay administration and teachers in the matter of planning syllabi and imparting the knowledge of good methods and practical helps. The Sisters involved in the school also see to the religious education of the children by means of catechism classes, devotions, and retreats. Sister Rashmi Toppo has charge of youth groups and strives to promote their moral and spiritual development.

Social and educational activities are combined in the night schools, which are directed and coordinated by the Sisters. Sister Malini Manjoly, assigned specifically to this work, traveled by cycle from village to village in order to promote the night school. Under her direction, Mahila Kalyan Kendra, merged into a kind of mobile *grihini*. As a result of village visiting by the Sisters, some of the young women have been induced to take a residential course in sewing. At the same time, health instruction is given, and basic skills in reading, writing, and arithmetic are taught. The program is checked through visits to the village, and its scope can be enlarged.

In all the work of the Sisters there is cooperation and unity, with each one involving herself, insofar as she can, in any work taken on by the others.

Rolling an incense stick

NAZARETH CONVENT, BASSEIN
1972

Sister Bridget Kappalumakal and Teresita Theruvankunnel (deceased) visit with school children in Bassein.

Sister Premila Parackattu prepares for liturgy at Nazareth Convent.

Chapter Ten

NAZARETH CONVENT, BASSEIN
1972

Bassein has a history steeped in Catholicism since the time of the Portuguese domination of the western coast of India. Although forced conversion of the native population to Christianity is a part of history, the astonishing fact is that so deeply was the faith implanted that even to this day Bassein is one of the most thoroughly Catholic areas of India. Not only religion but also the culture, the customs, and the very way of life were indelibly stamped on the people.

Bassein lies beyond the municipal limits of Bombay in what is known as the Thane District. A famous historical landmark is the old Bassein fort, a bastion of the conquering and colonizing Portuguese. A number of hills to the south, north, and east form part of the horizon. To the west is the Arabian Sea. The area is gradually building up into a residential and commercial district, but fields and open stretches of land still provide an escape from the congestion of Bombay. Even in the limited area of Bassein, Catholics are so numerous that they fill to overflowing three or four parish Masses on Sunday in as many as twenty large churches.

The SCNs came here in 1972 to take positions on the staff of Thomas Baptista High School. The first contact with the SCN community occurred at Bhopal in 1970, when Father Peter Paul Fernandes, assistant priest at Our Lady of Grace Church in Papdy, met Sister Margaret Rodericks. He expressed a need for Sisters to become staff members of the high school. He also wrote Sister Teresa Rose, the provincial. About the same time, he sent an official invitation to enlist the Christian Brothers for the same purpose.

Thomas Baptista High School, begun in 1894, had continued as an English medium coeducational school for many years. Because of the development of convent schools for girls, it evolved into a boys' school. It passed through several other phases—*Marathi* medium and then back to English with a simultaneous *Marathi* stream. Eventually a new school, built on a different site, was begun as an English medium branch of Thomas Baptista, known as St. Augustine High School.

The faculty in 1972 included the following: Father John Rumao, headmaster, Sister Mary Scaria Menonparampil, Brother Murphy, and Brother Whiting as teachers in the high school. Sister Mary Scaria taught biology for the most part. Sister Teresita Theruvankunnal taught Class 4. Sister Roselyn Karakkattu later joined the staff. Prior to the arrival of the Brothers and Sisters, the standard of the school had somewhat deteriorated, but as a result of their combined efforts, a decided change for the better became evident. In 1975 Sister Teresita was appointed mistress of novices and was replaced at Bassein by Sister Mary Thomas Parakulangara.

The Bassein community was subject to a number of transfers and replacements. Sister Mary Scaria, who was a pioneer at St. Augustine and later at Thomas Baptista Junior College, was given a farewell party on 22 April 1978 after six years of devoted service. At the same time Sister Mary Thomas was transferred. They were replaced by Sisters Josita Eniakattu and Ann Scaria Menonparampil, the sister of Sister Mary Scaria. Sister Ann Palatty had a short stint of service at Thomas Baptista College in July 1977, but left to pursue an M.A. degree at Sophia College. Sister Ann Palatty completed the M.A. in 1979 and the M.Ed. in 1980, after which she was transferred from Bassein. June 1979 brought Sisters Geeta Kochettonnil and Cassilda Castell to the staff of St. Augustine. In July, the school lost one of its very competent teachers, Sister Josita, when she left for Baroda to pursue a B.Ed. degree. Sisters Stella Chullyil and Stella Kaiprampatt joined the teaching staff, as did others in subsequent years.

The community history of Bassein was marked by a unique feature—the constant struggle to find a suitable place to live, a struggle that continued from the arrival of the Sisters in 1972 until they moved to their own newly built house in 1980. The first Sisters, through an arrangement made by the parish priest, Father Andrew Dias, and the principal of the school, Father John Rumao, were housed with Mr. Roshan D'Mello, who gave the top floor (consisting of one room) of his house for lodging. Subsequently the Sisters lived in various houses, among them the house of Irene Pereira, then Casabella in Mulgaon parish (where they had some terrifying experiences with fellow tenants), and lastly a house belonging to a Noronha family.

During these trying years of househunting, steps were taken to buy land, and by the first of March in 1978, deeds for the land at Barampur, the site of St. Augustine High School, were drawn up and the plans for building were under way. Father Rumao officiated at the groundbreaking for the future convent on 27 December 1978. On 20 March 1979, Father John Lobo blessed the site and laid the foundation stone in the presence of Sister Josita, Sister Mary Scaria, Brother Murphy, Irene Pereira, Joe Pereira, the contractor, and workers.

The big moving day to the new house, 27 January 1980, was spent in preparation. After an affectionate farewell to the people of the neighborhood, the Sisters left for their new convent at 7 p.m. A warm welcome awaited them from their colleagues, the Christian Brothers. Very valuable assistance had been given by priests, Brothers, neighbors, and good friends. Mass offered by Father Prakash Gokhale on 28 January brought Christ to Nazareth Convent to dwell in their midst. The official blessing by Father Hubert Pereira, S.J., took place on 2 March 1980 with a good number of visitors for the occasion: Sister Margaret Rodericks, provincial (Sister Margaret had made her first visitation to Bassein in September 1977), Sisters Olive Pinto, Reena Theruvankunnel, and Rosita Kavilpurayidathil, other Sisters of local communities, relatives, priests, and friends. All were welcomed by the four residents—Sisters Cassilda, Geeta, Ann Scaria, and Ann Palatty.

Convents always have some unusual anecdotes to relate. One night in September 1977, near panic seized the community when the church bell began to sound a tocsin at ll p.m. All the men from the neighborhood rushed to the church, to find that Father Dominic Fernandes had been beaten by four young men of the parish. By God's grace he had been spared serious injury. On an adventurous day of the same year, 2 December, Sisters Margaret and Ann Palatty, returning at different times from Bombay on the suburban trains, encountered an accident between Mira Rose and Bhayander and had to walk the remaining distance to Bassein, across railway tracks, through fields, hedges, and thorny bushes. One arrived at 9 p.m, the other after midnight.

In 1978 a new girl who had come for kitchen and housework unfortunately proved deficient in every facet of such employment. The climax was reached when, after receiving instructions on the ringing of the doorbell, that worthy young lady did her practice on it while the Sisters were sleeping.

A blessing came upon the SCN community when young women of the area began to show an interest in joining the Sisters. Sister Blanche Correia became the first candidate of Bassein in 1979. Sisters Dolcie D'Mello and Rena Fernandez followed in 1980, and Sister Gracy Gamcha in 1983.

An official episcopal visit was made on 7 December 1980 by Archbishop Simon Pimenta, accompanied by his secretary, Father Alex Rebello. Other episcopal visitors were Bishop Joseph Rodericks, S.J., of Jamshedpur, brother of Sister Margaret Rodericks; Bishop Telesphore Toppo of Ranchi; and Bishop James Toppo of Raiganj. The pro-nuncio, the ambassador of the Pope, was received in February 1985 at a public reception in Bassein. The climax, a landmark in the religious history of Bassein, however, came on February 1986 when the Holy Father, Pope John Paul II, visited this ancient bastion of Catholicism in the East. The Sisters and other friends crowded the terrace of the convent, as the helicopter bearing the Holy Father landed right in the compound of St. Augustine School. Thousands and thousands of people from far and near came to be present for the historical occasion.

The ministries of Sisters Blanche and Cassilda were of a pioneering character. Early in October 1978 Sister Blanche participated with Sister Ann Palatty in several vocational camps for students. Again in 1983 she visited Bassein in the interest of vocations. In 1984 when she became a member of the Bassein community, she took full-time work in various youth movements—Jeevan Darshan Kendra (youth center), YCS/YSM, and by joining the Legion of Mary she broadened the horizons of sociopastoral ministry. She was frequently engaged in vocation and youth camps and rallies. In September 1985, Sister Blanche organized an altar boys' rally that brought together about 800 altar boys from a number of parishes. She represented the house in the next month on the Parish Council of Manickpur.

Sister Cassilda, coordinator of the house, was also busy in general church activities. In 1980, she joined the Quest Program, instituted for college and working girls of Bombay. At a meeting at Giriz for superiors on 30 June of the same year, she was one of three Sisters elected to serve on the pastoral committee of the Pastoral Centre of Bassein. In August, Sister Cassilda attended the Regional Vocation Convention and was elected to participate in the National Vocation Convention to be held in the following year at Pune. The Bishops' meeting of the Conference of Religious of India, to be held in Baroda, was set for 14-17 January 1981. Sister Margaret deputized Sister Cassilda to attend the meeting in her place. From 2 to 3 May 1981, Sister Cassilda attended the National Convention for Vocation Promoters. During the ensuing months she was often engaged in vocation promotion programs and other allied projects.

Summing up the mission of Bassein, we see many changes of personnel and the adoption of types of ministry other than the original work. The Sisters have been teaching in college, high school, middle, and primary schools. Pastoral and social work has become an integral part of life in Bassein. Student Sisters have had the advantage of living in their own community while studying in various colleges and institutions across Bombay.

Bassein has many possibilities for the future. Perhaps one of the greatest responsibilities of the Sisters will be to maintain and foster the strong faith implanted in the minds and hearts of the people so many centuries ago by the colonizing Portuguese.

NAZARETH BHAVAN, SOKHO
(Kerwateri)
1972

Sister Jayanti Lakra shines a light on a catechetical chart during the village prayer, Sokho.

Chapter Eleven

NAZARETH BHAVAN, SOKHO
(Kerwateri)
1972

The history of the Sokho mission is perhaps one of the most complex of all the foundations of the SCNs in India. Its remoteness and its austere, barren terrain seem to set it apart both geographically and chronologically. There is a certain other-world quality about the place. The nearest railway station is, paradoxically, on the main Delhi-Calcutta line at Jamui, but once Jamui is left, the remoteness begins.

Missions to the Santhals were long ago established in the areas around Sokho both by the Jesuits of Patna and by the Franciscans of the Bhagalpur region. Several groups of Sisters had also been working in various missions of the Santhals. On 6 July 1972, the first group of SCNs—Sisters Maria Palathingal, Sheela Palamootil, Jean Kulangara, and a candidate, Philomina Hembrom—came to join Father Dan Rice, S.J., in the work of his mission. Their new "people of God" would be predominantly Santhals living in this huge area in sight of high hills, with a river nearby that would be dry most of the year, but often in flood and impossible to ford during the monsoon. They would be working with a people whose everyday life is made up, warp and woof, of poverty, sickness, high mortality, oppression, and injustice.

What was the direction this mission would take? In its beginnings it followed the general pattern of the work of the SCNs—health care, education both formal and informal, help with social problems, sociopastoral with village visiting, teaching of religion, and efforts to overcome exploitation of a disadvantaged people.

The memorable day of departure for Sokho was 5 July 1972. Communications had failed, and the Sisters' imminent arrival was announced only two days ahead, by means of a messenger carrying a mango branch with two leaves on it, which indicated that after two days the Sisters would arrive. Sisters Teresa Rose, Maria, Sheela, Mary Frances, and the driver of the Bakhtiarpur jeep, weighted down with piles of luggage, met Sisters Jean and Philomina at Jamui. The whole party, which now had annexed the Sokho trailer, proceeded to its destination. Because Sister Mary Frances had to return in the jeep, the rest of the party rode in the tractor-trailer and finally arrived to a tumultuous welcome by the 800 villagers on hand—the beating of feathered drums, the singing of school children, the washing of the feet in respect and welcome—young and old coming to greet the Sisters who would live in their midst and work with them.

The first Mass was offered in the chapel that evening. A tour of the school and adjoining areas the next day ended with the Sisters standing under the *neem* tree where Father Dan Rice had sat and meditated for three days, deciding what his future mission would be. At Kerwateri, two miles away, they saw the work of the people on the dam under construction. The specter of starvation became a reality to the Sisters when a small child was admitted in an advanced stage of starvation. Fourteen children living in Sokho died of starvation in 1972 alone.

The 16th of July was a typical Sunday in Sokho, with Mass taking three to four hours with five or six instructions, teaching of catechism, singing of hymns—truly a Sunday spent with God and God's people.

The different streams of ministry in Sokho developed separately. In an area where disease and malnutrition were endemic, the medical and health ministry took priority. Under Sister Maria's guidance, a substantial medical setup soon began to function. In November 1972 Sisters Ancilla Kozhipat and Bridget Vadakkeattam came for the first health clinic, which was successfully inaugurated with sixty patients. To extend the Sokho clinic, Sister Maria made regular calls at various mission stations and villages. Besides procuring the services of doctors, she also referred patients to the hospital when necessary. Two Grail Extension workers gave a seminar on baby care, smokeless stoves, peanut milk, nutrition, vitamin deficiency, etc. Early in the Sokho clinic's existence, 1975, interest was taken in ways and means to spread the medical work into the far-flung villages of the mission. Mr. Reddy, a representative of CARITAS (India), came to study the feasibility of a mobile medical unit for Sokho. Patients there were often of an unusual type. In late August of 1975, a patient who had been mauled by a bear was brought in—along with the bear hide and the meat. It seems vengeance was immediate and effective.

During the first several years, the public health team from Mokama continued to visit Sokho on a regular basis. In 1975 a number of personnel changes took place, including the replacement of Sister Maria by Sister Lucia Thuluvanickal. A more drastic development took place in 1976 when the medical ministry gave way to a healing ministry through prayer, an outgrowth of the developing charismatic movement in Sokho.

In 1977 and 1978, the general emphasis was on healing through retreat and prayer over the sick. Simple villagers were taught to take care of the immediate needs of the people. This type of self-help was also promoted through the staff and students of the school. Actual medical help was given to school children and those in the hostel. Both the health ministry and the sociopastoral ministry supported government efforts to eradicate malaria. Programs for adult literacy and natural family planning were also part of the Sisters' ministry.

By the end of the first decade, this almost imperceptible changeover had altered the health ministry. Material benefits, such as medicine, food, etc., were dispensed with. This development affected all the ministries and ultimately resulted in serious tension in the community and all connected with the mission. After a series of meetings in 1980, some of the problems were finally resolved. Nevertheless, several years passed, during which a certain amount of confusion prevailed.

Sisters Vandana Velleringatt and Teresa Velloothara were hard at work by 1983 on projects relating to health, social, and economic needs. The medical ministry gradually resumed its former role; a dispensary was again set up and continued to be open daily to alleviate the needs of the sick and suffering. As a result, there was a perceptible decrease in the death rate.

As in any underdeveloped country, the ministry of education assumed a place of high priority. In Sokho the fortunes of the school rose and fell and rose again. When Sister Sheela supervised the reopening of a school that had been closed because of the scarcity of food, the admissions rose to eighty in Classes 1, 2, and 3, with many boarders. The opening was on 31 July 1972, but unfortunately the school was again forced to close by mid August because of another shortage of food. Students, teachers, and workers had to be sent away. When the situation improved, the school was reopened.

In 1975 Sisters Sheela and Josita took over the school. As major changes in the mission development began to emerge, the school was also affected. The next year Sister Josita was transferred to the novitiate ashram at Kerwateri, and Sister Ann Muthukattil took charge of the school. About this time a program of adult education, called Pushpa Krishi Vidyalaya, was inaugurated in Nirmala Tola and Todimachua. When this school began to ask nominal fees for admission and study, and later when the midday feeding program for the school children was discontinued, the enrollment dropped considerably.

By the end of 1978, there were fifty-seven enrolled in school from kindergarten to Class 5, with seven teachers. Importance was given to classes in agriculture and cultivation. Children participated in programs for national and religious celebrations. Great difficulty was experienced in collecting the fees—Rs 2 per month and 40 kg of rice per year per child. The crisis was reached in 1979, when the school, with only fifty-five students, forty of whom were in the hostel, was showing a severe loss. By the end of the year, Father Dan Rice decided to close the hostel and, later, the school. With the closing of the school the nature of the ministry also changed. Sister Amala Valayathil took up the work of nonformal education. Tension prevailed in the community over the closing of the school and the hostel. Meanwhile, by late January 1980, Sister Amala began teaching children in Kerwateri, and by 1981 a small school was started there.

Each phase of the Sokho mission saw extraordinary changes, and so it was with the education ministry. As early as 1982, after meetings with the bishop, with Father Rice, with the Sisters, and with parents, the Sokho school was once more reopened. On 6 January, thirty children were admitted to school, all ready with Rs 5 admission. Actual classes had to be postponed until 1 February because of the serious illness of

Sister Jayanti Lakra, the headmistress, who was transferred in March and replaced by Sister Suma Muthukattuparampil. In August, a school lunch program, financed by Bishop Osta, was inaugurated.

Throughout the subsequent years, the school continued to flourish. By the end of 1985, the enrollment had reached 200, eighty-eight of whom were in the hostel. A great deal of encouragement had been given to education, including night classes. By 1990 education was on a firm foundation.

SOCIOPASTORAL

The first entry into the sociopastoral ministry was on Christmas Day 1972. At midnight Mass fifteen catechumens were baptized—five Ravidas and ten Santhals. After Mass there was dancing until almost dawn. After the morning Mass attended by 600 people, a feast was served to 1200. In the early part of 1975, the Sisters were fortunate to be guided by Sister Geralda, IBMV, a veteran of the Santhal missions from the 1930s, who came to stay with the Sisters for three months to help them in their work. When Sister Francine Moozhil joined the mission in Sokho, she spent ten days with Sister Geralda at Bardom, while the experienced missionary prepared a group for baptism.

The all-purpose hall was emptied of *bidi* leaves and straw and became Sokho's first church. By 29 January, Mass was offered there for the first time. Two-week cate-chetical programs were set up in several places, with two Sisters engaged in each. Father Rice and Sisters Francine and Sheela attended the anniversary of the first Santhal missions in Bandel in August of 1975. The great feasts of Easter and Christmas were celebrated with solemnity and joy, with people coming to Sokho from far and near. In 1974 Father Pat Rebeiro, S.J. became a permanent assistant to Father Rice.

On Holy Saturday night, Easter Sunday night, and Easter Monday night of 1974, the people experienced what they believed was a Satanic visitation. Stones were thrown on the roofs of the houses and even near some of the men, although no one was struck. Upon investigation, an idol used in devil worship was found in one of the houses. After removal of the image, the blessing of the houses, special prayers, and the installation of the picture of the Sacred Heart of Jesus, the evil spirit finally left the place.

The major changes that took place in the general setup and development of the mission in 1976 had its impact on the sociopastoral ministry. The trend was toward charismatic renewal and development. The Food-for-Work program was stopped, so that the people could learn to take responsibility for themselves and their families. Retreat work was taken up, and many individuals and groups came from outside to make retreats. A new retreat house was built.

On the political side, there was trouble beginning in September 1976, when police harassed some of the village people, even to the extent of putting innocent victims in jail and abusing the Sisters who tried to help them. After quite a few people were in jail and court a number of times, the harassment decreased somewhat. At the same time, the Block Divisional Officer (BDO) approached the mission for help on projects to give flood relief at Khaira, a nearby village. The BDO and his coworkers promised to help rebuild the dam at Kerwateri, which had been damaged by the flood.

From 1977 to 1979, the main thrust of the mission was in spiritual projects: retreats, village visiting for contacts, prayers, consoling the sick, listening to problems, instructing, marriage counselling, and catechetical work. Literally hundreds of people from outside sought peace in Sokho away from the toils and confusion of the world. Two Sisters and a few catechists cared for the 460 Christians of Sokho. Father Rice and Sister Lucia took care of the retreats not only in Sokho but also in many other places.

As mentioned earlier, tension slowly began to develop between those members of the community who favored the changes in the mission and those who opposed them. In mid March of 1980, the SCN provincial, Sister Margaret Rodericks, the Jesuit provincial, Father Abraham Puthumana, S.J., Father Dan Rice, S.J., and the Sisters involved had a joint meeting in which they tried to search out and settle points on which the two sides were at odds. Some decisions were agreed upon at this time. Later at the first coming of Bishop Osta to the mission, further meetings were held with him, the Sisters, the priests, and some of the people to discuss the setup of the mission.

Difficulties arose in 1981 in regard to accusations by the police for the felling of trees and also for thefts, often amounting to nothing but harassment of innocent people. Certain civilians also gave trouble to Father Rice and the Sisters. In July of 1981, Sister Lucia, who had long been in service in Sokho, moved to Jamtara, where she continued in the ministry of giving retreats and of healing. Sister Lucia returned to the Sokho mission again in 1982 for parish ministry. Sister Xavier Valiakunnackal, assisted by Sister Evelyn D'Souza, began a retreat for eighty-two people of the parish on 2 January 1982.

From 1981 on, the Sisters engaged in a number of activities to help the people of Sokho who were economically disadvantaged and who had long been oppressed and exploited because they were tribals. Projects and programs of assistance varied. On 2 February 1982, the SDO (subdivisional officer) distributed land deeds for the poor and much neglected people of that area. This distribution was the result of persevering efforts of Sister Vandana Velleringatt, assisted by Sister Teresita Theruvankunnel, to press the claims of the poor people by making use of existing laws that had been ignored. In March of the same year, a tractor driver, who was a next-door neighbor of the Sisters, died because of careless treatment after an accident. Sister Evelyn got busy on the case and succeeded in contacting officials, who arranged that compensation be given to his wife and children.

May is the season for gathering *bidi* leaves, which are used in making a substitute cigarette. In order to save the poor people from exploitation by the contractors, Sister Vandana began the collection of these leaves, paying the people in cash. She had to face challenges from the contractors about the legality of the procedure as well as enquiry from government sources, but Sister Vandana and her coworkers went on courageously and were eventually able to make an investment to aid these poor people. When the rain came, the work automatically ceased, but the Sisters experienced a sense of satisfaction for having been able to assist people who would otherwise have been oppressed and cheated.

As the stage began to be set for a new phase in the history of the Sokho mission, new personnel had also been taking the places of Sisters transferred to other missions. In August of 1982, the general arrangement was: Sisters Teresa Velloothara and Vandana in village, social, and health work; Sisters Lucia and Evelyn in pastoral work and retreats; Sister Suma in the school.

The year 1983 saw more projects going forward for the progress of the poor people. Government aid was given for T.B. and leprosy patients. Also from the electricity department came a transformer, another long-awaited benefit. The Food-for-Work program for the building of the dam at Kerwateri was resumed. This project and the reconstruction of the two wells were under the direction of Sisters Vandana and Teresa. Along with this work Sister Vandana also worked tirelessly on land claims, which, because of so much red tape and all kinds of government deliberations, seemed never to get fully settled. During this period Sister Evelyn was busy visiting villages and making contacts.

The most important event of 1984 was the transfer of the Sokho mission from the Patna Diocese to the newly-erected Bhagalpur Diocese. Father Dan Rice, whose memory and name will ever be enshrined in the Sokho mission, was replaced by Father Joseph Mulloor, a priest of Bhagalpur Diocese, whose experience for a number of years in the neighboring parish of Mariampahari had prepared him well for work among the Santhals of Sokho. The bishop of Bhagalpur, Most Reverend Urban McGarry, paid his first visit to Sokho on 5 October 1984.

By 1985, after many astonishing vicissitudes, Sokho had come full circle to its original style and structure: health care—dispensary and village health service; catechetical work— instruction in preparation for the sacraments and celebration of feasts for the moral life of the Christians; and social service— involvement in several projects and efforts to ensure the civil and legal rights of the poor of the region and the school.

A community event of extreme importance to Sokho was the opening of the novitiate ashram on 25 March 1975. Its history has been treated in the general history of the novitiate.

One of the most important celebrations was the 175th anniversary of the founding of the SCNs and the 15th of the Sokho Nazareth Bhavan, celebrated on 26 July 1987, with Mass followed by singing, dancing, feasting, and all the good things that make for a gala village festival.

The SCN mission in Sokho is still (1990) firmly structured according to its original vision. Medical work in the mission and in the village has helped to bring up the level of health considerably. The school and hostel flourish, and the effect of education on the general standard of living is visible. Social projects and methods of securing civil rights have brought new hope to people long suffering oppression and injustice. Above all, through the power of Christ living in their midst, generated by the persevering efforts of Sisters, priests, and other Christians, the people are mindful of their faith and its ultimate goal—eternal life.

Village school, indoors

Village school, outdoors

NAZARETH NILAYA, KUTUDERI
(Mahuadanr)
1974

Sister Rosemarie Lakra counsels a parishioner after Sunday liturgy at Kutuderi.

Chapter Twelve

NAZARETH NILAYA, KUTUDERI
1974

K utuderi, a village in the Chotanagpur Plateau, lies just five miles northeast of a very old mission, Mahuadanr, not far from the border of Bihar and Madya Pradesh. Originally founded by the Belgian Jesuits of Ranchi, Mahuadanr passed into the hands of the Australian Jesuits of the Hazaribagh region. Eventually Mahuadanr and its offshoots, one of which was Kutuderi, became incorporated in the newly formed diocese of Daltonganj. At Kutuderi the SCNs founded a new mission in late 1974.

Correspondence among the bishop of Daltonganj, Most Reverend George Saupin, S.J., the Jesuit regional superior, Father Philip Crotty, and SCN provincial Teresa Rose concerning this new mission was begun as early as July 1971. Pros and cons emerged as to the possibility of taking up this mission, but by July 1973 the pros seemed to be prevailing and long-range planning began in earnest.

The ministry envisaged was primarily education through administration of the principal school of the parish of Sale. It was already an operating school of some 300 students, 90% of whom were Catholics. Catechetical work was also included in the plan. After visits to the site and discussions of arrangements, an opening date was set. Sisters Marianne Puthoor, Jean Kulangara, and Rosemarie Lakra were assigned to begin the mission. The original opening date had to be postponed but was finally fixed for 13 October 1974.

The advance party, Sisters Teresa Rose, Rosemarie, Jean, and Marianne, arrived on 11 October with considerable luggage and were welcomed at the Holy Cross Convent in Mahuadanr by the Holy Cross Sisters, Jesuit Fathers Crotty, Barry, and McNamara, and the students of St. Theresa's School of Mahuadanr. The Sisters, having stayed with the Holy Cross Sisters the previous night, were welcomed on 12 October by the people of Kutuderi and also at St. Michael's School, Sale. The tribal customs of ceremonial washing of hands and feet, dances accompanied by song and drums, a parade, and welcome speeches were observed.

On the official day set for the inauguration and blessing, 13 October, about three thousand people gathered from three parishes: Mahuadanr, Gotgaon, and the newly erected Sale. Priests and Sisters of the area, along with the new SCNs and visitors, Sisters Eula Blandford and Mary Bennet Cecil from the United States mission office, Sisters Mary Frances, James Leo, and Ann Roberta all took part in the happy celebration. After the blessing of both convent and parish house, Mass followed. A welcome program of about two hours' duration brought out the talent of each village in song and dance. Gifts of wheat, rice, pulse, and corn were presented. As a sign of acceptance into the group, a shawl was put on each Sister. Money amounting to Rs 350 was presented to Sister Marianne, with the ceremonial giving of rice beer. The first Mass was offered at Nazareth Nilaya one or two days later. All too soon the visiting Sisters departed.

Almost immediately the Sisters plunged into the work, the first assignment being to assist with a retreat for the girls of St. Theresa High School in Mahuadanr. This enterprise proved a good means of communication with these girls with whom they would soon be closely connected. Within days, the Sisters began to move about from village to village. This project entailed walking miles and miles on foot through forest and jungle, climbing hills and mountains, crossing rivers, eating berries and fruits on the way, drinking from streams. Everywhere they found people who, though very poor, were ready to share what little they had with the Sisters, asking only that the Sisters in turn would be ready to share the people's cares and worries. At the end of the Puja holidays in October, Sisters Marianne and Jean joined the teaching staff of St. Michael's School, Sale.

The first Christmas Mass in Sale parish was offered by Bishop George Saupin himself. A large congregation celebrating the feast with traditional tribal customs made it a memorable Christmas for the new Sisters. Since Sister Rosemarie's immediate relatives reside in the Mahuadanr area, she and Sister Marianne set out on 29 December to visit Sister Rosemarie's mother at Rantasali in Madhya Pradesh. On their return trip, they walked to Bihar from Madhya Pradesh in one day—quite an achievement.

As the Sisters became more and more involved in the work of the mission in 1975, they participated in a number of activities: a meeting of catechists, superiors, headmasters/mistresses, Sisters, and parish priests to present and discuss matters of concern and of interest in deepening the faith of the people—teaching in the school, conducting guidance and marriage courses and retreats, working with women especially through Mahila Sangh, and preparing children for First Holy Communion.

The first monsoon brought a unique experience. On Independence Day, while the Sisters were returning from a school sports event, the jeep got stuck in deep mud. By clutching bamboo poles provided by men of the parish, the Sisters were able, with great difficulty, to wade across the swollen river.

Work in the school continued under the guidance of Sisters Jean and Marianne. In tribal schools, sports held a prominent place in the curriculum. In 1976, Sister Marianne escorted a group of girls from St. Michael School to Khunti to take part in the Bihar Women's Hockey Tournament. Although they were the only middle school students participating, they reached the semi-finals. On the return trip, the party of forty-two, consisting of one boys' team and two girls' teams, made a hike of fifteen miles after leaving the bus at Netarhat.

At the end of the first term in 1976, Sister Jean left for Lucknow to earn a B.Ed. degree and was replaced by Sister Stella Chullyil, who had previously substituted at Sale in 1975.

Several important developments took place in 1976. Preliminary discussions were held and plans were drawn for a new school building. A school complex meeting of Sale Center was held in August, with ten schools represented. An important proposal was the exchange of teachers to alleviate the teaching shortage.

The year 1977 marked the beginning of a long, hard struggle between the school and the government, in which the teachers of Sale were actively engaged. In July, the minority school teachers went on indefinite strike. Their demand from the government was: "Equal pay for equal work." Sister Marianne joined the *gherao* (holding an official hostage) and *dharna* (strike) in Ranchi to press the demand. All the teachers took part in the strike, which continued until 14 October, when it ended with the promise of the education minister that the demands would be met. After ninety-five days, the schools were finally reopened.

Plans for the school building went forward in 1978. A site had been chosen, an architect brought in, and groundbreaking was held in December, in the presence of lay teachers, Sisters, and workers, with Father Barry officiating. On 24 February 1981 the finished construction was formally blessed by Bishop Saupin. Among SCNs present were Sisters Margaret, Shalini, Mary Scaria, Mary Joseph, and Marianne. The school staff offered a Mass in thanksgiving for the gift of the new school by the Jesuits of the Hazaribagh mission.

At a special meeting of the diocesan education board in Daltonganj in June 1979, Sister Marianne and Theodore Kujur, headmaster of St. Joseph School, Mahuadanr, were appointed to work for the payment of the teachers in the mission middle schools of the diocese. This work continued throughout the ensuing months. On 4 October Bishop Saupin, Sister Marianne, and Mr. Kujur met at Patna with the chief minister, Ram Sunder Das, to present a memorandum concerning the payment of teachers in the minority schools. A case was filed in the High Court in Patna against the government in Sister Marianne's name, representing the diocese of Daltonganj. After several hearings of this case in January, the good news that the case had been won was brought on 27 January by Sister Marianne and Mr. Kujur.

New Sisters who had joined the school staff were Sister Philomina Hembrom in 1979 and Sisters Ann Palatty and Rekha Kerketta in 1980. At the same time, two pioneers of the mission—Sisters Marianne and Rosemarie—left.

The school developed to such an extent that by October 1982 it was decided that a high school would be added in 1983, the SCNs providing a headmistress. In April 1983 the managing committee appointed Sister Ann Palatty headmistress. Various changes in personnel were pertinent to the school as well as to other ministries. In 1976, Sister Sabina Mattappallil joined the community to assist Sister Rosemarie in parish work. In 1981 Sister Philomina became a pioneer in the new mission of Jamtara and was replaced by Sister Seema Monipallicalayil. Sister Priya Kalapurayil spent 1982 and 1983 on the teaching staff of the school and was replaced in January 1984 by Sister Mary Scaria. Sister Rajni Hembrom joined the community in 1982 for parish work. Sister Ann Palatty was transferred in June 1984, and the following November Sister Jean returned as principal of the school, having finished the B.Ed. degree.

The housing problem actually began in June 1983, when the owner of the land on which the Sisters' house was located addressed a letter to the *Panch* (the village council), asking that the Sisters vacate the premises within a month. Later, the villagers withdrew the demand and granted permission to the Sisters to stay on as long as they wished. Later incidents in 1984 indicated, however, that the many instances of harassment directed toward the Sisters and their occupation of the house—the beating of children connected with the Sisters, stone-throwing, and other abuses—were caused by teachers who had been dismissed recently. The unrest continued through a great part of 1984, and the people insisted that the Sisters should leave the house.

The housing problem was solved, but not without a struggle. When the provincial, Sister Shalini D'Souza, paid her first official visit in April 1984, this issue was reaching a critical stage. The Sisters expressed their desire to move from the house because of the harassment by village boys. Sister Shalini and the community tried to probe the cause of the trouble and eventually decided that a move should be made. The ultimate solution was the building of a new house completed at the end of 1986. The first Mass was offered on 29 November 1986 by the parish priest, Father Dungdung. Once in the new house the Sisters at last found peace. On 14 December, the concelebrated Mass with Bishop Saupin and five priests brought a gathering of fifty Sisters and about 150 lay people. After the Mass the bishop blessed the house. The rest of the day was spent in feasting, dancing, and singing. Christmas of 1986 in the new house was a happy and peaceful feast for all.

During all the years of the mission, other ministries besides education have been of high importance. Constant and persevering work was done in both the pastoral and health ministries. In 1976, Sisters Sabina and Abha Beck had succeeded in bringing about a change of heart among the villagers of Khapartala, whose church had been closed the previous year. After a moving seminar and retreat of three days, the church was reopened, a cause for rejoicing and thanksgiving to God.

There was constant visiting, instruction, and preparation for the sacraments. The celebration of feasts was ever a matter of interest and enthusiasm. A number of hitherto non-Christian feasts, which were very much the life of the tribal people, were included in the Christian calendar and fittingly celebrated according to tribal custom. The following are examples:

1) The sixth of January, the feast of the Epiphany, emphasized the Kingship of Christ. As many as 3000 participated in the grand procession.

2) In September, the feast of Kharma, which arose from tribal worship of the tree, was converted into the Exaltation of the Cross.

3) In October, the feast of Tuago, the new harvest, became thanksgiving for the gifts of the earth.

All these feasts are religious/social celebrations that are deeply appreciated by the tribal people.

From the time of Sister Rosemarie Lakra, a pioneer of the mission, health work had been carried on faithfully. Therefore, it was not surprising that in 1986 Bishop Saupin made a formal request, in a letter dated 22 September 1986, for a health program in Kutuderi, to be sponsored and financed by the diocese. Sister Shaila Vettamattathil, who had joined the community that year, pioneered the project.

In November 1983 Sister Teresa Rose visited Kutuderi, accompanied by her brother and sister-in-law, Charles and Charlotte Nabholz, who were visiting from the United States. The students of the school held a reception in honor of these guests, as Mr. and Mrs. Nabholz were special benefactors of the school, having donated a large portion of the furniture. As a mark of the school's appreciation, the guests were presented with traditional shawls, and the teachers held a tea party in their honor.

Mahuadanr mission has always been well known as a place rich in religious vocations. One of the pioneers, Sister Rosemarie, was herself from Mahuadanr. During the first decade three young women joined the candidacy—Jermina Kujur, her sister, Albertina, and Victoria Kujur. Thus the community itself began to grow as a result of the seeds planted in the garden of Kutuderi.

Nazareth Nilaya has been a place of varied activity, of new experiences, of both joyful and sorrowful events, abounding in the work of human interest as well as human woes. As in most SCN missions, the Sisters were dedicated to education, social work, the care of the sick, and the teaching and spread of Christ's Gospel, especially among the poor.

The location of the mission, a very short distance from one of the oldest missions in this tribal area, made it far less remote than other isolated mission stations. The work of education, too, had been established long before, with two large schools in Mahuadanr—one for boys and one for girls. Already there was a very large Catholic population dispersed through the surrounding villages.

The labors of the pioneers of the mission—the Belgian and Australian Jesuits and the Swiss Holy Cross Sisters—have borne abundant fruit. There is plenty of scope, however, for more "laborers in the vineyard." In Kutuderi there is need for the presence of the Sisters in the growing schools, for village visitation, for religious instruction, retreat work, marriage counseling, parish affairs, and basic medical and health instruction.

The Sisters share in the life of the people; they maintain a living standard as close as possible to that of the people, and they labor side by side with the lay people who are engaged in teaching, in catechizing, and in carrying on medical and social work. God's blessing is on them as the mission expands and becomes strong with faith in Christ, the center of their lives.

BETHEL HOUSE, GOMOH
1977

Leprosy patients in Gomoh rejoice at Sister Janice Rathappillil's visit.

Chapter Thirteen

BETHEL HOUSE, GOMOH
1977

Most new missions have a remote beginning and then an immediate one. In the case of Bethel, the remote beginning was a request in December 1975 from the Damien Social Welfare Center (DSWC) in Dhanbad, through Jesuit Fathers Joe Lacy and Walter Kongari, for the SCNs to come to Gomoh to join in the work of the center.

The geographic status of Gomoh is interesting. Although it is a small town, it is a place of importance because of its strategic position as a junction on the Grand Cord Railway line that runs from Calcutta across northern India. As a result, many important east/westbound trains as well as southbound trains to Ranchi and beyond pass through Gomoh. It lies in a region of natural beauty, with hills on its perimeter and a rolling terrain that leads into wooded jungle with a few small streams flowing here and there. One might say it is a sort of haven between two big industrial cities—Dhanbad to the east and Bokaro Steel City to the south.

As a follow-up to the request of December 1975, Sisters Margaret Rodericks and Sarita Manavalan visited Gomoh in July 1976 to assess the situation. They were impressed by the need for Sisters, which they categorized as follows: 1) work in De Britto House, a home for 300 boys who were for the most part children of leprosy patients, and also in "The Nest," a hostel run by Seva Sangh Samiti (a civic organization of Calcutta) for young girls and boys; 2) parish work; 3) social and medical work in the nearby villages.

From that time on, the project at Gomoh seemed to be assured. Work went forward with the purchase and preparation of a dwelling—Bethel House, an old English-style bungalow owned by Protestant missionaries. The community was assigned: Sister Bridget Vadakkeattam (coordinator), nurse; Sister Shanti Kappalamackal, teacher; Sister Marcelline Indwar (novice, former social worker at this center), and Sister Teresa Rose Nabholz, director of temporary professed Sisters, who would reside at Bethel. In later years, Sister Anne Marie Thayilchirayil, having succeeded to the post held by Sister Teresa Rose, took up residence at Bethel.

The advance party moved out of Mokama by the Pataliputra Express at 5:15 p.m. on 2 July 1977, bound for Dhanbad. Father Lacy, Father Kongari, Brother

Wency D'Souza, and Lalitha Abraham, a former SCN, welcomed them, and after a midnight dinner, the Sisters spent the night at Nirmala Leprosy Hospital, run by the Samaritan Sisters, located at nearby Govindpur. The next morning, a tour was made to Gomoh, where the Sisters were welcomed by the boys of De Britto House, along with their band, and by the children of "the Nest." They found Bethel House humming with activity, as all kinds of workmen and technicians tried to make it ready for the Sisters. The workers were ably assisted by Brother Wency and Sisters from nearby convents—the Samaritan Sisters, Apostolic Carmelites, and Notre Dame Sisters.

For the next two weeks, the Sisters spent the time visiting various institutions in the area—hospitals, leprosy clinics, rehabilitation centers, schools, and the like. Several communities of Sisters were in the area, and the work of the Damien Social Welfare Center had branched out into a number of dispensaries, clinics, and centers for treatment, including those village clinics held only under trees. The Sisters became acquainted with the types of people with whom they would work, and they learned the skills of caring for leprosy patients. Sister Crescentia Wise, who had started leprosy care in Mokama so many years before, must have smiled upon them from heaven.

By 16 July the house at Bethel was ready for occupancy, and a Mass was offered there. The actual first day of occupation was 18 July. An interesting and harrowing experience the previous day was the discovery by Sister Bridget of a deadly snake (krait) under the pillow of the bed on which she had been resting shortly before. God's protection was clearly visible.

The official day for the blessing of Bethel House and the inauguration of the new community was 6 August 1977. A large number of guests arrived, including Bishop Rodericks, Sisters, Brothers, priests, Protestants, DSWC officials, parishioners, villagers, hostelers, workers, and friends. The house was blessed, Mass was offered, and entertainment followed. Thus the Sisters were officially and warmly welcomed.

As work got under way during the ensuing months, many visitors came and went. Various retreats, workshops, and courses were held, and Bethel shared its facilities and its quiet with workers and participants. This phase in the life of Bethel continued for several years, and although it did not exactly take precedence over the original plans of the mission, it did hold great importance. Retreats and religious meetings were frequently held, and Bethel House became something of a haven for persons seeking solitude and peace.

The work in De Britto House, as sketched out in the original plan, had two phases—one of teaching, the other of caring for the health of the boys, especially those in the hostel. One Sister and sometimes two have been engaged in teaching in the school. In later years, the teaching program has been much enhanced, especially under the able guidance of Sisters Deepa Thekkecheruvil and Sophia Kalapurackal. Besides learning many skills and technical trades, the boys have a regular program of primary, middle, and high school classes leading up to the Board Examination of the State of Bihar.

The boys of the hostel were given skilled care by the ministrations of the nurses—Sisters Bridget Vadakkeattam, Pushpa Paruvananickal, Anjali Olickal, and others who came for short periods. Sister Mary Juliana Tuti gave a short health education course for the outgoing senior class of the De Britto House in 1985. The facilities of a regular clinic were available to the boys, and when necessary, the sick boys were taken to an infirmary area for care. Nursing care and medical aid were available not only to De Britto House but also to villagers who came for help and treatment and especially to leprosy patients in the vicinity and to a group of disabled leprosy patients who live in a small section called Amar Jyoti, where they are given medicine and external treatment of their wounds. A number of Sister nurses coming there to work have taken special training at the Nirmala Hospital at Govindpur.

The Sisters also visited the villages. In this work, Sisters Teresa Madassery and Elsa Ezhaparampil, members of the Catholic Relief Service, gave some valuable information on possible diocesan programs for the villages. Village work was fostered by a week's stay with the *mukhiya* (headman), Bipin Soren, of Laxmipur. Sisters Bridget, Priya, and Marcelline lived with the family, prepared their own simple food, bathed in the nearby river, visited the other families, and had classes in the evening for various groups. Sister Marcelline took the youngest group, Sister Bridget had health and hygiene classes and writing with the older girls, and Sister Priya gave tutoring classes. The evening usually closed with a chat with the *mukhiya* and his wife.

The unique feature of the mission in Gomoh is the connection it has with leprosy patients. From the early days of the community in India, when Sister Crescentia inaugurated the service to leprosy patients by establishing the clinic in Mokama, up to the present day, ministry to leprosy patients has been an important part of the SCN India mission. Even in Gaya, Sister James Leo had been able to give a small service to leprosy patients at the hospital and the village of leprosy patients on the outskirts of Gaya.

Bethel in Gomoh, however, presented a more direct approach to leprosy patients and the problems of leprosy as it affects the unfortunate segment of society who are the victims of the dread disease. In Bethel there were several approaches to this ministry. De Britto House provided a home as well as a school, with technical training for about 400 boys ranging in age from Class 1 to 10, most of whom were leprosy patients (cured cases for the most part), the disabled, or the children of leprosy patients. As previously chronicled, Sisters in school, infirmary, and dispensary contributed much to the welfare of these boys.

The second approach is through the ministration of the Sister/nurse to any needy patient and particularly to the disabled adults, both men and women, who occupy the section of the Damien Social Welfare Center known as Amar Jyoti. These patients, often in advanced stages of leprosy, are the blind, the lame, and the deaf—the "lepers" of the Gospel whom Jesus cured. How much even a kind word, the touch of a loving hand, the friendly joke, the blessing invoked, are tokens of esteem for these afflicted and often forgotten members of humanity.

Scope for social work abounds in the areas in and around Gomoh through such projects as adult and children's education, health education, mobile health care, religious instruction, advice on family and community problems, aid in development, and promotion of social justice through contacts with government officials. The present personnel is not adequate to handle so many areas of need. It is hoped that strong shoulders will emerge to carry some of the burdens and thus spread the City of God.

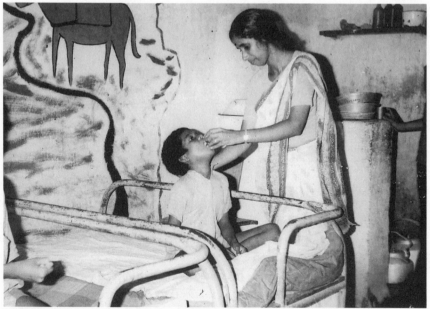

Sister Bridget Vadakkeattam administers medicine to a sick boy in the infirmary at De Britto House, Gomoh, a school for children of leprosy patients.

NAZARETH SADAN, BIHARSHARIF
1977

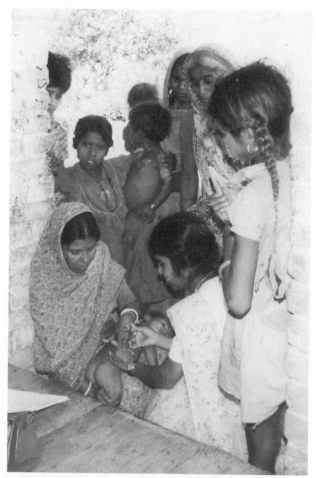

Sister Kiran Kaniyamkandathil immunizes a small child at
Tiyari village in Biharsharif.

Chapter Fourteen

NAZARETH SADAN, BIHARSHARIF 1977

Situated about thirty kilometers due south of Bakhtiarpur, Biharsharif is yet another link in the chain of missions founded fifty years ago by Father Marion Batson, S.J., under the leadership of Father Peter Sontag, S.J., one of the first superiors of the Patna Jesuits.

With the development of indigenous Sisterhoods in the missions of northern India during the 60s and 70s, more and more convents were established, thereby bringing the Sisters into active participation in the work of the missions. Nazareth Sadan in Biharsharif became an integral part of the mission in 1977, when the SCN community decided to participate in this work. The party of pioneers and accompanying Sisters, headed by the provincial, Sister Margaret Rodericks, left Mokama on 29 September, stopped at Bakhtiarpur, and continued its progress to Biharsharif, where the group was heartily welcomed by the parish priest, Father A. D'Costa. The pioneer Sisters, Grace Androth and Shaila Vettamattathil, were housed temporarily in the old parish house that had been remodelled as much as its limited capacity would allow. In later years, a two-story addition provided satisfactory living quarters and a chapel. Because the kitchen was not ready, the Sisters ate for some time in the dining room of the rectory.

The opening of the new mission on 3 October was a joyous occasion. Bishop Wildermuth was the main celebrant and official guest, assisted by twenty-three priests. Besides the contingent of twenty-five SCNs, other Sisters, Brothers, and about 1500 lay people attended the function. Mass under a *shamiana* (canopy) was followed by a reception for the two Sisters, during which gifts (some individual, many collective) were given by representatives of each of the villages belonging to Biharsharif parish. Speeches by the dignitaries and a cultural program followed. Heavy storm and rain did not dampen the spirits of the people, who considered it a sign of the blessings brought by the Sisters.

By early October Sisters Grace and Shaila were already visiting their first village, Maghra. The Christian people welcomed them and later escorted them back to the mission. Another happy reception was accorded Sister Grace at Tiyari village. (Because of a malarial attack, Sister Shaila could not attend.) These village visits continued until the last week of October. Everywhere the reception was warm and enthusiastic.

The school, though rather small, was going well. A note in the annals for 8 December 1977 mentions the traditional sports day for Vimala Mata, the original name of the school. The next entry tells of the development of the school under the administration of Sisters Anila Monippallicalayil and Anjali Olickal. The name of the school was changed to Pushpa Vidyalaya, and a new step taken with the admission of non-Christians to the school. A further development was the opening of a girls' hostel under the supervision of the Sisters. The boys' hostel, under the care of the parish priest, had long been in existence.

When the second term of the school year of 1979 began in July, Pushpa Vidyalaya received its new principal, Sister Mary Chackalackal. Under her dynamic leadership, the school was to achieve a standard of education seldom attained in such ordinary surroundings. In the first term the students acquitted themselves well in an interschool cultural program with Bakhtiarpur, Barh, and Mokama. By October of 1981 a new school building was completed, a tribute to the shrewd planning and hard work of the parish priest, Father Augustine Dayanand, who had succeeded Father D'Costa in 1978. The new building was blessed by Bishop Wildermuth and Bishop Osta on 6 October 1981. This new two-story building, spacious and airy, was an outstanding gift to education in the area.

An event of great concern to all at Biharsharif was the kidnapping by *dacoits* (robbers) of Sister Mary's brother, Father Thomas Chackalackal, S.J., in north Bihar in June 1981. Father Thomas had spent Christmas in Biharsharif in 1980. The news was alarming, and since Sister Mary was at that time on a home visit, the Sisters could only wait anxiously to hear the outcome. Although Father was forced to live with the robbers for nine days in the open jungles of West Champaran District, he was not harmed, even though the *dacoits* are known to be quite ruthless. He was released before Sister Mary returned from her home.

Twenty-four years of zealous work by Father D'Costa had borne much fruit in the sociopastoral ministry in Biharsharif. The Catholic population increased to a remarkable degree, and the church had a strong and highly respected position in the town as well as in the whole district. Under the leadership of Father Dayanand, the Sisters joined fully in all the religious projects of the parish. December 1977 was a month for youth: a retreat for school children; First Holy Communion for thirty children prepared by Sister Shaila; and a youth seminar conducted by Father Philip Mantara, S.J. Also in December, Sister Pushpa Paruvananickal joined Sisters Grace and Shaila.

In 1978, the Young Christian Association was formed as a result of the youth seminar. An adult literacy program was also initiated at this time. During March, Sisters Grace, Shaila, and Pushpa were active in village visiting. They investigated the problems of the people, ministered to their health needs, and offered assistance and solace wherever possible. When floods came in September, the Sisters assisted in flood relief work, helping to feed three hundred people a day.

Important pastoral events toward the end of the decade included the religious profession of Sister Abha Shanti in the Sacred Heart Congregation of Bettiah, the first religious Sister of the parish. Sister Shaila accompanied Sister Abha's father, Bal Deo, to Bettiah for the celebration.

Just before Christmas in 1979, the boys of Class 8 participated in a catechetical camp. As part of the program, the boys visited the village of Tiyari under Sister Grace's guidance. In June 1980, Bishop Wildermuth retired and was succeeded by Bishop Benedict Osta, S.J., who was received with enthusiasm and joy by the people during his first pastoral visit in October.

Biharsharif became the scene of terrible and bloody communal riots between Hindus and Muslims in May 1981. All institutions were closed, and there was serious tension between Hindus and Muslims. No one could venture out, as curfew was rigorously enforced. Many lives were lost, and much property damage occurred. From Patna came Bishop Osta and Jesuit Fathers Paul Jackson, Norbert Rai, and Father Scaria Mamootil to see what the church could do for the victims of the stricken area. Sister Rose Plathottathil came to help Sister Grace in the peace ministry. Slowly and painfully, the wounds of division and hatred began to heal, and normal conditions returned to Biharsharif.

Because Biharsharif continued for a long time to be a potentially sensitive area for communal disturbances, efforts were intensified to bring about a permanent peace. One such project was a National Integration Day on 27 November 1982. The district magistrate, the superintendent of police, and the parish staff organized a prayer meeting stressing religious harmony. It was attended by representatives of the Hindu, Muslim, Sikh, Christian, Jain, and Buddhist religions. Father Jackson's book, *Sharfuddin Maneri, the Hundred Letters,* was presented to the district magistrate for the public library. An Australian Jesuit, Father Jackson specialized in Islamic studies. The function did much to promote good feelings among the varied religious groups.

On 5 February 1983, a second meeting of the six religions, with Bishop Osta as chair, was held in the school. Religious harmony was again the theme, with prayer, a talk by Bishop Osta, and a group discussion. Thus the Christian community took the lead in trying to secure "peace on earth among people of good will."

Religious events were very prominent during the 80s. The ordination of Father Jose Chirackal took place on 19 March 1984 and was witnessed by a throng of about a thousand guests. Two bishops and fifty-seven priests concelebrated. A few months later, on 30 September, Bishop Osta returned on the occasion of the inauguration of Batson Hall. The ceremony began with Mass, at which 189 persons received the sacrament of Confirmation, and eighteen school children received First Holy Communion. The hall, intended for both school and parish purposes, was initiated by the district magistrate. Other government officials present were the sub-divisional officer and the superintendent of police.

School events kept pace with other ministries. In March 1982 a Parents Day was held, bringing together parents, teachers, and students. This step led to the formation in 1984 of the Parent-Teacher Association, with the first meeting on 18 February 1984. Pushpa Vidyalaya took part in a number of competitions. The school achieved national prominence when, after having competed in a state level *Kho-Kho* match (a game common in India) in Patna on 27 September 1982, fifteen participants competed in the All India Rural Games held in Trivandrum, Kerala, in December 1982. They comprised over half of the Bihar *Kho-Kho* team of twenty-four members. Sister Mary Chackalackal, the principal, accompanied the team as coach and manager. Pushpa Vidyalaya continued to gain importance in the rural sports field. The district *Kabbadi* match (another game common in India) was held in the school compound in 1984 on 25-26 February. Pushpa Vidyalaya again won the *Kho-Kho* match.

In a poetry contest in Bakhtiarpur on 18 October 1984, two of the four students from Pushpa Vidyalaya who took part were selected. Fifteen students participated in a dance competition in Mokama on 23 March 1985. Another important event was the attendance of a group of school children at the National Integration Day held at Rajgir on 3 February 1985. The students were accompanied by Sisters Mary Chackalackal and Stella Kaiprampatt.

Pushpa Vidyalaya had a number of changes in personnel. When Sister Mary, the first principal, completed six years of untiring, dedicated service in May 1985, the school and the whole community expressed their gratitude and appreciation for her contribution to the cause of education in Biharsharif. She was succeeded by Sister Stella Kaiprampatt, who served as principal until 1987, when she was replaced by Sister Ann Scaria Menonparampil. Sister Rita Puthenkalem had joined the teaching staff in 1982, Sister Janice Rathappillil in 1984, and Sister Abha Beck in 1985.

To mark international youth year, the Nalanda District *Kho-Kho* Match was held at Pushpa Vidyalaya on 24 August 1985. One hundred one *sesam* (a local herb) plants were planted by the Girl Guides in the school compound, and the school children presented a cultural program. The event was attended by the district magistrate and other government officials and prominent citizens. Meanwhile the social, health, and religious ministries progressed with the school. Sisters Lucia Thuluvanickal and Rosemarie Lakra spent two weeks in October of 1984 giving retreats to the people. In March 1985 Bishop Osta opened a charismatic retreat for about 500 participants from Magadh and Nalanda deaneries. On 29 July forty-one women made their commitment to the Mahila Sangh at the close of a one-day seminar under the direction of Father Thomas Athazapadam, S.J., and Sister Alacoque of the Sacred Heart Sisters of Bettiah. Under the leadership of Sister Abha, students took part in a rally of the Krus Vir (a children's mission organization) in Patna, 6-18 November.

In the health ministry, two activities are especially noteworthy. In September 1985, when cholera was rampant in the area of Biharsharif, Sister Kiran Kaniyamkandathil did outstanding work in an anti-cholera vaccination program. In 1986 Sister Kiran attended the National Health Policy Workshop organized by the Bihar Voluntary Health Association of India and sponsored by the government of India.

The following is a sample of important events in the pastoral ministry: 1) Twenty-eight parishioners joined thousands of Christians as they gathered in Ranchi on 5 February 1986 to greet the Holy Father, Pope John Paul II; 2) A two-day seminar was given in March 1986 for high school and college girls and boys; 3) Father Anand Prakash, newly ordained priest of Bakhtiarpur parish and former student of Biharsharif, offered Mass in Biharsharif and was honored by a program given by the hostel boys; 4) Nalanda brides and bridegrooms had a four-day marriage course given by Sister Mercy Thundathil, Brother James, and Father Matthew Uzhathal.

The greatest event of the Biharsharif parish was the celebration of its golden jubilee on 21-22 November 1986. Months of preparation preceded the observance. The twofold celebration marked the fifty years that had passed since the day when six newly baptized Catholics formed the nucleus of the new parish. On 21 November, a reception was held for a multireligious gathering attended also by civil officials and other eminent persons of the district. The following day, the main religious celebration was observed. Blessings were given by Bishop Osta on the new Jubilee Memorial Shrine with its beautiful statue of Our Lady made by one of the parishioners. The new prayer room in the school was blessed, and Mass was celebrated by two bishops and fifteen priests. Fifty children received their First Communion. The whole celebration, a result of the work and sacrifice of the Christian people, was a great success.

It is evident that the Sisters accomplish a great deal for education, for social welfare, for medical care and the promotion of good health, and for the moral and spiritual growth of the people. Their presence, their zealous work, and the example of their dedicated lives help to spread Christ's word among the many non-Christians of the area, bringing them ever closer to the understanding of God's plan of salvation for all people.

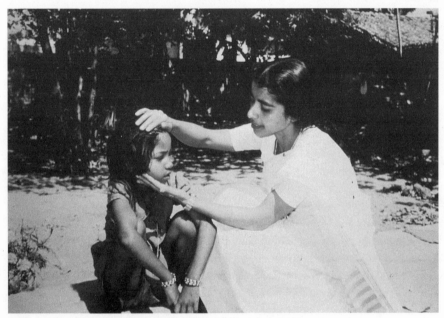

Sister Pushpa Paruvananickal comforts a patient at Biharsharif.

NIRMALA NIKETAN, JAMTARA
1980

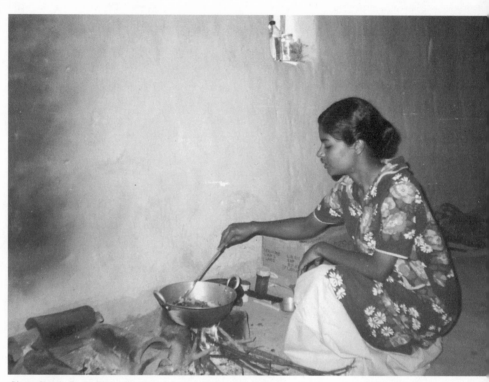

Sister Leena Padam, an expert cook, prepares the evening meal over an open fire stove in Jamtara.

Chapter Fifteen

NIRMALA NIKETAN, JAMTARA 1980

Jamtara, although not a very large town, is a regular railway stop for trains on the main line running to and from Calcutta. Before the new mission of the SCNs was established in 1980, there had been a Catholic presence in Jamtara. The house occupied by the Sisters is an enlargement of an older religious house formerly belonging to the Jesuits of the Maltese Province, who have long worked among the Santhals. With its quaint Gothic windows, its extraordinarily thick walls, and its solid structure, this old "Loyola House" is an example of a building style of bygone days. The entrance room still serves as a church on Sundays and feast days. With a spacious second floor added, the old building has become the convent of the Sisters of Charity of Nazareth under the new name of Nirmala Niketan. Located in the Dumka Diocese, it has become the nerve center of a thriving mission to the Santhals.

On 8 December 1980, the bishop of Dumka, Most Reverend Telesphore Toppo, along with the provincial, Sister Margaret Rodericks, formally opened the new mission. Pioneer Sisters Sheela Palamoottil, Beena Chirackal, Philomina Hembrom, and novice Aisha Kavalakattu were welcomed in a traditional Santhal manner by a large gathering of Sisters, lay people, and priests from all the surrounding areas. The following days were spent in exploring the location, which was near the railway station and the market, in arranging the rooms, and in getting needed utensils and supplies.

Missionary tours began in collaboration with the catechetical team from Madhupar, a nearby mission. In some places there were very few Catholics. These welcomed the opportunity for Mass, confession, catechism, and in general a Catholic contact through the Sisters, the priests, and the team.

Through the ministrations and help given by the Sisters, a very sick 22-year-old Catholic man was brought to Mokama. His family, the Sisters, and the Catholic community prayed very hard for him, and almost miraculously he recovered, thereby strengthening the faith of all who had prayed so earnestly.

The first Christmas was observed in true Santhal custom. Midnight Mass, solemnly and joyfully celebrated, was followed by tea and puffed rice, then dancing and singing till dawn. The SCNs had their own quiet celebration later. From Christmas on, the Blessed Sacrament was reserved in the small convent chapel.

One of the first entries in the annals of the new year 1981 was that the Sisters had begun the study of Santhali, an essential element for communication. Almost immediately came mention of the first Santhal candidate from the Dumka diocese, Susan Tudu. A second candidate, Sabina Murmu, joined from this diocese in July 1974 but later withdrew.

The Sisters spent much time in visiting the villages, many of which were non-Christian. They were received hospitably, the people giving them whatever they had—rice, fruits from the forest, etc. Sister Sheela had a unique experience on Ash Wednesday. Until then, Jamtara relied on the services of priests from other missions for religious services. A crowd assembled for the services of Ash Wednesday, but no priest appeared. Sister Sheela took the matter in hand and led a prayer service, during which she used the ashes to sign the foreheads of all with a cross, distributed Holy Communion, and "sent the crowd away filled."

From 23 May to 2 June 1981, Sister Shalini and seven second-year novices held a village program at Raniganj, a predominantly non-Christian area. They stayed in a village home and had daily prayers, lectures, curing of the sick, shows, slides, etc., proclaiming Christ the healer, the lover of the poor, the divine physician. The project affected the faith and confidence in prayer of both the large number of people residing there and the Sisters conducting it. Contact with the village continued.

After seven months in Jamtara, the Sisters formed some concrete plans for evangelization. In the pastoral ministry they decided to develop through village visiting a firm Christian community, using various means: training village leaders and getting help from villagers, giving retreats and catechizing, preparing parishioners for Mass and the reception of the sacraments, promoting family and group prayer among Christians, establishing units of Catholic organizations—Mahila Sangh (women's organization) and Uvak Sangh (youth organization).

In the medical field the team hoped to bring healing to the sick through medicine and prayer: to establish clinic days for Jamtara and other villages that would provide medicine and treatment, to replace the Santhal beliefs in *Ojhas* and *Bonjas* (witch doctors) with sound medical practices, to obtain government grants and free medicines for tuberculosis, leprosy, typhoid, and malaria vaccines, and to cure the sick through prayer, trust, and confidence in God's power to heal, to promote the practice of naturopathy and the use of indigenous medicines, and to obtain a vehicle to cover long distances between villages.

In educational ministry the Sisters planned to establish health centers to educate children and adults, to develop night school for adults, and to provide academic and vocational training for the young.

In the social area the team hoped to uplift the Santhals socially and economically by establishing a workable system of saving for the people and by promoting cottage industries such as basket making, kitchen gardening, poultry and goat raising. They also planned to set up a system of *grihini* schools and to have community meetings to work out educational and social projects.

During the year of 1981, Sister Gracy Thombrakudyil joined the diocesan faith formation team, where she worked effectively for over a year. As the first year drew to a close, the Sisters evaluated their work with a certain satisfaction and yet with a desire to advance their goals. They could see some of the long-range plans they had made slowly developing—involvement in the spiritual and material life of the people through village visiting; instruction of the people for the reception of the sacraments; the renewal of Christian life and worship; and, side by side, medical and educational projects in the making.

Two noteworthy events were a retreat for the parishioners of Jamtara, conducted by Sister Lucia in January of 1982, and a mother/child health program inaugurated on 24 February, with thirty-one children brought by their mothers on the opening day.

A small act of human kindness happened about this time. Sister Beena and a novice, Sister Anjana Kunnath, who was temporarily in Jamtara, were left by a sudden bus strike fifteen kilometers from their village. Seeing them walking, two men brought their cycles and took them home, each taking a passenger.

By 1982 the scope of education began to be enlarged. The government primary school of the village needed revitalizing. With the help of the village chief and the other villagers, Sister Sheela began the process, although it had to move slowly. About the same time, Sister Philomina started a *balwadi* (nursery) school in a village called Raniganj. In May and June a group of seminarians, guided by Sister Sheela, held a ten-day camp in Rupaidy, a completely non-Christian village about seven kilometers from Jamtara. As a direct consequence of this enterprise, another village school was started by Sister Philomina with Sister Sheela's help. During 1983, two other schools were opened, one close to Jamtara at Bewa, where the people themselves began collecting money in order to construct a new school building. The other school was started in a room at a village called Danidhi. With this excellent work as a lasting remembrance of her stay in Jamtara, Sister Philomina was assigned to teacher training at the end of April. She was succeeded by Sister Anima Pullikkiyil in the education ministry.

The opening on 23 June of the *grihini* school, combined with a sewing center, brought further educational progress in 1983. Thirty-five Santhal women joined. The teacher, Miss Salomi Murmu, had been trained at Holy Cross Vocational Training Institute, Hazaribagh. Besides sewing, girls were taught reading and writing, health and hygiene, mother/child care, nutrition, etc. An effort was made to gain government stipends for the girls.

Jamtara acquired the status of a separate parish and mission with the arrival of Father Fabian, T.O.R., the parish priest, who was joyfully welcomed on 8 January 1983. The Sisters and people at the same time expressed gratitude to Father Joseph Tigga of Dumka, Father Richard Joseph, and Father Sammut of Madhupur, who had so faithfully come to Jamtara to minister to their spiritual needs.

A very effective social awareness program was held for five days in February of 1983, designed to bring the Santhal people to an understanding of their great heritage, their culture, and what they possess as a noble tribal people. The people were made aware of existing political, social, and economic conditions in contemporary society. This seminar had far-reaching effects as the Santhals became convinced of the need for action on their part and agreed to organize and to work toward their own social betterment, especially through education.

In the early part of 1983, two important health programs were organized. The first, a leprosy education program conducted by a team from Damien Social Welfare Centre, was held for the public, the chief guest being Mr. Singha, the subdivisional officer from Jamtara. It was also supported by the Lions Club. The second event was the organizing by Sister Sheela of a health workers' training program for village women. In September this program was followed by a schedule of regular meetings of health workers in the villages. An important addition to the medical/health work was a jeep/ambulance, which proved to be a great asset in reaching remote villages for clinical work and other health programs.

In June of 1983, Sister Margaret Rodericks brought for a visit Miss Jenny Jeter, a friend from the United States, who represented St. Peter Parish, Lexington, Kentucky, which had adopted Jamtara mission as a personal project. A few months later, Sister Shalini came for a provincial visitation. At the end of 1983, Sister Gracy, who had contributed so much to the mission by her efforts to bring the people to Christ, was transferred to the new mission in Dumberdih.

In June 1984, prompted by a general opposition to the mission, trouble arose concerning the new school building at Jarnadi-Bewa. By meeting with villagers and getting them organized, Sister Sheela was able to garner some support. In the midst of all this, Sister Anima, whose work in the school was much appreciated by the people, was transferred to Dumberdih. Eventually the new school was completed. On 2 September, in the presence of over three hundred people, the building was blessed following a Mass celebrated by Bishop Telesphore and seven priests. A large number of Sisters, headed by Sister Shalini, were present. The new school building provided both classroom space and living quarters for Father Fabian and his assistant, Brother Alphonse.

In October of this year, Jamtara welcomed Father Rice, a famous veteran of the Santhal missions. The fourth anniversary of the SCN mission in Jamtara, 8 December 1984, was marked by a Mass celebrated by Bishop Telesphore, at which ten people were confirmed and a unit of Krus Vir inaugurated. On the previous day a whole family had been baptized.

Jamtara mission bade farewell to Bishop Telesphore in February 1985, when he was appointed coadjutor to the archbishop of Ranchi. The new bishop of Dumka, Most Reverend Stephen Tiru, was ordained in Dumka in 1985. His first visit to Jamtara was on 26 October. Having offered Mass for the people, he conferred his blessing and was feted with song and dance.

In 1985 and 1986 a number of personnel changes took place. Sisters Sudha Puthoor and Prabha Tirkey had taken up duties at the end of 1984. In early 1985 Sister Beena, one of the pioneers of the mission, left for Chaibasa, the land of the Ho tribe, after four years of devoted service in the medical field in the land of the Santhals. She had done inspiring work among the people and was greatly missed by all. In June, pioneer Sister Aisha returned as a professed Sister. The great social pioneer Sister Sheela left the mission on 1 August, bequeathing a noble legacy of untiring and dedicated service. Sister Anila Monippallicalayil came in May 1986 as headmistress of the school. A further move in education was made on 19 May, when Sister Sudha initiated a new *grihini* school at Janardy village about six kilometers from Jamtara.

To add a light note to the chronicle, it seems that the *mukhihya* (head man) of Bewa had been invited to hoist the national flag at the school on Independence Day of 1986. When he did not appear in time, Father Fabian mounted his motorbike and hastened to the *mukhihya's* house. There he found him plowing his field. He had quite forgotten. Quickly that worthy gentleman washed, dressed, and returned with Father to preside at the function.

From the very beginning of the mission in December of 1980, the pioneer Sisters and all who have come and gone—professed Sisters, novices, candidates— had worked, toiled, and suffered in order to bring Christ and the Gospel to the people who belong to one of the most numerous of the tribal peoples of Asia—the Santhals. Both successes and failures have been experienced in the course of events, opposition encountered, and obstacles of all kinds faced, but certain it is that the efforts have not been in vain and that progress is evident. More often than not, the troubles and trials have been balanced by interest, friendliness, cooperation, and an awakening to what is possible in the future.

Mixed feelings in Jamtara: Sister Beena Chirackal, with head slightly bowed, is sad to be leaving the village where she has served; Sister Sudha Puthoor, who is to take her place, is in a happier mood.

BETHANY, JAMSHEDPUR
1980

Sister Deepti Ponnambal talks with a parent at Jamshedpur.

Chapter Sixteen

BETHANY, JAMSHEDPUR
1980

As in the case of most beginnings, the seed was planted and germinated, and finally the flower and fruit sprang up. The seed of Bethany can be found in the work of Sisters Teresa Madassery and Mary Juliana Tuti, who administered health programs in town and village for four years before Bethany in Jamshedpur became an SCN mission.

The formal opening took place on 28 December 1980. Sister Margaret Rodericks, the provincial, opened the new convent; her brother, Bishop Joseph Rodericks of Jamshedpur, blessed the convent and offered the first Mass in the presence of about sixty-five guests, including the SCN Council members and SCNs from neighboring convents. The other pioneer members of the community were Sisters Sarala Anithottathil and Blanche Correia.

The convent, located on a busy thoroughfare of Jamshedpur, is a comfortable Company house owned by Tata Electric Locomotive Company, consisting of six or seven rooms, just a five-minute walk from St. Joseph Cathedral on the same side of the road. Between the cathedral and Bethany is the convent of the Sacred Heart Sisters, who staff the large school of the Cathedral parish. Although Bethany is one of many convents in Jamshedpur, its area and sphere of action often take the Sisters outside these limits into nearby villages.

The Sisters spent the first days of January 1981 "settling in." Sisters Teresa and Mary Juliana collected their belongings from Mercy Convent, where they had been living during the years prior to the establishment of their own mission. Part of the process of initiation into their new surroundings entailed getting acquainted with people and places in and around Jamshedpur. For Sisters Teresa and Mary Juliana the work was a continuation of what they had been doing for four years, but their base of operation was changed. At the end of January, they went to Maluka where they began a new village dispensary. In that area, they were to work in health care and health instruction. Sisters Sarala and Blanche had meanwhile begun teaching in the Rohargora village school, a branch school of Parusudih parish. To this school they traveled daily on cycles.

A diversion at this time was the series of elaborate birthday celebrations for Jamshedji Tata, founder of the steel industry. All Jamshedpur celebrates this event annually for three days. The special feature is the beautiful illumination of Jubilee Park.

Many of the activities in the first part of this year were applicable to all of the Sisters. A development orientation program at the Welfare Centre, organized by the diocesan director of Catholic Charities, proved very beneficial. Varied programs occupied the Sisters during the month of April—vocation days, health visits, social studies in local surroundings by students and workers, ordination of new priests, and the evaluation of the Catholic Relief Service Centre. In May the Sisters participated in a two-week youth camp in Jodhpur, Madhya Pradesh, a place at an elevation of about 2000 feet, of great scenic beauty and pleasant surroundings.

The first Christmas was a quiet but happy and joyful feast. Sister Margaret Rodericks celebrated the first anniversary, 28 December, with a five-day stay. As the year 1982 wore on, the Sisters continued their ministries. Sisters Teresa and Mary Juliana joined the diocesan team for the seminar on marriage, the first of its kind in the Golmuri parish. In May, Sister Teresa started a new project—a literacy program, with seven mothers of the Mother/Child Health Program at Mercy Hospital, Baridih. Working with the Catholic Relief Service, the two Sisters attended many meetings and participated in numerous village projects. Meanwhile Sisters Blanche and Sarala continued their very successful work at the school in Rohargora.

By January 1983, Sister Sarala was replaced by Sister Premila Parackattu, who began teaching with Sister Blanche at a different site, Gyan Deep Vidyalaya, a primary school belonging to the Golmuri parish located at Birsanagar. This new venture opened 15 January. The Sisters cycled to and from Birsanagar also, having left Rohargora in the hands of well trained personnel.

The health team suffered a disruption when Sister Teresa's serious illness kept her confined for a month in Mercy Hospital. Sister Mary Juliana carried on alone and was quite relieved when Sister Teresa was again able to join her in the health work and the nutrition programs undertaken in collaboration with the Catholic Relief Service. At the same time Sisters Blanche and Premila continued to be fully occupied with the school at Birsanagar. All the Sisters took part in various works within the parish, in the villages, and in outlying districts administered by the parish.

From 1984 on, frequent changes of personnel took place. In February, Bethany bade farewell to one of its founding members, Sister Mary Juliana, who became a pioneer at Khorimahua. Her work in Jamshedpur remains a living memorial to her pioneer spirit and indefatigable labors. Sister Elsa Ezhaparampil replaced Sister Mary Juliana. Sister Blanche, another pioneer in the field of education in Jamshedpur, left Bethany in June and was replaced by Sister Victoria Kujur. Also in June, Sister Premila left the Birsanagar school and was succeeded by Sister

Deepti Ponnambal. By July 1985, the last of the pioneers, Sister Teresa, departed from Jamshedpur after seven years of zealous labor in the health ministry. In the same month, Sister Marietta Saldanha joined the community. Sister Stanisla Hembrom replaced Sister Victoria in June 1986, and in the same month, Sister Deepa Thekkecheruvil joined the community while attending XLRI B.Ed. College, the first SCN to enter that institution.

The work of the Jamshedpur mission resembles the hidden life of Jesus. Through the years it has gone on steadily, perseveringly, without fanfare, without external pomp. Yet the hard labor and sacrifice of the Sisters have borne good fruit. Through their health ministry they spread the knowledge of Christ, the Divine Physician. Education beckoned to the Sisters in a rural setting. Having begun at Rohargora, they left their work in competent hands and moved on to Birsanagar. The health programs are no longer in the hands of the Sisters, but the school goes on, and the Sisters engage in all diocesan projects that are possible with their limited personnel.

Sisters Elsy Vettickal, Ann Roberta Powers, and Margaret
Rodericks look on as Margaret's brother, Bishop Joseph
Rodericks of Jamshedpur, officiates at the blessing of Bethany.

NAZARETH DHAAN, BARAUNI
1983

The river at Mansi where Sister Sandhya Baxla was drowned as she set out to give medical aid to flood victims in Barauni.

Chapter Seventeen

NAZARETH DHAAN, BARAUNI
1983

Nazareth Dhaan, the first SCN mission in the Muzzaffarpur diocese, was established at Barauni in the Begusarai District in 1983. Barauni is a small but important town lying just north of the Ganges about a one-hour drive from the SCN mother foundation in Mokama. It is dominated by the railway junction that connects most of the parts of India in the hilly northeast stretching up into the Himalayas, and by its vast industrial installations that comprise the Indian Oil Company, the Hindustan Fertilizer Corporation, and the huge complex of the Barauni Thermal Power Company.

Because the industrial complex is much more recent, the railway junction is largely connected with the history of the mission. It was for the employees of the railway, many of them Catholic Anglo-Indians, that the mission station was founded, but until recent times there was no resident priest. Barauni had long been a sub-station of Samastipur, and from there a priest came to Barauni for Sunday Mass. Jacob Jageshwar (Jacob Master), a catechist residing at the mission, served the station and helped with the teaching of religion. A school had been started, which remained in the hands of lay people until after the arrival of the Sisters.

With the advent of the large industrial companies, more Catholics were added to the congregation in the persons of Anglo-Indians and South Indians, all of whom were traditional Catholics. Thus it was that the Sisters were invited by Bishop John Baptist Thakur, S.J., of Muzzaffarpur, to serve in Barauni. As provincial, Sister Margaret accepted the invitation, and Sisters Rita Puthenkalam, Abha Beck, and Latika Kottuppallil were assigned to the new foundation.

After a week's last-minute preparation of the convent, which had been the house of Jacob Master, the big day of the formal opening arrived, 7 February 1983. Among the notables present for the opening were Bishop J.B. Thakur, Father Joseph Marianna, S.J., pastor; Sister Dorothy MacDougall, SCN superior general; SCNs from Mokama, Sacred Heart Sisters from Samastipur, people from nearby villages, and a number of priests. Sister Margaret, who had been called away because of the death of her father, was not present. After the celebration of Mass by the bishop, the house was blessed and the Blessed Sacrament enthroned in a small room at the end of the veranda. Thus a new SCN mission came into being.

During the first three weeks, Sister Sarita Manavalan, who had come for the opening, remained with the Sisters and helped them in various ways. They began visiting the people to find out their needs and living conditions, attended Mass at the Indian Oil Company and the Fertilizer Corporation of India, made short tours of nearby missions, and also shopped for various needs as they felt them. By 2 March, the Sisters were teaching part-time in the school. In June, Sister Amala Valayathil joined the community, having just finished B.A. examinations. At the same time Sister Latika left for a new mission in Gaya. Another teacher arrived in the person of Sister Nalini Mecharil, a second-year novice. In early July, Sister Abha was transferred to the school in Mokama.

On 8 July an important move was made when the Sisters took over the administration of the school. Sister Rita assumed the office of headmistress, while Sisters Amala and Nalini were assistant teachers. The first public function under the new administration consisted of the flag hoisting on Independence Day, 15 August. This was soon followed by the celebration of Teachers Day on 5 September. At Mass on the first St. Vincent's Day, 27 September, Sisters Rita and Amala renewed their vows. Then the day was spent in a grand tour of Barh and Bakhtiarpur provided by the pastor pro-tem, Father Jacob Kunnankal, S.J. They returned by way of Mokama, where a tasty supper was provided for them.

In preparation for First Communion, children from Indian Oil Company, Behut, and Godhara came for two days prior to the event. Under the guidance of Sisters Rita and Amala, they spent the time in prayer and instruction for this solemn religious celebration, which took place on 23 October.

The first Parent-Teachers meeting was held on 3 December. Grievances were brought forward by the *sarpanch* (head of the local council of the village), but certain guardians ably defended the school administration and the teaching. After various discussions, the meeting ended amicably. Another difficulty, a dispute with a teacher who was to retire at the time of the annual examinations, was finally resolved.

Christmas in Barauni was a happy one. Sisters Rita and Nalini accompanied Father Tony Grollig, S.J., to Indian Oil Company for Midnight Mass, while Sister Amala attended Mass at Barauni at 10 a.m. Just after Christmas on 27 December, Sister Nalini returned to Mokama after her six-month experience at Barauni.

During the ensuing years, the work of the Sisters in the mission continued in the school, the social welfare programs, and the religious instruction imparted through parish projects. A number of changes of personnel took place, with Sister Rita the only one remaining throughout those years. In 1986 Sisters Rita and Pratima took part in the education meeting in Mokama. With them was Mary Bodra, a pre-novice, who was to stay in Barauni for three months. Just two weeks later, Sister Rita, the last of the pioneers, was transferred. At that time Sisters

Pratima Tuti, Sandhya Baxla, and Mary Bodra comprised the staff. In June Sister Lilly Luka Vayampallitharapel joined the group; at the same time, however, Mary Bodra had to return to base after her temporary mission.

The year 1987 brought a number of thefts. Early in the year, quite a few valuable things were stolen, and fear was engendered in the hearts of the Sisters. No action was taken by the law, and nothing was recovered. In December, a group of seven *dacoits* entered the compound, tied the watchman, Ajay, to a tree, and demanded the keys, which Ajay refused to hand over. The *dacoits* walked around until about 3 a.m. and then left. The unfortunate Ajay could not arouse anyone with his cries and had to remain in the cold until 5 a.m. The police were informed and made an inquiry.

The 175th anniversary of the SCN foundation was celebrated on 15 February 1987 with a Mass celebrated by the pastor, Father Tobin, and by Father George and Father Pat Rebeiro. It was a memorable day for the Sisters. Two other religious events of importance were the confirmation day for thirteen children on 10 May and Sister Lilly's renewal of vows on 18 May.

The history of the SCN Barauni mission will always be especially memorable, because it was this mission that offered the first SCN as a victim of charity, Sister Sandhya Baxla, who gave her life in the service of the suffering poor. Sister Sandhya, a native of Bihar, just 38 years old, was the first SCN to die in India. Detailed accounts have been written elsewhere, but a summary must be included in any history of Barauni.

When the Ganges River was seriously flooded on 20 August 1987, a relief team from Barauni consisting of Father George, Sister Sandhya, Sister Antoinette (a Bon Secour Sister from Begusaraia), a catechist Peter, a volunteer engineer, Celine Minj Sah, and Helen Enoch Jha (the latter two were among the first nursing graduates of Nazareth Hospital) set out to give medical relief at a village where 10,000 suffering people awaited them. They were joined by two police constables and were provided with medical supplies and a boat to transport them to the villagers who were marooned because of the severe flooding of the Ganges and its tributaries.

The boatmen were none too skillful in the strong currents. When wind and rain increased, the situation became acute. The boat became uncontrollable and dashed against the pillar of a bridge and was shattered. There were five victims: Sister Sandhya, Sister Antoinette, Helen, Peter, and one of the constables. Although days passed before the bodies were found, the victims were all eventually laid to rest in the cemetery of Mokama except the constable, whose body was cremated according to the Hindu rite. God had claimed them all as victims of charity. They had gone in mercy to serve the suffering poor and had sacrificed themselves completely. Barauni will always remember Sister Sandhya and will ever realize the great blessing her life and death have brought to the community.

Sister Teresita Theruvankunnal joined the Barauni community on 1 October to replace Sister Sandhya. The trio of members was once more complete—Sisters Teresita, Pratima, and Lilly. On 2 November the whole community with Raj Kumari, the housekeeper, and Father Tobin went to Mokama for the blessing of the graves, to pray there and pay special tribute to Sister Sandhya. Bishop Thakur con-celebrated Mass with Fathers Tobin and George.

Celebration of Parents Day as well as the jubilee of the school were held on 13 November. It was a highly successful function despite bad weather. A number of guests were present, including Bishop Thakur, who with Fathers Tobin and George offered the thanksgiving Mass. The superintendent of police of Begusarai presided as chief guest at the cultural program.

The Sisters' presence in Barauni continues to be far-reaching. Besides teaching in the school, they are busy in catechetics among both children and adults who are living in the various colonies connected with their place of employment. They also go to outlying villages where they engage in adult education and in any kind of necessary social work that comes to their attention. Through their influence and advice they try to solve problems and to alleviate suffering wherever they can. Except for the industries, the area is in general economically deprived and poorly developed, which results in a population that is prone to all the physical and moral evils that extreme poverty tends to engender. Thus the Sisters come to the people to do as Jesus did, to heal the sick, to comfort the afflicted, and to preach the Gospel to the poor.

NAZARETH DEHRA, MANDAIR
1983

Sisters Josephine Kisku and Aisha Kavalakattu serve the evening meal they have cooked to the village family with whom they are living.

Chapter Eighteen

NAZARETH DEHRA, MANDAIR
1983

A quiet village about fifty kilometers from Hazaribagh on a large plateau, seemingly near the sky, from the southwest to the northeast a high hill broken only by a cleft on the northern end; a place of scattered houses and large fields, among them the Catholic mission, the school, and the Sisters' convent indistinguishable from the other houses except for the blue shutters and doors (the result of the purchase of a big tin of paint for everything)—all this is Nazareth Dehra, beautiful, peaceful, and simple.

As an SCN mission, Mandair has its roots in Chatra. From there the Sisters involved in social work went out into the forests and jungles near Chatra to ascertain the needs of the villagers. Thus the mission of Mandair came into being. Among the early itinerant pioneers from Chatra were Sisters Francine Moozhil, Jane Karakunnel, and Pushpa Paruvananickal, who lived in the villages, instructed the people, and helped with basic medical care. In 1981 the Jesuits of the Hazaribagh mission established residence in Mandair, and by 1983 the Sisters joined the mission on a permanent basis.

On a memorable day, 11 July 1983, the first Sisters, Olive Pinto and Pushpa, set forth from Hazaribagh in St. Xavier's jeep, accompanied by Father A.T. Thomas, Sister Reena Theruvankunnel from Mokama, Sisters Sophia Kalapurackal, Sarala Anithottathil, and Dolcie D'Mello (novice) from Chatra. By 4 p.m. they reached their destination and were welcomed by Brother Albert Dakra. Within two days of their arrival Sisters Olive and Pushpa began active work in the villages. They helped several seriously sick patients, and people began to trust their ability.

The Sisters lived in very simple conditions, sharing quarters with others in the same school building—one room for everything—without indoor bathroom facilities. During the first few months they had to assess their situation and to make decisions concerning their work and the way it could be implemented.

Father Robert Slattery, S.J., and Father Gyan visited at Christmas. About two hundred people attended the Midnight Mass, a joyful and solemn celebration. A great bonfire was lit to keep warm, and dancing continued until morning.

In January 1984 another move was made, this time to a small house in Kowathary. Here a number of visitors were received in the same month: Sisters Shalini D'Souza, Elizabeth Nadackal, Bridget Kappalumakal, and Marianne Puthoor; and Bishop Saupin, who came for the first time and conferred Confirmation. In January Sister Olive began teaching in the school on a part-time basis. During February Sister Pushpa directed the establishment of village health programs; unfortunately, she was forced to leave in April for a prolonged stay at the hospital at Mokama. It was June before she was able to return. Sister Anice Vattakulam also arrived in June to begin teaching in the school.

Life in Mandair had its peculiar features. When the rains came in June and July, rivers became flooded, roads impassable, and eventually the house in Kowathary could no longer be reached. Father Thomas provided a room in the parish house from which the Sisters started teaching in the school. Wading through flooded rivers, sloshing through mud, collecting firewood, getting lost in the jungle, having a heap of white ants fall upon them as they slept, experiencing heavy rains that soaked everything and left in their wake more white ants, joining the villagers in transplanting rice—these and other experiences enlivened the day-to-day life of Mandair.

Early September 1984 brought Sister Sophia Kalapurackal from Chatra to help the teachers with new methods and various teaching aids. Heavy rains prolonged her stay, as she could not cross the river. The difficulties of transportation caused by terrible roads and the lack of bus service created many problems. In order to improve the situation, cycles were purchased in November, and all the Sisters began cycling back and forth.

At the beginning of 1985 after several transfers, the community consisted of Sisters Pushpa, Anice, and Joyce Kalapurayil. Their ministries were medical, educational, and social, although there was always a sharing, especially in the pastoral aspects. Development occurred in each field of endeavor: the activation of the Catholic *Sabha* (council); more frequent staff meetings for the school; increased participation of students and teachers in the Children's Mass; health education classes in the school at least once a week; and involvement in village ministry. Sisters Pushpa and Joyce began contacting government officers who could help them in various development projects. They met the Child Development Project officer and the doctor in charge of the Primary Health Centre, both of whom were very cooperative. In May, as a result of Sister Joyce's efforts, the first school health checkup was given, and the children received polio and D.P.T. vaccination.

A new house for the Sisters was completed in July of 1985. Moving day was 22 July, the second anniversary of their arrival in Mandair. Auspiciously, planting of fruit trees and corn took place that same day. The Sisters, unaccustomed to such space, all slept in one room. A few days after the move on 16 July, the faithful pastor, Father Thomas, left Mandair. One of his last good deeds for the Sisters was to kill a snake, a deadly krait, in the new convent.

The Sisters' life at Mandair at this time was seriously disturbed by the request of the Catholic *Sabha* that the catechist and the Sisters be removed. This was a painful experience. The Sisters decided to refer the matter to the bishop. In August further tension arose between the Sisters and the Catholic people, instigated by the masters, Isidore and Raphael, who had been asked to resign from the school. When Sister Shalini was informed, she sent Sister Marcelline to assess the situation. When Sisters Shalini and Elizabeth came for a visit in September, they were able to clear up much of the tension and misunderstanding.

By the end of 1985 the community had again undergone changes. The Sisters had bade farewell to Sister Pushpa, one of the pioneers, who had won the love and respect of all. Sister Anice, who had worked faithfully in the school, was assigned to study. The membership at the end of 1985 consisted of Sisters Philomena Kottoor, Archana Valiaparambil, Joyce Kalapurayil, and Philomena Bading.

Two important visitors, representatives from the Tandwa Adult Education Offices, appeared on 4 January 1986. They wished to know more about the night school the Sisters had been conducting and promised to give recognition and necessary help. With the cooperation of the government, Sisters Philomena and Archana accompanied the subdivisional officer, the block divisional officer, and the chief officer to a few villages to meet the people and to discuss the programs for women.

On the pastoral side, a great day came for the people on 3 February when a group accompanied by Sisters Joyce and Philomena went to Ranchi to join the huge reception for Pope John Paul II. Another important event was a three-day retreat for women in March.

Sister Joyce continued her activities in government projects. In February she was accepted as one of the nonformal education staff of Tandwa Block. She also received two kits for the "Each One Teach One" program. In May she attended the regional activist meeting in Hazaribagh. The group studied and analyzed the social reality of India, especially that of Bihar, and pledged to support one another in the social ministry.

The formal blessing by Bishop Saupin of the parish, school, and convent took place on 29 October. It was well attended by people from nearby stations, relatives, friends, and even local government officials.

In retrospect, it is evident that the Sisters at Mandair have adapted to the life of the people with extraordinary flexibility, good will, and efficiency. Their house, modeled on those of the surrounding area, is a structure of brick, mud, and cement with the simplest amenities, yet it encloses within its walls a great deal of love, homeliness, and warmth that flows out to the people with whom they work.

The varied ministries are accomplished with limited personnel. The school of about 120 children ranges from preschool to Class 6. Evening classes are held for children who work during the day tending cattle or helping with crops. Additional pursuits include the supervision of schools in neighboring villages and involvement in adult education programs. All is in conformity with the government education policy of 1985.

Medical aid is given through a dispensary conducted in the convent. The Sisters plan to build a dispensary nearby that can be made more efficient and practical. Through a mobile medical/health care program, a different village is visited each week. Medical aid is given and health instruction imparted. A program of health care and basic medicine is planned to prepare villagers for such work.

A third and most important ministry is the spread of the faith through instruction to Catholics, involvement in church activities, and the visiting of people, both Christian and non-Christian, in order to bring them the knowledge of Christ and His love.

Through village visiting, the Sisters have learned the problems of the people, of their exploitation by the powerful, and of the injustices inflicted on them. As a result, the Sisters have not only given the people sympathetic support but have also endeavored to take up their causes with government officials to get assistance in righting the unjust treatment so often meted out.

Only two to three Sisters are usually assigned to Mandair, so it is obvious that they have a herculean task before them. It is one that they accept, however, with love and fervor in the true spirit of Catherine Spalding, bearing in mind the SCN motto: The Charity of Christ Urges Us.

NAZARETH JYOTI, HILSA
1983

Sister Amala Valayathil talks with village children in Hilsa.

Chapter Nineteen

NAZARETH JYOTI, HILSA
1983

Hilsa is a small town twenty kilometers south of Fatwah, which is a railway station on the main line between Patna and Mokama. Hilsa has been a mission for more than fifty years, served by itinerant priests who came from other mission stations. Finally, as it developed a school made up of forty-eight hostel boys, a parish, and an increase of Christian people, the time seemed ripe for enlisting a group of Sisters to take part in the life of the mission.

The choice of the Sisters of Charity of Nazareth was an apt one, since the SCNs had first come into this area at the request of Father Marion Batson, S.J., who had himself been a pioneer of the Hilsa mission. The arrival on 18 December 1983 of the first Sisters, Pauline Paraplackal and Nalini Mecharil, brought joy to the hearts of the people of Hilsa. The Sisters were welcomed by the parish priest, Father Andrews Thambi, the students of the school, the parishioners, and even the people of the town. The temporary house, Nazareth Jyoti, which consisted of two good-sized rooms with baths, veranda, and outside kitchen, made comfortable living quarters for the Sisters.

The Sisters quickly made themselves at home and adjusted to their new surroundings. By Christmas they had already made the acquaintance of their neighbors, as well as people in the nearby villages. This Christmas was marked by a great celebration, with Midnight Mass and plenty of fireworks afterwards. The deputy superintendent of police, hearing the explosions, came hurrying to see whether a robbery was taking place.

On the last day of the year, the Sisters visited the closest mission station, Fatwah. The Missionary Brothers of Charity, along with their founder, Brother Andrew, received the Sisters cordially. They attended Mass and enjoyed a feast before returning to Hilsa.

With the first days of January 1984, the work of the Sisters in the school began in earnest. During the admissions process on 5 January, the Sisters made an important observation. By and large the non-Christian parents knew how to sign their names, but many of the Christian parents did not. This fact made the Sisters realize the need of education among the Christian people. The school, Kristh Jyoti Vidyalaya, opened on 16 January 1984. Students, teachers, parents, Sisters, and the manager, Father Andrews Thambi, assembled on the school veranda, where an opening program was held. Father Thambi and Sister Pauline, the headmistress, gave speeches of welcome and thanks, which were followed by songs and prayers. Then the school was dismissed for the day. The next day, which marked the end of the first month of life in Hilsa, brought distinguished visitors from Fatwah in the persons of Bishop Osta, Father Augustine Mundoly, and Brother Albert Lakra, M.C. On the next day, Sister Shalini and her councilors arrived. The first Republic Day, 26 January, was celebrated by the school with drill and parade. As chief guest, the District Superintendent of Education hoisted the flag.

Life in Bihar is never complete without some experience of robberies. The new residents of Hilsa were initiated into the robbers' activities on the night of 2 February. About 10:15 p.m. *dacoits* entered the mission compound, fired off bombs, broke open doors, and entered the rectory and the boys' hostel. Although the *dacoits* stood watch at the doors of the convent and flashed lights in the windows, they did not enter. The priest and the watchman escaped over the back wall and informed the police. By God's mercy no one was seriously injured, although two hostel boys were beaten. Father lost his coat, tape recorder, and radio. On the night of 9 February, the Sisters again heard a suspicious noise at the back of the house and found that an attempt had been made to break a bamboo door there. These harrowing incidents caused much fear and anxiety.

At the SCN education meeting in Gaya on 24 March, Sister Pauline gave the first report on Kristh Jyoti Vidyalaya to the community. Just after the meeting Sister Marianne Puthoor, the director of education, came from Mokama to give a seminar for the teachers of Hilsa.

On Thursday, 19 April, electricity was installed in time for the celebration on Holy Thursday. Easter Sunday was a joyful feast, blessed with a little rain to make the weather cool and pleasant for the Easter Vigil. During the Easter season the Sisters made several trips on foot to more distant villages to visit a few scattered Christian families.

Bishop Wildermuth, the bishop of this mission for many years but now retired, visited Hilsa once more, accompanied by Sister Teresa Xavier. Sister Sushila Palatty joined the community on 17 July, bringing the number to three. She became involved in the pastoral ministry. Through her efforts, the Mahila Sangh was begun in November.

Flood waters entered the compound on 23 August. Because their hostel was flooded, the boys had to be brought to the school. The school and the Sisters' kitchen escaped inundation, but difficulties of transportation caused the school to be closed for five days. Annual examinations were held for the first time in December.

Changes in personnel occurred early in January of 1985. Sister Nalini was transferred to Gaya. School and parishioners gave a fitting farewell to the Sister who had been with them from the beginning. She was replaced by Sister Mary Manimala. The school suffered another loss because of Sister Pauline's illness and surgery, which resulted in a four-month absence. Much to the joy of all, she returned in September. An event of great interest to the Sisters was the arrival in September of a group of novices, who lived in a nearby village and worked with the people. Sister Marcelline Indwar accompanied them.

A double celebration was held on 10 October. The new school building was blessed by Bishop Osta. At the Mass of the day, Confirmation was also administered. Two groups from Hilsa attended rallies and meetings in Patna. Representatives of the Mahila Sangh conducted by Sister Pauline participated in the convention held on 11 November. In the same week, on 16 November, Sisters Sushila and Cornelia Ekka brought children to Patna for the Krus Vir rally.

The new year of 1986 was welcomed at Banares where the Hilsa community— Sisters Pauline, Sushila, and Mary—had gone to make a retreat at Maithridam Ashram. The three Sisters returned on 10 January, and school reopened. A new step was taken with the opening of the girls' hostel. Sister Mary was in charge of the ten girls, who seemed to enjoy their new home.

During Lent Sister Sushila spent much time in the villages preparing the Catholic people for Easter, explaining the meaning of the feast, and instructing them about Confession and Holy Communion. An immediate preparation for Easter began on Palm Sunday with a retreat given by Father William Goudreau, a pioneer of the Hilsa mission, who led the people in a joyous celebration.

More personnel changes took place in the middle of 1986. Sister Mary entered the B.Ed. course at Madras and was replaced by Sister Susan Tudu. Sister Nisha Chemmanam also joined the school staff. Hilsa became the contact community for Sister Mercy Thundathil. Farewells, however, often coincide with welcomes: Sister Sushila left Hilsa at this time after having accomplished much fruitful work in the mission.

A big event of July was a second, more serious flood. Water came rushing into the compound on the first of July. The kitchen was flooded, and all the equipment and supplies had to be moved. The school office was converted into the kitchen and dining room. The Sisters thought with pity of the poor people who had lost home and belongings. Despite the flood, it was possible to open the school on 8 July.

The work of the Sisters in Hilsa is mainly in three areas: administration of the school and service to the teachers; social service through village visitation to both Christians and non-Christians; and the teaching of religion to Christian children and adults and to anyone else who expresses a desire for information and knowledge. When the Sisters first took over the school, there were only forty-eight students, all of them boys of the hostel. By 1988, there was a fine school building with more than three hundred girls and boys—well ordered, well taught, and well disciplined—who studied from Class 1 to Class 7.

Work in the villages continued with active participation in the various organizations connected with school and church. As the Sisters worked side by side with the parish priest, there were many avenues open for Catholic development. The future of the mission is filled with hope and will ever be blessed by the great efforts of its early zealous pioneers.

Children at Hilsa prepare for a celebration.

MARIA SADAN, KHORIMAHUA
(Dumberdih)
1984

Sister Mary Chackalackal gathers a group of students at a village school in Khorimahua.

Chapter Twenty

MARIA SADAN, KHORIMAHUA
(Dumberdih)
1984

Khorimahua, a new mission in the Bhagalpur diocese, is situated only forty-eight kilometers from Jamtara. It is far from any sizeable habitation, somewhat remote and inaccessible, having only one bus daily going back and forth between Jamtara and Giridih. The land around is barren, with scarcely any cultivation, dry and bleak, lacking any natural beauty. The inhabitants are Santhals, a tribe special in its culture, ethnic characteristics, language, and customs.

The Sisters' house at first was a small mud-brick structure built in the style of the local village, composed of small rooms and possessing barely the basic amenities. Moreover, the whole building was subject to the problem of leaks in the rainy season and the invasion of white ants to destroy what little was there.

In this humble dwelling, on 11 February 1984, four Sisters took up their abode—Mary Juliana Tuti, Francine Moozhil, Gracy Thombrakudyil, and a candidate. The day before they had been escorted to their new mission by Sister Shalini and seven other SCNs. Father Matthew, parish priest of Maheshmunda and Khorimahua, hosted a "family" welcome dinner in Maheshmunda for twenty-two priests and Sisters, in addition to the SCN party. About seven hundred people from Khorimahua and the surrounding villages welcomed the Sisters with the beating of drums, washing of hands, and garlanding. The Mass was offered and the house blessed. A catechist expressed the joy of the people at having the Sisters and pledged their collaboration in working for the spread of Christ's gospel. Sister Gracy's response in Santhali to this speech was very touching. The next morning at 4 o'clock the women from nearby houses roused the Sisters and inquired how they slept and whether they needed help for cleaning, cooking, etc. Father Xavier came to offer Mass for the first time in the convent chapel.

During the next few days the Sisters took part in the work of completing the house, carrying cow dung for floors, bringing dung cakes for making the fire for cooking, and collecting white mud for decorating the walls of the house. The first water from the new well was blessed by Father Matthew. Unfortunately, the Sisters still had to carry drinking water from the streams near the fields to the house. After five days the Sisters began to explore their surroundings by visiting some of the villages both near and not so near. About fifty Christians of Dumberdih village, where the parish church used to be, welcomed them heartily. Although the church had been moved to a place near the convent, it retained its former name of Dumberdih. The Sisters continued to visit many places, both Christian and non-Christian. A heavy rain on 20 February brought the realization of what such a rain does to a village house. After the rain Sister Francine succeeded in making a vegetable garden.

Sister Gracy's work in pastoral ministry began immediately. Her extraordinary grasp of Santhali enabled her to enter more fully into the lives of the people. She began to help in the adult catechumenate in Maheshmunda and later started one in Khorimahua in preparation for baptism at Easter.

Sister Gracy called the villagers to Maria Sadan for a penitential service in preparation for Ash Wednesday. Since the priest could not come on that day, she conducted a service and initiated the Lenten season. The villagers began to gather daily for evening rosary. On Holy Thursday and Good Friday, Sister Gracy again held relevant Bible services and prayer for good crowds. Father Xavier was present for Easter Vigil Mass. The people were prepared for confession, and a large congregation participated fully in the Mass. Singing and dancing went on until morning. Another very joyful day came the following week when nineteen people were baptized, the first fruits of the mission in Khorimahua.

Sister Mary Juliana had spent some time in Jamshedpur and, upon her return before Easter, had set up a dispensary in the sacristy of the church. Patients began coming, gaining confidence in *Maran Didi* ("older Sister"). In Maheshmunda, on 6 May, Sisters Mary Juliana and Gracy launched the Mahila Sangh with about sixty women. The meeting closed with Mass, and the women received the badges of the organization. A program with Mass, house blessings, and rosary procession drew good crowds and provided a worthy religious celebration for the people.

Sister Francine left the mission on 12 May. Although she had been assigned on a temporary basis, she had contributed greatly to the establishment of the mission. Sister Anima Pullikkiyil arrived at the end of June, an answer to the prayers of all for a Sister to organize the school. Together Sisters Mary Juliana, Gracy, and Anima visited their bishop, Most Reverend Urban McGarry, T.O.R., to discuss with him their plans for the mission.

The thirteenth of August was an important day when both regular school and *silai* (sewing) school were opened. Sister Anima welcomed twenty-seven children to the school, and Sister Gracy began *silai* with fifteen Santhal girls. By the week's end, admission to the school had risen to sixty-five and *silai* admission to seventeen.

The really big day in Khorimahua was 19 August. Bishop McGarry, five priests, Sister Shalini, a number of Sisters of various communities, and a congregation of Santhals numbering about 1200, gathered for Mass and the official opening of the house, Maria Sadan. The whole group enjoyed the *swagatam* (welcome), which included dinner for all. Already it was evident that the work of the Sisters had made a great impact on the people.

Medical, health, social, and pastoral work progressed. In September, Sister Mary Juliana succeeded in getting some government doctors to come to the clinic for service among the people. A project was launched on 14 September in the form of a night school under Sister Gracy's direction. Five girls and twenty-five boys enrolled, and more members were soon added. The Bhagalpur college boys gave a drama dealing with superstitious beliefs and other social evils. A crowd of over one thousand witnessed the drama and were greatly impressed by the truths exemplified.

In mid November Father Matthew was transferred to Kharagpur and was succeeded by Father Thomas. Development continued in 1985 with the inauguration of the mother/child health program (MCH). The idea was proposed to the women by Sister Mary Juliana at a meeting of the Mahila Sangh and was enthusiastically accepted. Registration took place on 6 February 1985. Two important meetings were held in the same month. On the occasion of the visit of Sisters Shalini and Vinita, who had come for the first anniversary of the mission, a meeting was held with Father Thomas to evaluate the work of the year and to make plans for the future. A second meeting with Sister Gracy, Father Thomas, and the parents of the school children on 17 February was very profitable.

As has been previously stated, no mission in Bihar was ever complete without a *dacoity* (robbery). Khorimahua's was a costly one. On the night of 19 February the dispensary in the church building was broken open and practically cleared out—medicines, medical instruments, desk, bench, table, chair, and all the utensils. This was apparently done in revenge for the dismissal of the *darwan* (nightwatchman) by Father Thomas. Unfortunately, the villagers joined in this attitude of revenge.

As this feeling continued, Sister Gracy began a program of family prayers in March. A plan was made to go to each family for evening prayers. On Saturdays the families would gather at Maria Sadan for prayer and Bible service in preparation for Sunday. Sister Gracy had prepared the villagers for reconciliation at the prayer services, and at their request Father Thomas offered Mass. As a sign of reunion, the people contributed Rs 10 per family to buy a statue of Our Lady for the village.

In June the well that had been under construction was finished, and the Sisters no longer had to dig holes in the field to get drinking water.

By June 1985 the school enrollment had gone up to 163, with 120 in regular attendance. For the celebration of Independence Day, 15 August, there was a Mass, followed by flag hoisting and a program. The school children performed well, and many people attended. A visit by the SCN superior general Sister Dorothy MacDougall and the mission office director Sister Josephine Barrieau took place in

October 1985. These distinguished visitors were given a big welcome by about four hundred villagers from the area. In traditional Santhal custom, women washed the feet of the honored guests, garlanded them, and escorted them with dancing under decorated umbrellas. The reception was a memorable affair with entertainment by *silai* school, regular school, youth club, and night school. In January 1986 Sister Mary Chackalackal, veteran school teacher and headmistress, joined the mission and took charge of the school. A third year was added to the existing classes.

At Easter time in 1986 Sister Gracy and Father Thomas had an extraordinary and harrowing experience. They had gone to Nepal to engage in retreat work at a village called Sirsia, located between Damak and Dharan. Sister Francine shared the work with them. The Nepalese police harassed the Christians and eventually arrested the Sisters and Father Thomas, beat them, and jailed them for nine days. It was a dreadful experience for all, and even after the victims were released, the Christians were still harassed, and the trial of the catechists was not concluded. All were relieved and happy when Sister Gracy returned to Khorimahua. Eventually all charges against the Sisters, Father Thomas, and the catechists were dropped by the government.

In 1987 Sister Victoria Kujur joined the school, and in February Sister Mary began an individual mission on a trial basis. She took up residence in the room of a private house in Azimpur and was able to gather children from kindergarten, first, and second classes. Later she took on students of a higher level in the afternoon and evening. From Monday to Saturday she resided there. On Saturday she came by bus to Khorimahua, where she remained until early Monday morning. By this means she established a Christian presence in a non-Christian community.

The mission in Khorimahua continues to grow and develop in the fields characteristic of most SCN missions: medical and health care; vocational as well as formal and informal education; pastoral work through religious instruction, preparation for the sacraments, and training in faith and a life of prayer. The Sisters have worked together in all the ministries and have shown a wonderful spirit in helping one another and in working for the common good. Despite hardships, trials, and troubles they have continued to move forward, proclaiming the faith to those who have not heard and strengthening the faith of those who have heard and have received it.

PROVINCIAL HOUSE, PATNA
1986

Sisters Shobhita Panthaladickal and Shalini D'Souza converse outside the Provincial House in Patna.

Chapter Twenty-one

PROVINCIAL HOUSE, PATNA
1986

For a long time a plan had been forming in the community to move the provincial administration from Mokama to Patna to have a more central location. The plan materialized when space became available in 1986 in the house of Mrs. Leena Gough, which was located in a residential area called Fairfield Terrace within walking distance of St. Michael's School and the parish church of Kurji. Mrs. Gough, an elderly Catholic, vacated the upper two stories of her house for the Sisters, while she continued to reside on the ground floor.

The historic move took place on 21 July 1986, with the departure from Mokama of a heavily laden truck bound for the new administration headquarters. Evening found Sisters Shalini D'Souza, Josita Eniakattu, and a group of novices ensconced in the new dwelling, enjoying hot food brought by Sister Mercy Thundathil from Nav Jyoti, the diocesan catechetical center, and relaxing eventually in a well earned sleep. The second day was spent unpacking and arranging all the furnishings needed to begin housekeeping in a new place. Sister Josita and the novices departed, while the pioneering community began to assemble: Sisters Shalini D'Souza, Vinita Kumplankal, Ann Roberta Powers, Teresa Madassery, and Reena Theruvankunnel. The faithful Notre Dame Sisters visited them, bringing fruit, bread, cake, and flowers. Father Jerry Drinane, S.J., rector of St. Michael's, also paid a visit, while Father James Kavakatt, the parish priest, welcomed the new community to the Kurji parish. Final farewells to Mokama were paid on 31 July. Bishop Osta presided at the official blessing of the new convent on 4 August 1986. The new chapel was opened, Mass was celebrated, and the Blessed Sacrament reserved.

Soon a systematic daily program evolved, although deviations were often necessary according to circumstances. Because Patna is centrally located, there has always been a constant flow of visitors coming and going—Sisters on business with the administration, travelers interrupting their journey, friends and relatives stopping to see their dear ones—the total number could never be estimated.

The personnel of the provincial house consisted of those Sisters directly involved in administration, the Sisters who managed general finances, and those in charge of the management of the house. Sisters Ann Roberta and Teresa had the taxing ministry of attending to finances and of dealing with the auditors at their regular visitations. Sister Reena was transferred to teach at Nazareth Academy in November 1986. Sister Shobhita Panthaladickal arrived in January 1987 and Sister Anima Pullikkiyil in May 1988. The latter, besides her other duties, taught in the minor seminary. In 1989 Sister Mary Scaria Menonparampil joined the community, teaching science at St. Michael's School.

It was soon evident that the administration had outgrown the house at Fairfield Terrace, and a search was initiated for a new place that could adequately serve the expanding administration. When a two-story house on East Boring Canal Road came up for sale, the community took advantage of purchasing a place already built and ready for occupancy. Thus the Sisters in administration experienced a sense of permanency. The move to the new dwelling was made on 15 August 1987, the fortieth anniversary of Indian independence and the feast of the Assumption of Our Lady into heaven. Bishop Osta blessed the house and offered Mass in the new chapel on 19 September 1987.

During the years 1986 to 1989, Sister Shalini, her successor Sister Sarita Manavalan, and their councilors received a number of requests for foundations. Some of these became new missions; others had to be rejected. Investigation into the possibilities kept the Sisters traveling long distances to interesting parts of India. Sisters Shalini and Vinita visited Sangsay in the Darjeeling district in 1986 and eventually sent Sisters to this mountain mission. The Andaman Islands beckoned in 1989, but after a visit by Sisters Shalini, Sarita, and Marcelline Indwar, the invitation was refused. After an exploratory visit in June 1989 by Sisters Reena Theruvankunnel and Sarita, a school at Kafligair in the Almora District of Uttar Pradesh was accepted. Another intended project was the opening of a house in Bangalore. Sisters Sarita, Reena, and Celine Arackathottam went to Bangalore "for a look" in September 1989.

In addition to these travels within India, the provincials also traveled abroad. In November 1987 Sisters Shalini and Ann Palatty went to the United States to attend the General Assembly of the SCN community. As provincial from 1988 on, Sister Sarita attended Executive Committee meetings in the United States.

In the last year of her office as provincial, 1988, Sister Shalini had the joy of celebrating her silver jubilee as an SCN. A less felicitous event of that year was the earthquake of 21 August. At the news that Dharan in Nepal was heavily affected, Sister Shalini, Sister Vinita, Sister Anima, Father Joe Knecht, S.J., and Brother Matthew from Loyola left on 23 August to offer assistance to the Sisters there. They returned in two days with the news that the Sisters were safe, but that the place had been badly damaged.

A provincial election was held in late 1988, and Sister Sarita Manavalan was elected provincial. In May 1989 Sister Sarita took up residence in Patna, and her installation, together with that of her council members, took place on 1 June 1989. The councilors were: Sister Reena Theruvankunnel, assistant provincial; Sisters Anne Marie Thayilchirayil, Teresa Kotturan, Teresita Theruvankunnal, and Ann Palatty.

The provincial house is ever a hub of activity, and while its history possesses no spectacular episodes to proclaim its fame, it continues as a powerhouse for the whole SCN community. Its residents have the awesome responsibility of guiding the lives and destinies of the Sisters who make up the institutions and who, under their direction, must carry on the various works of the community. It is truly a center, and from there must emanate the rays of charity that should motivate all that is done by the Sisters of Charity of Nazareth in India.

The Sisters of the Province bless Sister Sarita Manavalan, as she takes on her responsibilities as Provincial (1989).

NAZARETH LEE, SANGSAY
1986

Sister Vinaya Chalil teaches sewing in Sangsay, West Bengal.

Chapter Twenty-two

NAZARETH LEE, SANGSAY 1986

Each new mission usually has a distinctive character, and Sangsay is no exception. Situated 1500 feet down the side of a steep hill about eight kilometers from Kalimpong in the district of Darjeeling, it would seem almost inaccessible. It is a spot of great natural beauty, surrounded on all sides by lush green hills with the snow-capped Khanjchendzonga, the third highest mountain peak in the world, crowning the hills of Sikkim to the north. The final approach has to be made on foot after reaching the top of the mountain by motor from Kalimpong.

The mission of Sangsay was a substation of Mirick in the Darjeeling diocese. For some time there had been no resident priest, and the people were served by the priest of Mirick and by the priests of St. Augustine's Church in Kalimpong. The Missionary Sisters of Charity came on weekends for medical, social, and catechetical work. As the mission grew, a church and rectory were built, and a visiting parish priest was appointed. The time seemed ripe for founding a convent with resident sisters to take up the works that the visiting Sisters had been doing. By this time there were forty Catholic families in the parish and about 900 more families scattered about in the surrounding hills. The people manifested an open attitude toward religion that augured well for evangelization. The need for educational and health work was great. A few small schools—government and parish—were not sufficient to serve the needs of many children who were receiving little or no education. In addition, the general health of the people was poor because of malnutrition, with a high incidence of tuberculosis. General ignorance of good health practices and of the proper use of locally available food added to the problem.

Negotiations with Bishop Eric Benjamin of Darjeeling to provide the nucleus for a convent in Sangsay were completed by September 1986. At a special Mass in the chapel at Mokama on the evening of 20 September, the new Sangsay community, consisting of Sisters Maria Palathingal, Philomina Hembrom, Vinaya Chalil, and Cecilia Simick, was blessed and commissioned to go forth to this new mission.

On 21 September, the pioneer party, escorted by Sisters Shalini and Vinita, in a jeep loaded with trunks, suitcases, bedrolls, and all kinds of household equipment, departed for the ten-hour ride to Siliguri. Damien Madassery, brother of

Sister Teresa Madassery, and the driver, Shiv Kumar, did a good job at the wheel, and at 5:30 p.m. the party arrived at Seva Kendra (Catholic Relief Service) at Siliguri. The next morning, after Mass offered by Father Anthony Namchu, the party prepared for the next leg of the journey, this time in a Seva Kendra truck, to St. Augustine's in Kalimpong, a ride of two hours and twenty minutes. Disturbing news awaited them—the possibility of an 108-hour strike that would make travel to Sangsay impossible. Fortunately, a quick departure and ride through the area of tension and trouble brought them to the top of the hill where their descent had to be made. "Operation Down Hill" was successfully directed by the catechist Joseph, who had joined the group at Bimbong Dara. Down the 1500-foot descent came women, men, and children, carrying trunks, boxes, and household equipment to furnish the new convent of Nazareth Lee. When the Sisters arrived at 3:30 p.m., they were welcomed with flowers, ceremonial scarves, and the songs and dances of children. To quote from the annals written by Sister Shalini: "All was well—Catherine's daughters, Lawrencetta's tribe, was in mission once more."

The following days witnessed much activity in arranging the house, a seven-room building with kitchen and back veranda. A small chapel was fitted up, and Mass was offered for the first time on 25 September by Father Donald Lewis, the parish priest. St. Vincent's Day, 27 September, was fittingly celebrated with Mass, feasting, fun, and laughter. The Sisters began visiting the villages where the people received them happily. The sick soon came for medical services from Sister Vinita, a doctor, and Sister Maria, a nurse.

On the day of the official opening, 4 October, a good number of outside guests arrived, including the full SCN contingent from Dharan in Nepal—Sisters Sarita Manavalan, Anima Pullikkiyil, Seema Monippallicalayil, Rosita Kavilpurayidathil, and Francine Moozhil. Other guests included Bishop Eric Benjamin, Father Lewis, Father Albert Lobo, three Missionary Sisters of Charity, three Notre Dame Sisters from Darjeeling, four diocesan Brothers, and the parents and brothers of Cecilia Simick. A concelebrated Mass began at 11 a.m., during which the bishop gave an inspiring sermon. Children of Mirick and Sangsay gave a welcoming program, which was followed by an excellent lunch. Soon afterwards, mindful of the steep and long return, the guests began to depart.

The months of October, November, and December were filled with constant activity, as the Sisters became acquainted with their new surroundings and way of life. Like the disciples in the time of Jesus, they went out two by two to the villages of the hills, visiting families, identifying problems, ministering to the sick, conducting prayer services, and performing other related works. Each time they returned with joy, having found the people receptive and eager, happy that the Sisters had come to them. The *Yogda* school, St. Dominic Savio, became part of their ministry. Paramedics joined Sister Maria in the medical work, and volunteer workers also gave help in knitting and sewing classes. The first Christmas was spent in the midst of this happy, joyful people in a simple but profoundly spiritual way.

Trouble between the Gorkha National Liberation Front (GNLF) and the Communist Party of India (CPI) had long been brewing, and during the first half of 1987 the agitation reached its height. Despite eruptions in nearby hills, the work of the Sisters went on. Sister Maria was constantly involved in the healing ministry, receiving patients and making endless journeys, all on foot, to bring aid to the sick and injured in villages two, three, four, and five hours away. She was often accompanied by Sister Cecilia and Veronica, the paramedic, who gave invaluable assistance. Sisters Philomina and Vinaya were equally occupied with visiting the houses, conducting prayer services, and helping in the *Yogda* school, as well as doing private coaching during the holidays. They began promoting adult literacy classes through night school, in which all the Sisters joined. In the early months of 1987, because of serious epidemics of dysentery and measles, especially among the children, the resources of Sister Maria and the paramedics were strained to the utmost. Although a number of children died, yet many more survived as a result of the untiring work of the medical personnel.

In 1987 the agitation between the GLNF and the CPI affected even the remote area of Sangsay. Houses were looted and burned, and harassment and even killing took place. For the Sisters the climax came on the night of 28 June with a bomb blast just outside their house, which resulted in the shattering of a number of windows. Only Sisters Maria and Philomina were present, as Sisters Cecilia and Vinaya had gone to Ranchi to attend the Junior Sisters' program. The Sisters were shocked and frightened by this attack and spent the whole night sitting quietly in the chapel in prayer. In the morning the news was sent out, and the people of the parish, a few Brothers, and Father Donald came to assess the situation and to offer help and solace. Boys were appointed to guard the Sisters at night.

Father Donald announced to the people on 12 July that the Sisters were leaving Nazareth Lee. The people received the news with sorrow. The Sisters had decided to go to the Cluny Convent in Kalimpong for a few days. After a week's stay, Sisters Maria and Philomina were joined by Sisters Cecilia and Vinaya. The four then returned to Nazareth Lee. On 10 July, Sisters Shalini and Vinita arrived to investigate the situation. A meeting was held on 12 July with people from all the region, both Christian and non-Christian. When the Sisters' feelings were explained to them, their response was open and generous; they wanted to share the Sisters' joys and sorrows. The people replaced all the broken windows, and the confidence of the Sisters was restored with these assurances.

The health program steadily progressed. Beginning on the first of August, Sister Joel Urumpil gave a very successful week-long health program for the women, attended also by a few men. At this time the first paramedics—Veronica, Anna, and Renuka—completed their course at Hayden Hall in Darjeeling. This institution, founded by the Canadian Jesuit, Father Hayden, is a multifaceted organization providing facilities in many fields of social development. On 26 November, in the Sangsay area, a large number of sleeping kits were distributed to needy villagers. The Seva Kendra and Hayden Hall have done yeoman service in assisting the needy in the hill tracts.

Also in November the Sisters began planting a garden on the irregular terraces near the house. The first year closed with a happy celebration of Christmas, even though the Gorkha land problem remained unsolved.

By the beginning of 1988 the general character of the Sangsay mission was evolving. More and more contacts were made through home visiting, which was vital in reaching the people in such a scattered mission. In the pastoral ministry there were some special events. Sister Cecilia conducted a marriage retreat for a young couple, the first of its kind. On the negative side, a unique marriage took place in which the bride and groom and the whole wedding party arrived at the church in a drunken state. Insults were heaped upon the priest and the Sisters. Father Donald went through the marriage ceremony and blessing, but the party went off without attending Mass. On the following day apologies were offered to the priest and the Sisters, and peace was restored.

The Sisters were called to the house of a very sick Catholic man. In the absence of the priest, Sister Cecilia anointed and blessed him with holy oil, and Sister Philomina gave him Holy Communion. After praying with him and the family, the Sisters returned to the convent. The next morning he died peacefully.

A retreat for about twenty-four boys was directed by Father Pius Marcus. Later a two-day retreat was given for about sixty mothers and fathers.

The fourteenth of December 1988 brought Father Pat Rebeiro from Patna and Father Cherian Namjali from Darjeeling. They immediately became involved in the mission. Father Pat remained through Christmas, the only priest present. He offered the Midnight Mass and a morning Mass in Nepali. After Mass there was joyful feasting and carol singing.

The medical and health ministry continued to progress. The dispensary ministered regularly to the sick. Sister Maria and the paramedics made frequent visits to surrounding villages as well as to far-flung *bustees* (groups of villages). Sister Maria was frequently called for house deliveries, even across the mountains in the dark night. She was never too tired to set out on long walks to help the suffering. The Mother/Child Health program (MCH) was very effective. Distribution of oil, bulgur, soybeans, and vitamins was made through the Catholic Relief Service. Health education did much to improve the condition of the region. When patients needed hospital care, however, it was necessary to transport them up the steep climb of 1500 feet to the motor road and to find a jeep to take them to the hospital in Kalimpong.

The political agitation continued to cause social problems. Long strikes brought untold hardship. Food supplies could not be obtained, and the people were reduced to eating roots and grass to prevent starvation. Many people were killed or injured. Several boys, badly beaten up by a hostile group, were brought to the dispensary for treatment.

To add to the people's woes, a massive earthquake struck India and Nepal on 23 August 1988. Sisters Cecilia and Vinaya, alone at Nazareth Lee, were awakened at 4:30 a.m. by a violent shaking and the sound of the roof groaning. *Almirah* (cupboard) doors flew open, and tins began falling. The Sisters rushed outside in fear. Their only loss, however, was a few chickens that died when they fell from an upper perch. Having heard of widespread destruction in Nepal, the two Sisters went to Dharan and were relieved to find the Sisters there safe and well.

St. Dominic Savio School continued under the leadership of the dedicated headmaster, Padam Subha, who had been teaching there for about twenty-five years. The Sisters, especially Sister Philomina, gave able assistance.

An auspicious day, 10 June 1988, witnessed the blessing of a new school building. Night school afforded a great benefit to those who could not attend at any other time. A first meeting with parents was held in November to discuss various school matters—fees, uniforms, sports days, etc. Sister Vinaya, though thoroughly occupied with social work, found time to enlarge the scope of her labors by opening a sewing class. She began with four students in what might be termed a "crash program," with three hours in the morning and three in the afternoon.

Continuing the pastoral ministry in 1989, Sister Sheela Palamoottil came early in January to give a seminar for both the youth groups and the mothers. Sister Cecilia gave invaluable assistance by translating the seminar sessions into Nepali. In May and October, rosary devotions were held in different houses. Frequently in these months when no priest was present, the Sisters under the direction of Sister Shobhana Kattuvallil, who had joined the community in June, held prayer services with the assembled parishioners. Sister Shobhana also conducted the funeral and burial service of a Catholic child. A boost was given to the spirits of the people by the official visitation of the vicar general, Father Thomas D'Souza, and Father Marianna. Later Father Walter Fernandes from Darjeeling spent two weeks in the parish, visiting parishioners and reaching out in every way to the people. Christmas was well prepared for, and the presence of Father Grassot from Kalimpong made the celebration complete with Midnight Mass and Mass the following morning. After dinner, caroling groups were formed to go to different areas to bring the message of Christmas to the people of the hills.

In the same year the medical and health ministers were always busy, treating the sick, bringing new life into the world, and providing food for needy persons. Sister Maria and the paramedics were on constant call, and Sister Vinaya was untiring in seeing to food supplies and to other social enterprises. Dr. Sanyukta Liu, a doctor working in Pedong, visited Sangsay in the month of March and became much interested in the work. Later, when she was transferred to Kalimpong, she continued to assist by helping with direct medical aid where possible and by adding liberally to the supplies needed in the dispensary. Dr. Liu, her four brothers, and her sister had all been students at Nazareth Academy, Gaya, and were well known to the Sisters.

In February 1988, Sister Cecilia, who was a native of these mountains and a pioneer of the mission, left to take up nursing in Mokama. She was given a touching farewell by the parish and the community. A newcomer to the scene, Prabha Minj, joined the household for cooking and for general work. She remained more than two years and was greatly missed when she left.

In late September Sister Philomina's mother had died. Returning from a brief visit home, Sister Philomina was accompanied by Sister Sarita, the provincial, and Sister Reena, the assistant provincial. This was their first visit to Sangsay since assuming their new offices.

Two important events at the end of the year were the very successful inter-school sports organized by Sister Philomina, assisted by Sister Vinaya, Sister Shobhana, and the school staff; and the laying of the foundation stone of the new community hall to be built beside the church.

In the new year of 1990, medical work went on as busily as ever. Regular clinic days had been scheduled, which comprised treatment of the sick or injured, injections for polio and other diseases, and health classes by paramedics. House visits to see the sick or to conduct deliveries continued.

A big gap was left when Sister Maria departed on 31 March for the United States. She was an elected delegate to the General Assembly at the SCN motherhouse. In her absence Sister Vinaya fell heir to heavy duty, supervising the building and distributing medicine and supplies. Sister Maria returned on 18 July, receiving a hearty welcome from one and all. In characteristic fashion she enthusiastically resumed her work.

Important personnel changes took place in 1990-91. Sister Arpita Mundamattathil joined the mission primarily for teaching in the school. She replaced a pioneer of the mission, Sister Philomina Hembrom, who joined the community in Dharan, Nepal. Sister Philomina's good work in Sangsay will long be remembered. Sister Vinaya left in August 1990 for a study leave in Manila and returned in 1991. In April 1991 Sister Maria, a pioneer of Sangsay, was appointed to teach at Nazareth Hospital Nursing School. Sister Beena filled her place temporarily with efficiency and devotion until July of the same year, when Sister Jyoti Thattaparampil, having completed the B.SC. in nursing, arrived to take over the medical ministry and to carry on the excellent foundation laid by Sister Maria.

During the early months, work was progressing on two structures, a parish hall and a new convent building. By 21 February the Sisters were able to move into a comfortable new house. The rooms for the dispensary were under the living quarters of the Sisters. The blessing on 11 March was attended by a large delegation that included the vicar general, Father Thomas D'Souza, Brothers, Sisters, and priests from far and near, many parishioners and Sisters Anne Marie Thayilchirayil, Marcelline Indwar, and Deepti Ponnambal.

Easter of that year was the occasion of a beautiful ceremony—the baptism of seven catechumens who had been instructed by Sister Shobhana, who had been preparing catechumens in both Sangsay and Pethong. Of great importance to the mission was the installation on 3 May of the first resident parish priest, Father Jerome Singh, in the presence of a large gathering.

Sangsay as a mission has great promise even though it is beset with many problems. The extreme poverty of the people, the low level of literacy, the indifference toward education, the general poor health of the people resulting from malnutrition and crushing labor, the large number of physically and mentally disadvantaged people caused by intermarriage with close relatives, and the widespread abuse of alcohol—all are serious social problems. On the other hand, there are many assets—openness in society with few barriers regarding sex, caste, religion, or status; a cheerful, happy, almost carefree attitude toward life; a sort of Gospel mentality ("Why are you fearful, oh ye of little faith?"); and an acceptance of whatever happens. The people are notably charitable to one another and to outsiders.

Largely Buddhist in practice, a good number of the people of Sangsay have embraced Christianity; many others are eager and ready to enter the Church. One of the difficulties is the means of communication, since the families are scattered all around the hillsides, sometimes two, three, or even more hours away. Many of the Catholics walk for several hours just to attend Mass on Sundays. They have a simple, genuine faith that supports and guides them in their struggles. Our prayer can be: "May Christ ever reign" in this beautiful Himalayan land.

Sister Maria Palathingal welcomes an elderly neighbor into the house at Sangsay.

NAV CHETAN, MADHEPURA
1987

Sister Bridget Vadakkeattam (upper left) and a co-worker vaccinate children in Madhepura.

Chapter Twenty-three

NAV CHETAN, MADHEPURA
1987

Madhepura had a slow beginning and also progressed slowly, but the progress it did achieve was due in large measure to the faith, courage, and perseverance of the Sisters who went there to minister. It was a hard, demanding struggle. Disappointments, suffering, opposition, and frustration abounded, but still the mission continued, and after several laborious years, light could be seen at the end of the tunnel.

Madhepura district was cut away from the Saharsa district, in which Shahpur, Santhali Tola is situated. This area was an outstation of Latonah, and the priest came here at intervals for Mass. In more recent years, the priest comes from Saharsa, from which station he serves a number of smaller ones.

Geographically Madhepura is in the northeastern section of Bihar, adjoining the Purnea District, which meets the bordering state of Bengal. The Sisters live in the middle of a small Santhal village in a two-room rented mud house. The Santhal people have accepted them as their own and help them in many ways, especially in the housekeeping typical of their particular culture and traditions.

The first SCN to come to Madhepura was Sister Rose Plathottathil, a homeopathic doctor. Prior to her coming, Brother Cyril, M.C., had come for only a short time, but is still remembered by the people. Others who had come for short periods were Joseph Mirandi, Father Abraham from Latonah, and Gunga Tudu, a catechist from Latonah, who left when he was threatened by the political party Rashtriya Sevak Sangh (RSS).

Having heard of this mission, Sister Rose came in March 1987, hoping to set up a medical facility for the people of the area. Realizing the need for a knowledge of the language, she left to study Santhali, returning in June with Sisters Agnes Tudu and Ann Muttukattil. Sister Rose began medical work, while Sisters Agnes and Ann began teaching.

The first house was very primitive, without flooring or bathroom, made only of mud and bamboo, built by the youth of the village. The house later occupied by Sisters Ann George Mukalel and Sunita Vayalipara was also constructed by the local people. It stands on ground belonging to Mohan Murmu, who has most generously allowed the Sisters to remain on the land and has treated them like members of his own family. In 1990 the Sisters moved to a new location where land was bought and a more permanent house erected.

In September 1987, the Sisters experienced a flood that kept them marooned for three or four days. They even sat on their beds to avoid the rising water. Survival was difficult. One redeeming feature was an abundance of fish.

The same year, through the efforts of Father Abraham Odalany, the Church acquired land for the Sisters. Unfortunately, under instructions from outsiders, this land was immediately occupied illegally by a Santhal family who remained on the land until 1992. At that time, under the initiative of the district magistrate of Madhepura, Mr. Ajay Kumar (a former student of Nazareth Academy), the people vacated half of the land and a peaceful settlement was reached.

Two ministries went side by side—medical work under the direction of Sister Rose and nonformal education supervised by Sisters Agnes and Ann. In addition to her medical work, Sister Rose engaged in other projects. She began the process of bringing electricity to the village, and by 1988-89 electricity became a reality there. She also succeeded in getting a number of young women and men into the Sadar Hospital in Madhepura.

Between 1987 and 1989 personnel changes took place. Sisters Agnes and Ann were transferred, and some time later Sister Rose also left the mission. In April 1988, Sisters Sunita Vayalipara and Bridget Vadakkeattam came to Madhepura. Sister Bridget took up the medical work begun by Sister Rose and continued it until early 1990. Sister Sunita became involved in a number of projects, some of which she had initiated, in the fields of nonformal education, adult literacy, and programs for self-employment.

Among the programs pursued during these years were the following: a course begun by Sister Sheela Palamoottil that developed into an adult literacy course especially designed for youth; a tailoring course for women to promote self-employment; and cultural activities for children, initiated by Sister Sunita.

In 1988 Sister Ann George joined the group at Madhepura. She took charge of the adult literacy courses and also coached high school and college students. By 1990 only two Sisters remained—Ann George and Sunita.

In cooperation with the government rural development program aiming at self-employment (TRYSEM), the Sisters continued the tailoring courses. They began a further project at Nayanagar, about seventy kilometers away. A poultry farm was begun in March 1990. Twenty-eight landless and unemployed women were trained in the TRYSEM program. The project cost Rs 198,000. Fourteen chicken houses were constructed and stocked with 2800 fowls. The proceeds provided good bank accounts for each laborer, and the recipients continued to raise chickens on their own. During this period Sister Ann George was living at Nayanagar in a very dilapidated house without even the most essential amenities. Sister Sunita remained with the projects at Madhepura. At last, in 1990, a new house was built—simple and small, made of mud, bamboo, grass, and fiber. In August 1991 classes in nonformal education for children were begun. The teachers were Arjun Murmu and Devlal Mirandi, local youths who had completed the Intermediate Arts certificate in college. These young men were trained by Sisters Ann George and Sunita, who continued to teach.

The Sisters' work had the firm backing of Bishop John Baptist Thakur, S.J., of Muzzaffarpur, who has continually encouraged the efforts being made and who has also assisted the Sisters materially in their projects and used his own resources in promoting their work.

Among those who have served the mission well have been the Brothers and priests of the Indian Mission Society of Saharsa, who have provided food, shelter, hospitality, and every other kind of service. Lastly, tribute should be paid to Mr. Ajay Kumar, a former student of Sister Ann George at Nazareth Academy, who as district magistrate of Madhepura has done everything in his power to promote plans intended for the welfare of the people of the district.

The Madhepura mission, having survived many struggles and misfortunes, still keeps its head high and promises to continue the work inaugurated by the zealous Sisters who staffed it.

The community at Nazareth Convent prays over Sister Marina Thazathuvettil as she sets out for her new mission in Madhepura District.

SCN NIKETAN, BANGALORE
1989

Sisters Gloretta Gomes, Sabina Mattappallil, Sujita Muthalakuzhy, Regina Ekka, and Elizabeth Lobo celebrate St. Vincent's Feast Day at Bangalore.

Chapter Twenty-four

SCN NIKETAN, BANGALORE 1989

One more branch house was to be added to the list of SCN establishments in India before the end of the 80s. By a decision passed at the Province Assembly of 1988, a committee of three, Sisters Marietta Saldanha, Rita Puthenkalam, and Mercy Thundathil was created to find a suitable house for the new convent in Bangalore. A house of studies had existed in Bangalore between 1972 and 1977; it had not proved feasible, however, and had eventually been closed and the property sold. The committee's search resulted in the purchase of the home of an elderly couple, Mr. and Mrs. John Aroygamma, in June 1989.

The new members, Sisters Celine Arackathottam and Evelyn D'Souza, escorted by the provincial, Sister Sarita, and the assistant provincial, Sister Reena, left Patna for Bangalore on 21 September 1988, heavily laden with baggage. The long journey ended on 23 September when they arrived in Bangalore City station, where they were received by the eleven SCN students, Sister Evelyn's nephew, and Sister Celine's sister. The Sisters were surprised when Sister Sarita handed them the keys of the house, with the news that since the owner had already vacated it, they could immediately take full possession. How comforting it was to find it clean, freshly painted, and furnished with fans, tube lights, curtains, gas cylinder, and a single burner stove. The pioneers enjoyed some coffee and the food left from the journey and were refreshed by a good night's sleep on mattresses provided by kindly neighbors.

The first days and weeks were spent in preparing the house for permanent occupancy. All kinds of household appliances, furniture, and provisions had to be purchased. Slowly but steadily, the bare house was furnished and gradually became a satisfactory convent with all required facilities.

Before Sisters Sarita and Reena left, the Sisters made courtesy calls on the local priests, as well as to the archbishop's house, where the vicar general, Father Joseph D'Silva, received them in the absence of Archbishop Mathias. On the feast of St. Vincent de Paul, 27 September, the student Sisters arrived to celebrate the feast. At 6 p.m. the parish priest, Father Nicholas, offered Mass and blessed the house. The evening meal was thoroughly enjoyed by the assembled SCNs. On the following day, after the completion of all documents concerning the purchase of the new property, the final registration took place in the subdivisional office, and SCN Niketan became official SCN property.

During the months of October and November, development of the house and its surroundings continued. With the cooperation of all, the small backyard soon began to bloom with flowers and to provide vegetables for the table. Furniture was delivered, and all the rooms began to have a lived-in appearance.

Notable visitors began to arrive in November. Sister Mary Frances Sauer, a 1947 pioneer, and Sister Carmelita Dunn, both visiting from the United States, spent two weeks enjoying the delightful environment of Bangalore. Visitors in early December were Sister Marietta Saldanha, Bishop Osta, and Father Matthew Uzhutal, director of Jyothi Bhavan, Mokama. Sister Mary Stella Ambrose came to spend time in Bangalore after completing a four-month course of training for care of the blind, the ministry in which she was engaged.

Most of the SCN students gathered at SCN Niketan for the celebration of Christmas. The hostelers joined enthusiastically in preparation for Christmas by decorating the house, making special foods, and spreading the joy of Christmas with their lively activity. Christmas Mass was offered at St. John's Friary, and upon returning home the Sisters celebrated Christmas with heartfelt joy through singing, dancing, and partaking of tasty refreshments. During the day, they spread Christmas cheer as they went around singing and greeting their neighbors. The year closed with recollection and Midnight Mass at the parish.

As the new decade of 1990 dawned, SCN Niketan, though still in its infancy, showed signs of growth and development. Intended primarily as a house for students, it shows promise of things to come. It may be necessary to grope in the dark for a while, but God's light will penetrate the darkness and show the way to new opportunities for serving the suffering and the needy in both body and mind.

HIMALAYA VILLA, ALMORA
1990

Hills of Almora, showing how
they have been denuded by the
irresponsible cutting of trees.

Chapter Twenty-five

HIMALAYA VILLA, ALMORA 1990

The SCN community was first contacted in December 1988 about possible personnel for the AML (Almora Magnesite Limited) School in Kafligair, operated by the Delhi Jesuit Society. Negotiations continued through 1989. The provincial, Sister Sarita Manavalan, and her assistant, Sister Reena Theruvankunnel, visited the place in June 1989 and subsequently deemed the project acceptable. Final preparations were made.

The AML School is located in the Almora District, U.P. Hills, about 45 kilometers (two and a half hours by bus) from Almora, the district seat. The school is owned by the mining company and serves children of the mining personnel as well as children of the locality. The headmaster, Father Felix Abraham, S.J., Sister Ruth, a Medical Missionary who has been teaching in the school, the new Sisters, the teachers, and all employees are paid partly by the company and partly through the fees of the students. The classes at present range from preschool to Class 6. The medium of instruction is English, although strong Hindi programs have been retained.

By December 1989 two Sisters had been appointed for the new mission, Sisters Mary Chackalackal and Usha Saldana. For them it was like going to a new country, the vast Himalayas, and they began to prepare busily for the change of climate and the new culture of the *pahar* (hills). On 20 January 1990 the two pioneers of the new mission along with their two escorts—Sisters Eugenia Muething from Gaya and Sarala Anithottathil from Mokama—were sent off with all good wishes and blessings from the Provincial House, Patna, by Sister Sarita, Sister Reena, and all the community who had assembled there. The four Sisters and seventeen pieces of luggage were somehow stored into the second-class ladies' compartment of the Magadh Express, and the party was off for Delhi, the first leg of the journey.

Father Varkey Perekkatt, S.J., regional superior of the Delhi Jesuits, welcomed the Sisters at the Delhi station, took charge of the luggage, and transported them by Maruti van to St. Xavier's, where lunch awaited them. The evening closed with Mass at 9 p.m. The next day was spent in visiting and shopping, and by night the four Sisters and the luggage were packed into a bus by the able maneuvering of

Father Varkey. Promptly at 9 p.m. the bus departed on its eleven-hour ride to Almora.

From Kathgodam the bus began the final four hours, a climb of twists and turns, and, as the day dawned, the incomparable beauty of the Himalayas was revealed. Destination was reached at 8:30 a.m. on 23 January as the bus halted at the terminal in Almora. Waiting at the bus stand were two of the Delhi Jesuits, Father Felix and Father Joseph Matheikal, who worked in that region. The two priests took care of the luggage and conducted the party to their small quarters in Almora. With the aid of the priests' servant, the Sisters prepared a good lunch.

About 2 p.m. Father Felix and the Sisters departed for Kafligair. At 5 p.m. after more twists and turns as the taxi descended into the valley, the Sisters saw for the first time, nestled between the hills, the school where they would be teaching and finally the two-room quarters where they would live. The first to welcome them was the Catholic family of Mr. Joseph Nair—his wife Theresiamma, their two sons, John and James, Mrs. Nair's mother, affectionately known as Amajee, and Mrs. Nair's niece, Elsie. Mr. Nair is a company official in charge of all the blasting, a very responsible position, and Mrs. Nair is the chief staff nurse in the company dispensary. Elsie is the laboratory technician in the dispensary, and the two sons are in Classes 8 and 7 at St. Joseph's College, Naini Tal. Nightfall found everyone, after a pleasant supper, happy to settle down for the night, two in beds and two on the floor. Thus the new mission at Kafligair was begun.

The next five days or so became a program of initiation. The day after the Sisters' arrival, Mr. Nair invited them to see the company factory, its furnaces, and huge machinery. After the tour of the factory, one of the teachers, Mrs. Joshi, took the Sisters up to the site of the school, but because they had forgotten the keys, the inspection had to be done from the outside only. (School session begins in mid February.) This expedition provided a new experience in climbing, first up to the school itself and afterward up the nearby hills. In the afternoon Mr. Nair took Sisters Sarala and Eugenia to the mines, a nine-kilometer drive up a twisting roadway by company bus and truck. In the evening all the Sisters and Father Felix were guests of the Nairs for dinner. The whole party had visited Mr. Chandra, the general manager of the company, and were received cordially by him and his wife. Mrs. Chandra is a teacher at the AML School.

The following day, 25 January, was the beginning of a big tour of the hill stations. After meeting Father Joseph in Almora, the four Sisters, Father Felix, and Father Joseph left for Ranikhet. There they met the parish priest, Father Y. Raju, S.J., and the Sisters of the Canossian Convent School. These Sisters provided a bountiful lunch, after which all took a tour of the beautiful town of Ranikhet, important in military circles as the regimental center of the Kumaca Regiment. In the evening, Father Raju treated the Canossians, the SCNs, and priests to dinner. Then followed a peaceful and restful night at the Canossian convent.

Morning Mass was concelebrated by the three priests. The Sisters provided a delicious breakfast, after which the tour proceeded by bus to St. Mary's Convent (IBMV Sisters), Naini Tal, in time to enjoy a fine lunch. The afternoon was spent in a boat ride on the Naini Tal lake, shopping, souvenir and gift buying, and visits to St. Francis Home (Capuchins) and St. Joseph College (Irish Christian Brothers). Sister Beata, IBMV, had four cozy beds ready in the infirmary at St. Mary's, complete with hot water bottles to warm them. After this interesting day, the Sisters retired to a most comfortable night.

The following morning, the Sisters attended Mass offered by Fathers Felix and Joseph in the room of an elderly Sister (82 years old), who had been seriously ill. Shortly after breakfast, Sister Eugenia and Father Joseph left for Jeolikot and Kathgodam. They visited the IBMV convent school and orphanage in Jeolikot and then went on to Kathgodam, where they saw the social center conducted by the diocese of Bareilly and the old people's home that is supported and operated by the Ursuline Sisters. These Sisters also have a large school in the same compound. The bishop of Bareilly, Most Reverend Anthony Fernandes, happened to be present, and Sister Eugenia had the surprise and pleasure of meeting him and the new parish priest, Father John Baptist Macarenhas, after a lapse of more than thirty years. As young seminarians, the bishop and the parish priest had attended the same summer school of music that Sister Eugenia attended. Meanwhile Father Felix and the three other Sisters remained until afternoon in Naini Tal and then proceeded to Almora where they spent the night. When the whole party reassembled in Almora, they called on the topmost official of the Almora Magnesite Limited, the managing director, Mr. David Pichamuttu, at his lovely home high on a hill in Almora. He received the visitors most graciously, and during the ensuing conversation, he recalled his mission school days in Bangalore.

The breaking up of the quartet of SCNs who had come to Almora took place on 29 January when Sisters Mary, Usha, and Eugenia bade farewell to Sister Sarala when she departed for Delhi and the long journey back to Mokama. Sister Eugenia remained for an extended visit. On the 30 January, their first settled day in Kafligair, the Sisters began cleaning and arranging the house to suit their needs. Like all of the people of the mining colony, they had no domestic servant and took up all the work of the house, including the cooking.

The first visitors arrived on 31 January—eight Sisters from St. Mary's Convent in Naini Tal. Father Joseph accompanied them, and they kindly brought in their van the SCN luggage that had been left behind in Almora. As is their custom, the IBMVs brought plenty of food and a number of other goodies for the SCNs of Kafligair. Mr. Nair conducted the party on a tour of the factory and mines, and after a round of coffee and snacks, the party departed for Naini Tal. The first days in Kafligair ended with the successful baking of a cake on 1 February.

The mission in Almora is just beginning. How it will develop, what form it will take, what ministries will later be attempted are all unanswered questions. For the SCN community it is a place of challenge, a new ground on which to build. The God of the harvest will direct the way, and it will be for the community to follow courageously and to meet the needs of the ministries that may be presented for implementation and fulfillment.

Sisters Vinita Kumplankal, Bridget Kappalumakal, and Ancilla Kozhipat listen to the hill lore of a wise woman of Almora.

EPILOGUE

Nazareth Along the Banks of the Ganges is an account of the life of the Sisters of Charity of Nazareth in India, covering the years 1947 to approximately 1990. These were years of beginning and development but not of completion. It is a history of those years, of the original missions, of the growth of an indigenous sisterhood, of the founding of institutions and missions that spread out gradually to many parts of India, of the successes and failures, of the joys and sorrows, and of all the vicissitudes that make up the warp and woof of the history of any enterprise. Therefore, 1990 brings the narration only to an interval, a pause in the history. A look into the future assures us that there will be much more to be written.

May we who are familiar with Nazareth in India pray that progress, both material and more particularly spiritual, will be accomplished for many years to come, and that the glory of God and the good of souls will ever be the result of the work of the Sisters of Charity of Nazareth in India.

ADDENDA

Although the years following 1990 have been witness to much growth in the SCN community in India, only a brief account can be made here so that the publication may not be delayed. The following are a few developments:

1. Chatra, now more than twenty-five years old, has grown into a full-fledged primary, middle, and high school with hostels for boys and girls. Necessary buildings had to be added to accommodate its twelve hundred students.
2. A number of new places have been started in the Bombay area.
3. The character of the mission in Almora has shifted from education to social service projects.
4. New missions are now in the making, notably: Gumla in Bihar, Trichy in Tamil Nadu, and Banakal in Karnataka.

Thus can be seen the spreading of the SCN community in far-flung areas of India.

AN AFTERWORD: NEPAL

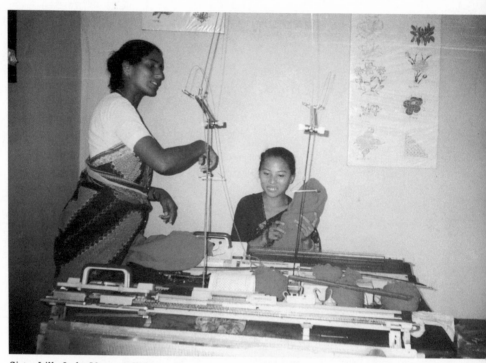

Sister Lilly Luka Vayampallitharapel supervises knitting by machine in Dharan, Nepal.

AN AFTERWORD: NEPAL

Although Sister Eugenia Muething's account of the Sisters of Charity of Nazareth in India does not include the story of the Sisters' work in neighboring Nepal, this volume would be incomplete without the recounting of that experience. Margaret Maria Coon, SCN, and Anna Catharine Coon, SCN, have studied the various accounts of the Nepal communities preserved in the Archives of the Nazareth, Kentucky, Motherhouse and provide here a brief narrative of the brave women who ventured into the Hindu realm, where some of them suffered greatly. Appended to the Nepal account is a brief first-hand telling of a part of the story by Joel Urumpil, SCN.

Nepal, the only Hindu kingdom in the world, lies on India's northeast border in the majestic Himalaya mountains. For almost two hundred years (1768-1950) it was governed by despotic rulers who enforced its complete isolation from the world beyond its borders. An early faint hint of change occurred in 1949 when the Prime Minister asked the Jesuits of Patna to establish a high school for boys in Kathmandu, so that the young men of his country need not go abroad for education. The Jesuits agreed, but before the preparations for the new mission were complete, the Revolution of 1950 in Nepal brought a new king to power. He opened the country to the outside world and encouraged the Jesuits to establish their school as planned. In 1951, Godavari High School received students in Kathmandu, and three years later Xavier High School expanded the mission. At about the same time, the German sisters of Mother Mary Ward's foundation, IBMV, founded a school for girls in Kathmandu, Nepal's capital city.

The country's need of missionary service of every kind was and is overwhelming. Eighty-five percent of its people are illiterate. Life expectancy averages forty-four years, and infant mortality is one hundred fifty-two per thousand births. One of every thirteen persons suffers from mental illness due to malnutrition. Extreme, pervasive poverty and oppressive social and cultural practices undermine progress in every area of human development.

Evangelization is forbidden by law, but schools, hospitals, and social service centers are acceptable as long as no attempt is made to convert anyone. The second Vatican Council called the Church in mission to promote itself as *sign* rather than *sanctuary.* As *sign* the Church is interested in perfecting its service simply as a testimony to the presence of God's saving love in the world.

The United Mission to Nepal, staffed by personnel from thirty-five Protestant mission groups representing a dozen denominations from fifteen countries of Asia, Europe, and North America, was the sponsoring agency for many mission projects. These groups were pledged to work as one Christian body in loving service. Nepal's laws posed no threat to Jesuit, Maryknoll, IBMV, and United Mission projects, thanks to the government's acceptance of the Church as *sign* and the wise directives of Vatican Council II.

In 1977, the SCN India Province, responding to the Jesuits' invitation to join them in ministry in Nepal, sent Patricia Mary Kelley and Olive Pinto to Kathmandu to assist for several months in the schools, health care, and social services while examining needs that a permanent SCN mission could address. Arriving at the capital city's airport on 26 January, the two SCNs spent the first two nights with the German sisters at St. Mary's convent because some repairs were necessary at their intended residence. Patricia Mary wrote, "Father Dressman met us at the airport and welcomed us with three oranges each, in lieu of a *mala* . . . . Kathmandu and the snows were lovely."

A few days later, Father Larry Brooks reported, "Patricia Mary helps at school—teaches a little speech. Olive works in the infirmary and the pre-vocational programme."

Bridget Vadakkeattam was assigned to three months' mission in Nepal, to begin 1 April 1977. She served as supervisor of student nurses at Shanti Bhavan Hospital, which was operated by Protestant missionaries and owned by United Mission to Nepal. Bridget accompanied nurses to the villages in their public health training program.

Barbara Thomas and the Executive Committee, in confirming the beginning of mission to Nepal, designated it a foreign mission of the India Province, as SCNs to go there were to do so on a volunteer basis. Sisters were invited in the India Newsletter of September 1977 to submit applications to Mokama by 1 December. In the first year, only sisters from India were to go. U.S. volunteers were to have some time in India before going to Nepal, and their final discernment would be with the India Province.

Anne Marie Thayilchirayil, Jean Kulangara, and Joel Urumpil received assignments in December 1978 to be the pioneers of the permanent SCN mission in Nepal. Margaret Rodericks, provincial, commissioned them at ceremonies in the convent chapel at Mokama on Easter Sunday, 15 April 1979; and each received her missionary cross from Sister Lawrencetta, who had led SCN missionaries to India more than thirty years earlier.

Two days later, 17 April, they departed with Margaret Rodericks, Ann Bernadette Ormond, and Sunanda Urumpil to spend the night in Bettiah before proceeding to Kathmandu and the warm welcome of Father James Dressman, S.J. Their home, Nazarethalaya, was a red brick building with a printing press on the ground floor, offices on the next level, and residence on top. The living quarters included a large bedroom, a central area partitioned for use as a chapel, a dining/sitting room, and a kitchen which opened on a terrace.

Father Tom Gaffney, S.J., the bishop's representative in Nepal, celebrated the Eucharist with the SCNs and blessed their home 20 April 1979. Guests included the Jesuits, the Maryknoll priests, the IBMV sisters, and lay friends.

The study of the Nepali language was urgently important and the sisters worked at it from the day they arrived in Kathmandu. Their teacher, Mr. Dutta, came from one of the language schools for daily two-hour classes with them. Their letters told of the experience.

Jean wrote, "He is an excellent teacher . . . only we don't find enough time for study. Almost every day we have visitors. Besides, we have been invited to different places. Yesterday we went to the Inter High School spelling contest. The queen and many ministers were present."

Anne Marie wrote, "Our Nepali classes are very good. Nepali is much harder than I thought it would be, but we have so much fun trying to talk in it. Mr. Dutta doesn't waste a minute of the two hour class . . . he doesn't speak English or Hindi unless he absolutely has to. He uses the role-playing technique, too, which is a big help."

For six months the sisters devoted themselves to study and to the investigation of the human needs that their service might address. Jean and Anne Marie in Godavari conducted literacy classes for women at Kitani and Mundaba, while Joel worked in the parish at Dhobi Ghat (translated "place of those who wash clothes").

Ann Kernen, SCN, the first American to join the Nepali project, had written in February 1979 that she hoped to reach India in January 1980. In the meantime she planned to enroll in Mission Studies at the Catholic Theological Union, Chicago, for the summer session, and to study language at the University of Wisconsin in the fall.

When Teresa Rose returned from the General Assembly at Nazareth in January 1980, Ann Kernen accompanied her to Mokama to continue her preparation for mission in Nepal. En route, they stopped for a "foretaste" visit at Kathmandu, and Ann was able during four days to absorb some of the beauty of the land and the cordial, happy spirit of its people.

At the time of Ann's visit, Jean was attending a workshop in India, but Teresa Rose, Anne Marie, and Joel shared with Ann, updating SCN/India news, visiting the Jesuits and their schools, meeting with the German sisters and the Maryknoll priests. Another very joyful contact was made with Alfreda Crantz, SCN, from Louisville, Kentucky. She was working for the Tom Dooley Foundation at Bir Hospital, and she gave them a glimpse of her ministry there.

At the completion of her orientation and discernment in the India Province, Ann Kernen flew to Kathmandu where Joel, Alfreda, Father Dressman, and Father Bill Gavin, M.M., met and welcomed her in June 1980. She wrote, "Joel and I will live together here in the city, and Jean and Anne Marie will continue at Mundaba Village, Godavari . . . . Ours is an apartment at Dhobi Ghat, a living room/dining area, two small bedrooms, a tiny chapel, a kitchen, and a tiny, tiny bathroom, Indian style . . . . Officially the Christian Church does not exist in Nepal, for it is not in any government records. There is a one-year prison term for a person who receives baptism; a six-year term for the baptizer."

Joel traveled to Darjeeling in July to contact young women interested in religious life. In September Bishop Osta visited each religious house in Nepal. Ann and Joel invited Alfreda to share his visit at their home. In his two hours with them they were impressed with his sensitivity and kindness, his "wonderful gift of openness." In June 1981 Ann returned to the United States because of illness, and shortly thereafter Rose Plathootthil, SCN, a medical doctor with the specialty of homeopathic medicine, joined the Nepal mission at Kathmandu. In August 1982 Ann Murphy, the second U.S. SCN confirmed for the mission in Nepal, arrived at Mokama and after orientation and discernment in India, joined the Nepal group in October.

During the five years of SCN presence in Kathmandu, the Church had become well represented, having twenty-eight priests and several communities of sisters in ministry. In the spring of 1983 the sisters decided to leave the Kathmandu valley and move eastward: Anne Marie and Ann Murphy to Ilam; Jean and Tara Ekka to Dharan; and Joel and Rose to Damak. Many workers in the tea gardens of this area were Catholic, and for them the SCNs would be the only visible presence of the Church.

Olive and Bridget Kappalumakal visited the sisters at their new location in late August to share the province news and discuss local community and ministry needs. At Dharan, the site offered for SCN permanent residence was a two-story building with lower level for ministry with the mentally retarded and upper level for living quarters. The property was owned and maintained by the Church. When Tara was transferred to India, Jean replaced her, and Sarita Manavalan came for adult education services in Jean's place.

Rosemarie Lakra and Joel moved in early July to a village near Damak, into a small house donated by a wealthy citizen who was interested in the development of the area. The property had been vacant for many years, so the sisters had to pull out grass, close rat holes, fill ditches, and chase snakes to make it habitable. In service to the people, Joel coached some of the school girls, and both sisters worked with groups of retarded children.

Ann Murphy arrived 9 November to join Anne Marie at Ilam. Father George Merick visited them, celebrated Mass, and promised to come to them from India once a month. Nepal's Education Minister visited their Mt. Michi school and was impressed by the welcome he received from its two hundred students and by the cultural program presented in his honor.

SCNs of Ilam, Damak, and Dharan held their joint area meeting 8 and 9 April 1984 at Ilam. Father Bill Robins, S.J., regional superior of the Jesuits in Nepal, joined them after having walked the last five miles of his trip because of a bus breakdown. Discussion treated of inculturation into Nepalese society, collaboration with other religions and the laity, planning for vocation promotion, ongoing development, and the upcoming celebration of Ann Murphy's silver jubilee.

The India Provincial Council, meeting in Nepal in June, 1984, recommended the following actions:

1. Appointment of a full-time Director of Faith Formation on the national level;
2. Vocation promotion in the Darjeeling area, India, by SCNs of the Nepal mission;
3. Discernment of future missionaries to Nepal in the context of a five-year plan for the Church there;
4. Agreements for Rosemarie's pastoral service and Joel's medical service to be formulated and signed;
5. Official approval for purchase of the Damak house to be obtained from Nazareth.

Because of legal complications, it was later decided that Father Casper Miller, S.J., ecclesiastical superior of the newly-created Nepal jurisdiction, would negotiate and sign the papers for the house in Damak. Anne Marie was appointed by Father Miller to be Director of Faith Formation in Nepal. She would be based in Kathmandu and assume duties in February 1985.

Official tolerance of Christians wore thin around the village of Sirsia in 1986, when local Hindus seized the land of a poor widow (not Christian) to build a temple to a goddess, and local Christians protested the injustice. After a Holy Week retreat, while blessing homes in Sirsia, SCNs Francine and Gracy, Father Thomas, and three catechists were accused and arrested on charges of proselytizing. They spent nine days in prison, where they were repeatedly beaten and verbally abused.

Released on bail from prison, the defendants remained under indictment and under orders to appear for hearings and the court's decision concerning the date for the trial. Amnesty International entered negotiations in their behalf in November 1988; Church officials brought their influence to bear; and British Members of

Parliament officially requested that the Nepal government allow Christian missionaries to carry on their work.

Francine alone finally remained accused, summoned to hearings, required to call witnesses, and informed of successive delays in scheduling her trial. Four years after the arrests a new democratic government in Nepal withdrew the case without bringing it to trial.

The January 1995 issue of *SCN Missions* carried news of Francine's death at Mokama's Nazareth Hospital, 10 November 1994, and a summary of her moving experience. Arrested in Damak for converting people to Christianity, Francine was working with Santhal women who were already Christian, converted in India before coming to Nepal to work in the tea gardens. Through the intervention of Church authorities she was released from prison after ten days.

Later diagnosed to have cancer, she worked at Mokama managing the farm and caring for the animals. It was reported that on the day of her death some of her animals refused to eat. She was conscious to the end, had a wonderful sense of humor.

Teresa Xavier Ponnazhath and Preeti Chalil were the first to serve in the mission at Tinkune, in a house purchased by Nav Jyoti Women's Center, Dharan, 1992. The following February Teresa Xavier was on an errand, and Preeti was working at home. When Teresa Xavier returned, she found tragedy. Preeti was dead, smothered with a pillow in an apparent robbery, in which two or three hundred dollars was stolen.

In early 1994, Sisters of the Nepal mission at Kathmandu helped to free six mentally ill women from the Central Prison there. In their visits to the prison the sisters had learned that mentally ill women were detained there with convicted inmates because Nepal had only one thirty-bed facility for the treatment of the mentally ill. Prison officials were pleased to release the six women judged most capable of rehabilitation into the care of the missionaries. The Jesuit Social Work Institute furnished legal status, financial support, and personnel at the Nav Jyoti Center where the women were received and cared for until they could be returned to their families.

As part of their second-year novitiate training, SCN novices in India live for an extended period among the very poor, not so much to give and do for the people as to learn from them the secret of their blessedness in the eyes of Christ. In Nepal, sisters have found the needs of women and children of that country even more urgent than ones they address in India. Nepal, having no resources that the people can hope to develop, is ranked Fifth World on a scale that ranks India Third World. Health needs are great; education is scanty; and mental retardation abounds among those who are malnourished.

SCNs train women to develop skills that will earn their living. In Kathmandu the sisters house and teach children who would otherwise be on the street begging.

They conduct a primary school in eastern Nepal and follow their students through high school and into the working world.

In one year of their prison ministry at Kathmandu (May 1993-April 1994), SCNs were instrumental in reducing the number of mentally ill women detained at Kathmandu Central Prison from forty-six to fourteen.

In 1996 there were five sisters in East Nepal and four in the capital city, Kathmandu. All were from the India Province and were engaged in education, health care, and social services in the towns where they resided and in the surrounding villages. Their efforts concentrated on the needs of women and children, although they were at the service of all, seeking to meet new needs as they became aware of them.

THE BEGINNINGS OF THE NEPAL MISSION
A Personal Account

On April 18, 1979, Sisters Anne Marie, Jean and I left for our mission in Nepal accompanied by the provincial Margaret Rodericks, Ann Bernadette and Sunanda Urumpil. We went in the Nazareth Hospital van. We reached St. Xavier's, Kathmandu, around 3 p.m. We had left Mokama the previous day and had spent the night at a mission station at the Indian side.

Father James Dressman, superior of the Nepal Jesuits, was waiting for us with garlands. He garlanded us, one after another, and immediately drove us to our new apartment. It was on the top of a press, a two-room dwelling with a tiny kitchen and a roof where we could relax and watch the snow-capped mountain! We asked Father to go and buy some food as we were too tired to cook. After the meal, Father left us for the night. We spread some linen and mattress on the floor, and soon we were fast asleep.

The next day, after unpacking, cooking, etc., we went to visit the religious communities in the valley accompanied, of course, by Father Dressman. At the time, three Religious groups—the Jesuits who were running two English medium schools, the IBMV Sisters who were running an English medium school for the girls, and the Maryknollers who had a school for the mentally retarded—lived there.

After two or three days, Sister Margaret and the team left us. Now we were by ourselves! Of course we felt lonely and homesick, especially since we didn't know the language. The first thing we did was to find out where the post office and the bus stand were. We were told by some sisters and fathers that the only way to travel back to India was by air. We decided to check it out and found out that most people travelled by bus!

We lived near the famous Pashupathi temple, and the locality in which we lived was called Maiti Ghar (home of goddess Maiti). The people were very friendly even

241

though we were "dark skinned Indians!" We noticed, unlike the people of India, the Nepalese are very religious and happy. Poor and rich alike went to the temple every Saturday, their holy day, with some offering, mainly rice and flowers and fruits.

The first thing we did was to find a Nepali teacher for ourselves. This man, Mr. Data, was a very good teacher. As soon as we reached his house, we would be served hot tea, only then he would begin the lessons. He taught us for an hour daily for two months. Since we knew Hindi, we didn't find Nepali too difficult. After the classroom preparation, he found for us two villages in which to live and to practice Nepali. Jean and I lived in one village, and Anne Marie in another. We lived in these villages for a month. The people in these villages never made us feel as if we were foreigners. On the first day in the village where Jean and I stayed, something frightening (but funny for us) happened. The family had given us one string bed (big enough for one person only). The young girl from the family insisted that she too wanted to sleep on that cot. So there were three of us! Since Jean and I were too tired, we immediately fell asleep. Suddenly we were awakened from our deep sleep by the girl who kept on shouting, "*Bhuichalo!!* Let us go out into the open space." We didn't know the meaning of "*Bhuichalo*" and thought that a wild animal must have come to attack us. But we were puzzled as to why we had to go out into the open if there was a wild animal. Once outside, we were made to understand that there was an earthquake! Everyone was so dead serious, but we could not stop laughing at our foolishness.

We returned from the village all enthusiastic about getting into ministry. The Jesuits wanted both Anne Marie and Jean to teach in their school. They had no job for me since I was a nurse. Jim Dressman took me to the Protestant hospital, but they didn't want a Catholic nun. Anne Marie and Jean didn't want to teach in the school either. Jean again was offered parish ministry. That too she didn't feel she could do. Finally we decided to go to a village called Godavari, 15 KM outside Kathmandu, and do social work. The Maryknollers were happy about our decision, and they said that they would support me financially if I did health work in the village. It was all decided to the disappointment of Father Dressman and the other Jesuits. Then one day the parish priest, Father Allan Starr, came to our place for supper. He talked about the parish, how scattered and lonely the people were, etc. My heart was being moved as he talked. The next day I visited some of these Catholics with the help of a parishioner. I was so sure that we could not avoid pastoral ministry, and I was ready for it. But that meant disappointing the Maryknollers who had promised financial assistance in the health work. It also meant that I had to commute daily from Godavari into town because we wanted to live in Godavari village, and we had been given a house by the villagers. We prayed, we discussed, and we listened to one another. We finally decided that we would take up pastoral ministry. The IBMV sisters were very kind to give me a room in their convent in the town so that on weekends I could stay in town for Mass, catechism, etc. The Jesuits gave me a moped to travel back and forth into the city.

We settled in the village Godavari. Anne Marie and Jean had two centers for women and young girls. They taught them literacy, knitting, and sewing. Anne Marie took some practical training in nursing, and together we took care of the emergency medical needs of the villagers. I went daily to the town in search of Catholics—in the gullies, in the slums, in the embassies and in five-star hotels; in schools and hospitals. They were all of Indian origin and scattered all over the valley. They were literally "sheep without a shepherd." We organized them into groups. The Jesuits built a place of worship. (Previously they were having Mass in one of the classrooms.) A couple was brought to India for leadership training. With their help we organized the youth, taught catechism to school children, conducted first communion, etc. The Maryknollers helped to initiate neighborhood Mass. Slowly the scattered flocks were forming themselves into a distinct, sizeable group!

Since we were the first religious group to live in the village amidst the people, we often had visitors from the church circle, to have first-hand experience of this novelty. But for SCNs this was nothing new. Once the Bishop of Patna had come to Kathmandu for a visitation. He wanted to come to the village. But some of the IBMV sisters tried to prevent him, saying that he would have to walk for half an hour uphill, and it would be almost impossible. Finally, he told them that if he could not return back from the village, please send a wheel chair and fetch him! He did come and spent half a day with us and enjoyed himself thoroughly.

When Sister Ann Kernen joined us in May 1980, I moved into town, and we both lived in Dhobi Ghat in a rented house. In 1983 we decided to move out of the valley into East Nepal. There were numerous tea gardens in which many Catholics (Indian Tribals) were living and working. And they needed spiritual care. Also all the Religious and priests were comfortably settled in the valley; greater need was outside the valley where the bulk of the population was residing under very primitive conditions. And so we all moved out with our new companions—Sisters Anne Marie and Ann Murphy went to Ilam; Jean and Tara went to Dharan; Rosemarie and I went to a village in Damak. The sisters in Ilam did non-formal education and also taught in the college. The ones in Dharan taught the mentally retarded children and also taught women sewing and knitting. In Damak I had a dispensary and a centre for sewing, knitting, and a literacy program. Rosemarie toured the tea gardens, contacting the Catholics and taking care of their needs.

After a year or two, Anne Marie returned to Kathmandu and took charge of the faith formation of the whole of Nepal region. Because of a lack of personnel, Ilam was closed. In 1985 Francine, who was working with Rosemarie and me, was imprisoned along with Sister Gracy who had come from India to help Francine conduct a retreat for the Catholics of Sirsia. In 1986 the Damak mission was closed, and I returned to India.

Joel Urumpil, SCN

Sisters participate in a liturgy at the convent in Kathmandu.

GLOSSARY

almirah—cupboard

balwadhi—nursery

badha khana—banquet

bidi—tobacco rolled in tobacco leaf

bonjas—witch doctors

bhuichalo—earthquake

bustees—groups of villages

chota—small

chowkidhar—nightwatchman

dacoit—robber

darwan—nightwatchman

dharna—strike

dhobi—washerman

dhoti—article of male clothing worn in India

ghar—home

ghat—hilly place

gherao—holding an official hostage

grihini—a programme intended to prepare young girls for marriage, home and health care, and family life

IBMV—Institute of the Blessed Mary Virgin (German Foundation)

IBVM—Institute of the Blessed Virgin Mary (Irish Loreto Sisters)

Jeevan Darshan Kendra—center

kabbadi—a game played in India

kho-kho—a game played in India

Krishi Vidylaya—agricultural school

Krus Vir—mission organization for children

kurta—tunic worn in India

Mahila Kalyan Kendra—women's handicraft center

Mahila Sangh—women's organization

Mahila Swastia Kendra—women's health center

maidan—playground

mala—necklace of flowers

maran didi-"older sister"

Marathi—language of Bombay

maund—eighty pounds

mistri—mason

mukhihya—headman

naruma—leafy roof

nasta—snacks

neem—medicinal tree

ojhas—witch doctors
pahadh—hill
paisa—smallest denomination of
    money in India
panch—village council
petromax—lantern fueled by petrol
sabha—council
sarpanch—head of the
    local council
sesam—an herb indigenous
    to India
Seva Kendra—service center
Seva Sangh Samiti—service
    organization

shamiana—canopy
silai—sewing
swagatam—welcome
tal—low-lying area
tum-tum—a flat-topped vehicle
    drawn by a horse or pony
Uvak Sangh—youth organization
yogda—school utilizing the
    principles of Hindu discipline
walla—suffix meaning "one who"

INDEX

The Congregation of the Sisters of Charity of Nazareth was founded in Kentucky in 1812. Catherine Spalding was elected first superior.

Established for the purpose of educating the children of the Bardstown, Kentucky Catholic Diocese, the community quickly expanded its ministries to meet the needs of the changing times.

Today, SCNs engage in diverse ministries in the United States, Belize, India, and Nepal. Continuing their tradition of involvement in education, SCNs serve as teachers and administrators at a variety of schools in Belize, India, and the States. In the area of health care, the SCNs sponsor a health care system in the United States and operate a hospital, nursing school, and hospital outreach program in Mokama, India.

The sisters engage in diocesan ministries as pastoral associates, retreat directors, spiritual directors, directors of religious education, youth ministers, and campus ministers in all the locales where they reside.

SCN social service ministries sponsor or work with agencies and programs to address the needs of those who are elderly, homeless, poor, addicted, or otherwise in need of assistance. They also address legal and ethical issues in the countries where they live and serve.

The Sisters of Charity of Nazareth, along with their Associates, are committed to serving the economically poor, especially women, and caring for the earth.